Core Principles of Group Psychotherapy: An Integra *Training Manual* lives up to its ambitious title. It su basic principles of group therapy, traditional and significant research, and applicability to a wide var will prove useful for beginning and experienced group therapists alike, and it is designed to provide a template for effective teaching of a group therapy course.

Eleanor F. Counselman, Ed.D., CGP, LFAGPA; president, American Group Psychotherapy Association

Although I am not given to sweeping statements, I find myself compelled to offer one here about this marvelous book. This is a remarkable compendium of valuable information about the theory and practice of group therapy along with the research support for various group therapy models. An expansive range of core principles and the techniques that derive from them are presented in a beautifully organized and eminently readable manner and will provide useful material for novice and experienced clinicians alike.

Joseph Shay, Ph.D., CGP, LFAGPA; Department of Psychiatry, Harvard Medical School; co-author, *Psychodynamic Group Psychotherapy* (4th & 5th editions); co-editor, *Complex Dilemmas in Group Therapy* (1st & 2nd editions)

Core Principles of Group Psychotherapy by Kaklauskas and Greene is an important and timely new group therapy manual that balances being comprehensive and accessible. It provides an overview and comparison of various approaches to group therapy, inviting readers to identify the perspective that best fits them, which is a key component to effective therapy. Both pragmatic and thought provoking, this volume is an extremely valuable contribution to the group therapy literature.

Louis Hoffman, Ph.D.; fellow, American Psychological Association (Divisions 1, 10, 32, 36, & 52); editor, *Existential Psychology East-West* (Vol. 1 & 2)

Core Principles of Group Psychotherapy provides both entry and advanced level group therapists the current essential knowledge and skills needed for effective group leadership. The enduring and modern group theories and evidence-based practices and applications that are presented should serve to help therapists hone their own leadership styles and facilitate their ongoing professional growth. *Core Principles of Group Psychotherapy* is highly recommended for group leaders who want to advance their knowledge and applications of effective and evidence-based group leadership understanding and skills.

Nina W. Brown, Ed.D., LPC, NCC, FAGPA; professor and eminent scholar, Old Dominion University; author – *Psychoeducational Groups* (4th edition), *Conducting Effective Psychoeducational Groups*

Francis J. Kaklauskas and Les R. Greene's book, *Core Principles of Group Psychotherapy*, is a wonderful addition to the growing literature on group psychotherapy. Its uniqueness emerges in its being grounded both in practice and research, and its serving as a practical manual. The editors have made a huge effort to include many core topics in group therapy and beyond. I was especially impressed by the extended and detailed chapter on a multicultural perspective in group work, which is very attuned to current crucial issues in the USA. Another important chapter is on the ethical group therapist.

This book will become very valuable to teachers and students, practitioners and scholars alike.

The new *Core Principles of Group Psychotherapy,* is a must have guide to the latest in group psychotherapy research and practice. Clearly written, scholarly, and grounded in clinical experience, immediately applicable to group practice in all settings. We highly recommend this insightful new resource manual for anyone interested in group psychotherapy!

Core Principles of Group Psychotherapy

Core Principles of Group Psychotherapy is designed as the primary curriculum for the Principles of Group Psychotherapy course in partial fulfilment of the Certified Group Psychotherapist credential awarded by the International Board for Certification of Group Psychotherapists. The text is divided into five modules: foundations, structure and dynamics, formation and development, leadership tasks and skills, ethics, neuroscience, and personal style.

The book is part of the AGPA Group Therapy Training and Practice series. This series aims to produce the highest quality publications to aid the practitioner and student in updating and improving their knowledge, professional competence, and skills with current and new developments in methods, practice, theory, and research in the group psychotherapy field.

In addition to helping group psychotherapists bolster their skills so as to ensure the availability of quality mental health services, this guide is an essential resource for students and clinicians interested in learning more about group psychotherapy, as a text in academic courses, or as part of a practicum or internship training curriculum.

Francis J. Kaklauskas, Psy.D., CGP, FAGPA, has worked extensively as a group clinician in a wide variety of settings. He leads the Existential/Humanistic doctorate program at Saybrook University, and teaches group psychotherapy at the University of Colorado and Naropa University. He has published widely on the pragmatic integration of theory and research into actual clinical practice.

Les R. Greene, Ph.D. CGP, LFAGPA, is a past president of the American Group Psychotherapy Association and a Distinguished Fellow of AGPA. He has served as editor of the *International Journal of Group Psychotherapy*. He is on the clinical faculty of Yale University School of Medicine and the staff of the VA CT Healthcare system where he teaches and supervises group, couples and individual psychotherapy.

AGPA Group Therapy Training and Practice Series

Series Editors: Les R. Greene, Rebecca MacNair-Semands, and Martyn Whittingham

The American Group Psychotherapy Association (AGPA) is the foremost professional association dedicated to the field of group psychotherapy, operating through a tripartite structure: AGPA, a professional and educational organization; the Group Foundation for Advancing Mental Health, its philanthropic arm; and the International Board for Certification of Group Psychotherapists, a standard setting and certifying body. This multidisciplinary association has approximately 3,000 members, including psychiatrists, psychologists, social workers, nurses, clinical mental health counselors, marriage and family therapists, pastoral counselors, occupational therapists and creative arts therapists, many of whom have been recognized as specialists through the Certified Group Psychotherapist credential. The association has 26 local and regional societies located across the country. Its members are experienced mental health professionals who lead psychotherapy groups and various non-clinical groups. Many are organizational specialists who work with businesses, not-for-profit organizations, communities and other "natural" groups to help them improve their functioning.

The goal of the AGPA Group Therapy Training and Practice Series is to produce the highest quality publications to aid the practitioner and student in updating and improving their knowledge, professional competence and skills with current and new developments in methods, practice, theory, and research in the group psychotherapy field. Books in this series are the only curriculum guide and resource for a variety of courses credentialed by the International Board for Certification of Group Psychotherapists. While this is the series' original and primary purpose, the texts are also useful in a variety of other settings including as a resource for students and clinicians interested in learning more about group psychotherapy, as a text in academic courses, or as part of a training curriculum in a practicum or internship training experience.

For more information about this series, please visit www.routledge.com/AGPA-Group-Therapy-Training-and-Practice-Series/book-series/AGPA.

Core Principles of Group Psychotherapy

An Integrated Theory, Research, and Practice Training Manual

Edited by Francis J. Kaklauskas and
Les R. Greene

NEW YORK AND LONDON

First published 2020
by Routledge
52 Vanderbilt Avenue, New York, NY 10017

and by Routledge
2 Park Square, Milton Park, Abingdon, Oxon, OX14 4RN

Routledge is an imprint of the Taylor & Francis Group, an informa business

Library of Congress Cataloging-in-Publication Data
A catalog record for this title has been requested

ISBN: 978-0-367-20308-5 (hbk)
ISBN: 978-0-367-20309-2 (pbk)
ISBN: 978-0-429-26080-3 (ebk)

Typeset in Sabon
by Swales & Willis, Exeter, Devon, UK

Visit the eResources: www.routledge.com/9780367203085

To all those - leaders and members – who with courage and compassion create, join, and work together in healing groups.

Contents

Guidelines for Students

This training manual was designed as the primary curriculum for the *Principles of Group Psychotherapy* course in partial fulfillment of the Certified Group Psychotherapist credential awarded by the International Board for Certification of Group Psychotherapists. While this was its original and primary purpose, the text can also be useful in a variety of other settings, including as a resource for students and clinicians interested in learning more about group psychotherapy, as a text in academic courses, or as part of a training curriculum in a practicum or internship training experience.

The original training text by Robert Weber was published over a decade ago, and this present version is designed to incorporate and integrate recent advances in theory and research with the contemporary practice of group psychotherapy. Our goal was to be inclusive of the variety of approaches, clinical needs, and treatment settings where group psychotherapy is practiced today. Each of the authors combines scholarship and academic teaching experiences with decades of actual clinical group practice in a variety of clinical situations. The focus and breadth of the information presented is intended to be useful across varied settings and with many differing clinical populations, and to have multicultural applicability.

While the manual covers a comprehensive range of topics, readers are encouraged to pursue areas that match their interests or needs of their clients that extend beyond the text recommendations. This manual attempts to provide the core **foundational knowledge** and **functional skills** that will assist in making the groups you lead more efficacious and enjoyable regardless of setting.

Acquiring competence in practicing group psychotherapy is best achieved through both study and experience. Accordingly, students are encouraged, not only to read and discuss the material presented, but to wholeheartedly participate in any experiential group work that accompanies this training. The combination of formal study and personal experience, as well as clinical supervision, continues to be regarded as the most comprehensive way towards acquiring and increasing one's group leadership skills.

If this manual is part of a structured course, please ask questions of the instructors to clarify the information and feel free to share your experiences. Students are encouraged to think freely for themselves and not to passively accept the presented material without comparing it to their own experiences and beliefs. Only through the ongoing refinement of ideas and theories can group psychotherapy continue to expand and grow. No one manual or training can be sufficient to master the intricacies of group work and continued training and supervision is recommended throughout one's career.

Guidelines for Instructors

Thank you for using this manual. Our hope is that it provides a supportive base from which your pedagogical style can be both effective and enjoyable for you and the students. While the manual covers a wide range of information essential to understanding the contemporary conceptualizations and practice of group psychotherapy, it is best viewed as a starting point from which you can blend the needs of your students and the setting with your own ideas and experiences. While we attempted to incorporate multicultural perspectives throughout the text and with a particular focus in Chapter 2, the manual is primarily grounded in the traditional views of group psychotherapy represented within the United States and Canada. If using this manual in other countries or cultures, culturally informed adaptations are encouraged.

The manual has been designed to fulfill the curricular requirements for group psychotherapy certification awarded by the International Board for Certification of Group Psychotherapists. Depending upon the setting and time frame in which you teach this material, the depth and range of areas to be covered will vary. As an instructor, many choices are available to facilitate student learning. You could have students read the entire manual or the chapters to be covered before the lecture, discussion, and experiential exercises. As you will notice, we have formatted the material into five modules with groupings of chapters within each module. While the chapters have been logically organized starting with foundational knowledge, to functional skills, and then to other core group parameters, in certain situations you may find it best to change the order to emphasize certain sections over others. The exercises and questions are designed to have students reflect on the material as they may apply to their own personal and professional experiences; feel free to select some and disregard others due to circumstances of class length and needs of the students. While the readings and resources are varied and extensive, including seminal and classic clinical-theoretical papers, video material, and research studies, you may find resources better suited to increase student learning or to provide needed emphasis. And while we have provided some case examples, we also hope that you as the instructor and your students will bring personal experiences with groups to the material to create a lively and relational collaboration in the classroom. Finally, as you see by the new subtitle of the manual, we have aimed at offering an approach that integrates research with theory and practice; appreciating the importance of empirical study is an important component of building competence as a group psychotherapist.

Acknowledgments

As the editors, we would like to thank, first, our primary work group, the American Group Psychotherapy Association, and its leadership, particularly Marsha Block, Angela Stephens, and Diane Feirman, for their support and guidance throughout this project. The American Group Psychotherapy Association's Science to Service Task Force shepherded this project and we would like to thank their membership and the co-chairs, Rebecca MacNair-Semands and Martyn Whittingham, for their ideas, reviews, and expertise. Moreover, we would like to acknowledge Josh Gross, Molyn Leszcz, Jill Paquin, and Michele Ribeiro for their reviews of the manuscript, helpful ideas, and encouragement. We also feel tremendous gratitude to the additional authors and co-authors of specific chapters (Sally Barlow, Susan Gantt, Reginald Nettles, Elizabeth Olson, and J. Scott Rutan) who graciously shared their wisdom and knowledge gathered over decades of clinical practice and rigorous scholarship. We also want to thank all our group members, group leaders, supervisors, mentors, teachers, and friends who encouraged our personal and professional growth. And we especially want to express our deepest gratitude towards members of our primary groups – our wives, Elizabeth Olson (FJK) and Michelle Collins-Greene (LRG) for their consistent, loving support and wise and tactful feedback about our work and our characters, and our sons Levi (FJK) and Joshua (LRG) for providing inspiration and optimism about the future.

We hope that the readers find the manual beneficial to them and valuable in their work.

Contributors

Editors

Francis J. Kaklauskas, Psy.D., CGP, FAGPA Dr. Kaklauskas is a fellow and former board member of the American Group Psychotherapy Association and a founding board member of the Colorado Group Psychotherapy Society and the Rocky Mountain Humanistic Counseling and Psychological Association. He has worked extensively as a group clinician over the last 25 years leading multiple types of groups across a variety of clinical and academic settings. His publications cover a broad spectrum of topics including the integration and application of transtheoretical perspectives and empirical findings into actual clinical practice, the utilization of spiritual and philosophical perspectives in therapy, and the goals and techniques of process groups. He has co-edited several books with a cross-cultural focus including *Brilliant Sanity: Buddhist Approaches to Psychotherapy, Shadows and Light: Theory, Research, and Practice in Transpersonal Psychology - Volumes 1 & 2*, and *Existential Psychology East-West*.

Les R. Greene, Ph.D., CGP, DLFAGPA Dr. Greene is a past president of the American Group Psychotherapy Association and a distinguished fellow of AGPA. He has served as editor of the International Journal of Group Psychotherapy and currently co-chairs the Science to Service Task Force of AGPA. He is on the clinical faculty of Yale University School of Medicine where he teaches and supervises group, couples, and individual psychotherapy. He has published extensively on the dynamics of group psychotherapy and the relationship between psychotherapy research and practice. He is a three times recipient of the Alonso Award for Excellence in Psychodynamic Group Psychotherapy Theory, most recently for the paper, Group Therapist as Social Scientist, with Special Reference to the Psychodynamically Oriented Psychotherapist.

Authors

Sally Barlow, Ph.D., ABPP, CGP, FAGPA Dr. Barlow has served in many leadership roles in the American Group Psychotherapy Association, American Board of Professional Psychology – Group Specialization, and the American Psychological Association's Division for Group Psychotherapy and Group Psychology. She is widely published, including co-editing the book, *Critical Issues in Psychotherapy: Translating New Ideas into Practice* and authoring *Specialty Competencies in Group Psychology (Specialty Competencies in Professional Psychology)*.

Susan Gantt Ph.D. ABPP, CGP, DFAGPA Dr. Gantt is a distinguished fellow of the American Group Psychotherapy Association and Board Certified in Group Psychotherapy. She is the director of the Systems-Centered Training and Research Institute and is Emerita Faculty in the Department of Psychiatry and Behavioral Sciences at Emory University School of Medicine where she continues to teach group psychotherapy. She has co-authored the books, *Autobiography of a Theory* and *SCT in Action* (with Yvonne Agazarian), as well co-edited The *Interpersonal Neurobiology of Group Psychotherapy and Group Process* with Bonnie Badenoch. She has received the Alonso Award for Excellence in Psychodynamic Group Psychotherapy Theory for her work editing the special issue of *International Journal of Group Psychotherapy*, Neurobiology and Interpersonal Systems: Groups, Couples and Beyond.

Reginald Nettles, Ph.D., CGP Dr. Nettles is a former member of the Board of Directors, American Group Psychotherapy Association, past president of the Mid-Atlantic Group Psychotherapy Society, and has served in leadership roles within the American Psychological Association and Maryland Psychological Association. He is on the faculty of the National Group Psychotherapy Institute and founding chair of the Center for the Study of Race, Ethnicity, and Culture at The Washington School of Psychiatry. He has taught group counseling and psychotherapy at The George Washington University, University of Baltimore, and Uniformed Services University of the Health Sciences, and Cultural and Minority Issues in Psychology at The American University. He served as Director, Counseling and Health Centers, University of Maryland - Baltimore County, and on the counseling staffs at Howard University, and American University. Among his publications is his co-edited volume (with R. Balter) *Multiple Minority Identities: Applications for Practice, Research, and Training.*

Elizabeth A. Olson, Psy.D., MSW, CGP Dr. Olson is past president of the Colorado Group Psychotherapy Society and directs the Group Psychotherapy Training Program at University of Colorado – Wardenburg Health, Counseling, and Psychiatric Services. She has published on a variety of topics including group psychotherapy, mindfulness, and parenting, and co-edited the book, *The Buddha, the Bike, the Couch, and the Circle: A Festschrift for Dr. Robert Unger.* She has led a wide range of groups throughout her career from multi-family groups and Dialectical Behavioral Therapy with adolescents to long-term psychodynamic oriented groups and training groups with clinicians. She is founder and clinical director of The Collective for Psychological Wellness in Boulder, Colorado.

J. Scott Rutan, Ph.D., CGP, DFAGPA Dr. Rutan is a distinguished fellow and past president of the American Group Psychotherapy Association. He founded the Center for Group Psychotherapy at Harvard Medical School (Massachusetts General Hospital) and co-founded the Boston Institute for Psychotherapy. His publications are diverse and include the widely utilized text, *Psychodynamic Group Psychotherapy*, currently in its fifth edition.

Course Objectives

Chapter 1   To recognize the influential historical figures and early contributions to the field and survey the current state of the field.

Chapter 2   To demonstrate increased sensitivity and proficiency in multiculturalism and diversity related to group psychotherapy.

Chapter 3   To identify structural dimensions and conceptual levels in understanding group phenomenon, behavior, and processes.

Chapter 4   To explain the group level factors, processes, and mediators that lead to therapeutic change.

Chapter 5   To recognize problematic group processes and identify ways to successfully manage them.

Chapter 6   To identify the requisite tasks in successfully forming a psychotherapy group.

Chapter 7   To compare and contrast the various models of group development and to explain why a developmental perspective helps the therapist in selecting interventions and focus.

Chapter 8   To identify the basic and universal therapeutic skills in conducting therapy groups.

Chapter 9   To identify the advanced skills needed to optimize group therapeutic work.

Chapter 10   To master the essential ethical principles in practicing group psychotherapy.

Chapter 11   To review the relationship between brain functioning and group psychotherapy interventions.

Chapter 12   To demonstrate increased appreciation and care for oneself in the role of group psychotherapist.

Preface
The Joys and Challenges of Group Leadership

Carl Rogers once remarked that good therapists are born, not made, so we should spend our resources on recruitment rather than training. While training is obviously an essential part of becoming a competent therapist or group leader, Rogers' point may speak to certain dispositional characteristics. Being a therapist is not for everyone, and group leadership likewise may only be attractive to those who welcome a capricious flowering of cognitive, emotional, and relational complexity.

Group psychotherapy can be a polarizing pursuit among students and clinicians. Some say they dislike groups, and others profess a deep love of group work. Even Wilfred Bion (Bleandonu, 1994), one of group therapy's pioneers, alternated between deep appreciation and disparagement for this modality.

As people, we are social animals with our own histories and locations throughout the varied groups of our lives. In our childhoods, we start with our family of origin group and then move outward to elementary school classrooms, social clubs, and activity groups, teams, and so on. As adults, we join other groups as co-workers, neighbors, friend groups, new families, professional organizations, and so forth. Undoubtedly, the groups we are a part of throughout our lives can provide great sustenance, insight, and joy at times, while at other times they can bring forth painful experiences of feeling misunderstood, undervalued, rejected, anxious, and confused. As we look over the groups in our lives, how have we been supported, and how have we been disappointed? How have the groups of our lives impacted us?

Famed group therapist Lou Ormont used to say group leaders don't sleep as well at night as other people. He would go on to explain that groups are so stimulating, fascinating, unpredictable, and imprecise that they stay with us long after our workday is done. All of us have had thoughts about our groups after our members have left the room. Often, only on our commute home do the dynamics become clearer and our best interventions come to mind. On reflection, we may regret having said *this*, when we should have said *that*. But also hopefully at times, we reflect and feel that we did a good job as we see the growth in our members. Despite our level of training or clinical experiences, engaging in group leadership provides opportunities for an enlivening and interesting existence.

As leaders we become fond of many of our members and frustrated and annoyed by others. As members tell their stories, it can seem as if sometimes they are narrating our own thoughts, feelings, and aspects of our own stories. Through listening to our members, we gain knowledge and insight about a wide variety of topics, ranging from an insider's view of various careers, to new approaches for relieving stress, to the best dating strategies. We learn about the best local new restaurants and even the best way to cook samosas or mustard greens. We learn who is an honest local car mechanic and about what TV shows we may want to record. We can have full out belly laughs with our members about the absurdity of life situations or ridiculous miscommunications. But we also hear what it is like to be privileged or discriminated against, what it is like to live with physical limitations mental illness, poverty, trauma, loss, and all the varieties of human pain.

As they feel, we feel. When members talk about heartache or grief, these feelings are brought anew within us. With discussions of a new romance, a new job or other transition, we can feel excitement and hope. When our members connect with each other, we feel great intimacy, while at other times it feels as if each person in the group is locked in a separate world of isolation and loneliness.

And as leaders, we are in charge of all of this. Unlike the individual therapist, the group leader can feel responsible for the well being of a large family with conflicting needs and desires. With success comes great satisfaction, and with limited outcomes or failures we can feel shame associated with a sense of incompetence (Weber & Gans, 2003). We are also the object of multiple projections simultaneously. Sometimes these projections are off the mark, but at times our members see us all too clearly in our glory and limitedness. They can see our strengths, but also areas that need professional, or even personal, attention.

When we lead groups with adolescents, we can feel hopeful and creative, but impulsive and searching for an identity. When working with anxious groups, we may become worrywarts, and with depression themes, we can lose our energy. Feelings are contagious, and there are many feelings in the group room. Our members impact us and our lives, and in turn our friends and families. We learn self-care, coping skills, and professional distance, but the best leaders remain permeable to connect with their members and their experiences.

Group leadership can be more than a career; it can transcend to be part of a life full of feelings, explorations, reflection, and relationships. Working with groups helps us be effective and aware of relational dynamics, not only in the group therapy setting, but also throughout our lives. The entire world is a group, and we are merely group members in the various communities of our lives.

In this manual and course, The American Group Psychotherapy Association, the editors, and authors want to provide you with the core knowledge and skills that will assist you in leading your psychotherapeutic groups, and also potentially provide some inspiration for group work to become a wonderful and powerful addition to your career and life.

Francis J. Kaklauskas

Recommended Resources

Bleandonu, G. (1994). *Wilfred Bion: His Life and Works*. London: Free Association Books.

Rogers, C. R. (1951). *Client-centered Therapy: Its Current Practice, Implications, and Theory, with Chapters*. Boston, MA: Houghton Mifflin.

Weber, R. L., & Gans, J. S. (2003). The group therapist's shame: A much undiscussed topic. *International Journal of Group Psychotherapy, 53*(4), 395–416.

Module 1

Group Psychotherapy Foundations

Historic, Contemporary, and Cultural Perspectives

1 History and Contemporary Developments

Francis J. Kaklauskas and Elizabeth A. Olson

The history of group psychotherapy (Anthony, 1971; Barlow, Fuhriman, & Burlingame, 2004; Scheidlinger, 1994, 2000) bursts with happenstance discoveries, creative and courageous inventiveness, investigative fortitude, caring hearts, and interesting, passionate personalities. Despite being just over one hundred years old, group psychotherapy has branched out into many aspects of our contemporary world. Group dynamics are regularly acknowledged and discussed, from small workplace power struggles to global diplomatic dynamics. While the formal term of "group psychotherapy" only began to gain a footing with the rise of psychotherapy at the middle of the last century, the practice of people getting together to learn, grow, and support one another is timeless. Groups form the very base of our humanity and humanness.

Pre-Therapy Group Influences

- Anthropologists recognize the practices of human group identifications, conflicts, connectedness, and collaboration from our earliest historical roots.
- Many worldwide myths highlight the underpinnings of group psychological factors on human behavior. These stories tell timeless tales of interpersonal alliances, misunderstandings, mistreatments, and all shades of human relatedness.
- Gustave Le Bon's (1895) "The Crowd" described how one's thinking and behaviors change in unique ways in varied social situations.
- Charles Triplett (1898) discussed how cyclists perform better when riding in a group or peloton than individually.
- Some cite Sigmund Freud's Thursday night discussion group of psychoanalysts as the first group psychotherapy or group supervision meeting.

Joseph Pratt

Internist Joseph Pratt inadvertently started group psychotherapy in July of 1905. He began holding educational classes focused on hygiene with some inspirational religious readings for his patients suffering from tuberculosis. He noticed that patients often gathered together after his talks in dyads and small groups. Moreover, he suspected that patients who regularly attended his presentations, not only remained **optimistic and courageous** despite living with a chronic illness, but also appeared to have **fewer symptoms and better recovery**.

In Pratt's talks, the patients were taught about how to work with their attitudes and illness. Yet, after the class, they also got **emotional support and connection** from other patients. While Pratt initially thought that it was the information he was providing that was the magic in their improved health, his **patients** believed it was the **connection, support,** and the **increased hope** they felt through their conversations with others struggling with similar challenges (Pratt, 1907). Over time, Pratt further expanded the opportunities for his patients and their families to talk to each other during his presentations. The power of group psychotherapy was discovered.

- Pratt is usually considered the creator of group psychotherapy.
- First formal psychotherapy groups for people with tuberculosis started in 1905.
- Created out of necessity to see more patients simultaneously.
- Initially focused on lectures and providing medical information.
- Attendees reported most enjoying and benefitting from talking with one another, and Pratt increasingly utilized their between-member interactions in lieu of lectures.
- In 1921, the psychiatrist E.W. Lazell adopted and extended this group approach at St. Elizabeth's Hospital in Washington, D.C. for World War I veterans suffering with psychotic symptoms.

Jacob Moreno

Jacob Moreno was a Romanian psychiatrist who was always drawn to theater, the creative arts, and spontaneity. Well before completing his formal medical training, he engaged in spontaneous theater, ranging from forming acting troupes to impromptu performances in the parks of Vienna with children and marginalized individuals.

- Creator of psychodrama – a form of group therapy in which group members engage in spontaneous theater and roleplaying.
- Worked with the underprivileged in the parks in Vienna prior to World War I.
- Coined the term "group psychotherapy" in 1931.
- The following year (1932), the American Psychiatric Association held a conference that accepted this term and this new method of treatment.
- Valued spontaneity, creativity, and mutual sharing.

Psychodrama therapy enlists its group members to role-play a scene from a group member's (protagonist) historical past, dreams or fantasies, or anticipations of future events. With collaboration and input from the group, the group leader or director sets up the scene and group members enact the characters, psychological parts of the protagonist, and all the other elements of the scene.

Basic psychodrama techniques are:

- **Doubling:** Someone stands behind and speaks for a member.
- **Role reversal:** Characters switch roles in the middle of the action.
- **The Soliloquy:** At the end of a scene the protagonist speaks spontaneously.

While the focus in a psychodrama scene is on one group member, other participants and the audience (group members who did not take a role) can vicariously experience strong feelings and insights into their own lives.

Other Early 20th Century Developments

During this period, ideas about the psychology of groups gained interest in academic writing as reflected in the works of William McDougall (1908, 1920), Sigmund Freud (1921), and others. The practice of group psychotherapy also expanded into more mental health hospitals and clinics (Marsh, 1935).

- Trigant Burrow expanded psychoanalytic ideas into the group therapy format and first used the terms *group analysis* and *here-and-now*
- Post-Freudian theorists including Melanie Klein, Alfred Adler, and Carl Jung had increasing interest in interpersonal relationships and collectives.
- Kurt Lewin coined the term *group dynamics* (1947) in his innovative studies of group process and leadership roles

Samuel Slavson

Samuel Slavson was an engineer, journalist, and teacher who began conducting psychotherapy groups in 1919. He was a proponent of progressive education and the child guidance movement, wrote extensively on group psychotherapy, and founded the American Group Psychotherapy Association in 1942.

- Believed self-expression and self-acceptance increase adjustment and happiness.
- Started with **Activity Groups** using art supplies with children and adolescents.
- Moved to **Interview Group Therapy** which encouraged members to talk honestly with one another.
- Group members were prompted to focus on each other's positives and to have positive interchanges.

Mid Century Developments

Following World War II, group psychotherapy experienced a **rapid and dramatic growth** in **application, theory development, and research** as soldiers returned home with both physical and psychological injuries, and families dealt with grief and loss, and the general population struggled with ongoing fear and trauma. The need for psychological services greatly exceeded the systems that existed, and so health care workers increasingly relied on group approaches.

Clinicians and participants found benefit through connecting with others who shared similar experiences, hearing feedback and suggestions from a diverse collection of peers, experiencing one's vulnerability, and providing support to others. During this period two of the most prominent group practitioners and theoreticians, S. H. Foulkes and Wilfred Bion, developed their lasting seminal ideas about group work.

S. H. Foulkes

Foulkes was a German born psychiatrist who immigrated to England. He studied with many of the leading figures of the psychoanalytic movement including Helene Deutsch and Wilhelm Reich, and was colleagues with many individuals of the Frankfurt Institute of Sociology. He is noted for at times asking the patients in his clinic's waiting room to free-associate together, and went on to significantly contribute at the Military Neurosis Centre at Northfield Hospital in the areas of group analysis and therapeutic community.

- Prior to World War II, conducted private practice psychoanalytic groups.
- During and after the War, worked at Northfield Hospital to help with the mental health needs of soldiers and families.
- **Group-as-a-whole** – Group was seen as more than the sum of its parts (members, leader and setting), but also a whole unto itself.
- Each group has a unique pace, anticipation, defensiveness and work style.
- Identified group selection criteria.
- Group members benefited from having multiple transferences towards each other as opposed to just the individual therapist. He focused closely on how members responded to each other, and he asked about these choices or behaviors.
- Preferred the term "conductor" (as in an orchestra) to the term group leader, as he felt the title "leader" reflected negatively within the cultural context of the autocratic and destructive leaders of World War II.

Wilfred Bion

While Foulkes is remembered for his outward warmth, his sometime colleague Wilfred Bion was known for his passion and strong ideas and ideals. Bion studied under John Rickman and Melanie Klein, and made many significant contributions to psychotherapy and group psychotherapy. His book *Experiences in Group* (1961), a collection of essays based on his leading groups at the Tavistock Clinic in London, is a classic study in group psychotherapy.

- Used an unstructured group approach to study group processes and encouraged members to focus on the group dynamics that unfolded.
- Basic Assumptions (see Chapter 5) interfere with the work of the group.
- Bion ultimately became disillusioned with group work as he returned to focus more on individual treatment, developing a sophisticated theory of personality and an interest in psychotic processes.

Recommended Resources

Anthony, E. J. (1971). The history of group psychotherapy. In H. Kaplan & B. Sadock (Eds.), *Comprehensive group psychotherapy*, 4–31. Baltimore, MD: Williams and Wilkens.

Barlow, S. H., Fuhriman, A. J., & Burlingame, G. (2004). The history of group counseling and psychotherapy. In J. L. Delucia-Waack, D. A. Gerrity, C. R., Kalodner, & M. T. Riva (Eds.), *Handbook of group counseling and psychotherapy*, 3–22. Thousand Oaks, CA: Sage.

Bion, W. R. (1961). *Experiences in groups and other papers*. London: Tavistock.

Foulkes, S. H. (1990). *Selected papers of S.H. Foulkes: Psychoanalysis and group analysis*. London: Karnac.

Freud, S. (1921). Group psychology and the analysis of the ego. Standard Edition, 18. London: Hogarth.

Freud, S. (1922). *Group psychology and the analysis of the ego (1922)*, Trans. by J. Strachey. New York: Boni and Liveright.

Le Bon, G. (1960). The Crowd: A Study of the Popular Mind. 1895. *Reprint, New York: Viking.*

Lewin, K. (1947). Group decision and social change. *Readings in Social Psychology*, 3(1), 197–211.

Marsh, L. C. (1935). Group therapy and the psychiatric clinic. *The Journal of Nervous and Mental Disease*, 82(4), 381–393.

McDougall, W. (1908). Introduction to social psychology. London: Methuen & Co.

McDougall, W. (1920). *The group mind: A sketch of the principles of collective psychology, with some attempt to apply them to the interpretation of national life and character.* London: GP Putnam's Sons.

Pratt, J. H. (1907). The organization of tuberculosis classes. *Medical Communications of the Massachusetts Medical Society*, 20, 475-492.

Scheidlinger, S. (1994). An overview of nine decades of group psychotherapy. *Hospital and Community Psychiatry*, 45, 217–225. Available at http://ps.psychiatryonline.org/doi/pdfplus/10.1176/ps.45.3.217

Scheidlinger, S. (2000). The group psychotherapy movement at the millennium: Some historical perspectives. *International Journal of Group Psychotherapy*, 50 (3), 315–339.

Triplett, N. (1898). The dynamogenic factors in pacemaking and competition. *The American Journal of Psychology*, 9(4), 507-533.

The Origins of Cognitive Behavioral Group Psychotherapy

In the early 1960s, psychoanalysis was still experiencing clinical popularity. However, in academic circles, behaviorism and learning theories had already surpassed psychoanalysis in interest and acceptance. Psychology was still working towards gaining greater credibility and legitimacy as a science, and the observable changes in learning and behavior were easier to quantify. In animal research labs, psychology students were learning to link stimuli to predictable outcomes. This met the growing **logical positivist Zeitgeist** that science will lead to a new and better future. Psychoanalytic ideas were beginning to be criticized as too ethereal, abstract, difficult to research, and at times too disturbing for the general public to fully embrace. The behavioral ideas of Ivan Pavlov and John Watson re-emerged as central in psychology training and research. In academia, behaviorism took center stage again with the ideas and work of B. F. Skinner and Joseph Wolpe that were more easily researched. Newer complementary ideas were also on the horizon, as Albert Ellis and Aaron Beck ushered in the cognitive revolution that garnered enthusiasm in both academic and clinical work.

Behavioral Foundations

a. **B. F. Skinner** remains one of the best-known and (perhaps) most controversial figures in psychology. He formulated the model of **operant conditioning,** and demonstrated that behavior could be modified through post factum consequences.

Operant conditioning's model of measuring and controlling the impact of **rewards and punishments** provided optimism that eventually the right combinations could be ascertained to treat many behavioral challenges. While many praised his diligence in forwarding the scientific approach to understanding behavior, others believed that he overgeneralized from his animal research findings to human behavior. Some found his **challenges to freewill** and his mechanistic approach dehumanizing and distasteful. His behaviorist ideas continue to permeate segments of our approaches to **education, parenting, criminal justice, and organizational management.** Perhaps with the distance of time and reflection, we see that **conditioning principles** can be helpful in understanding and modifying behavior, but that operant conditioning is not a panacea for all individual and collective ills.

b. **Joseph Wolpe** is best known for his theories of **reciprocal inhibition,** of which **systematic desensitization** is one form. He believed that World War II soldiers could unlearn responses to traumatic experiences through this process, and his behavioral principles continue to serve as the basis for contemporary psychotherapeutic treatments of some forms of anxiety such as phobias and trauma conditions.

Cognitive Foundations

a. **Albert Ellis** is best known as the creator of **Rational Emotive Behavioral Therapy (REBT).** His approach focused primarily on **irrational beliefs** that were often framed in **absolutes,** such as, "Everyone must think that I'm perfect or I will be worthless." As early as the 1950s, he was conducting group treatment using his early form of cognitive-behavior therapy with a model termed the **ABCs:**

- **Activating event** (identifying some actual event in the individual's world that was stirring feelings and thoughts).
- **Beliefs** about the events (exploring the idiosyncratic and irrational meanings of the event for the individual).
- **Consequences** of emotional impact from these beliefs (identifying the emotional sequelae of these beliefs).

b. **Aaron Beck** moved away from psychoanalytic thought to become the central figure in cognitive-behavioral therapies. In the early 1960s, he proposed that it was **automatic pathogenic thoughts about self, the world and the future,** rather than the Freudian notion of an aggressive drive turned against oneself, that underlie depression (Beck, 1979). This cognitive focus expanded into the treatment of anxiety and other mental health challenges. Beck's cognitive model continues to be widely applied in treating many forms of pathology in group psychotherapy. Characteristics of automatic thoughts include:

- **Arbitrary inference** – the drawing of a conclusion that something is true despite the absence of supportive evidence or the presence of contradictory evidence.
- **Selective abstraction** – the focusing on only selected details of a situation, taking things out of context, and disregarding other information. Looking only for the negative and not recognizing the positives.
- **Overgeneralization** – drawing a conclusion from a single event or piece of information.

- **Magnification or minimization** – perceiving something as more-or-less salient than others do (e.g. making a mountain out of a molehill).
- **Personification** – taking things personally, or believing events were directed intentionally to oneself despite the evidence of a real causal link.
- **Dichotomous thinking** – categorizing experiences into two polar extremes, or all-or-nothing thinking.

For Beck (1996), while each client had a unique cognitive map, those individuals with similar clusters of symptoms were thought to have comparable maps. In this way cognitive therapy aims to **identify specific pathognomonic underlying beliefs associated with each kind of psychopathology.** While focusing on cognition is central to change, Beck also strongly endorsed behavioral work as a powerful companion.

Cognitive Behavioral Group Psychotherapy Today

Contemporary cognitive behavioral therapy (CBT) continues to integrate **a variety of techniques** including creative arts therapy, relaxation training, and behavioral practice. This integrative spirit of cognitive behavioral has allowed it to continue to change and grow over time, but also has left a central, widely accepted definition open to debate. Generally, Cognitive Behavioral Group Psychotherapy (CBGT) focuses on **distorted or maladaptive beliefs,** and places **less value** than psychodynamic approaches on exploring and gaining **insight** into clients' developmental histories and core **intrapsychic conflicts.** While valuing the therapeutic alliance, CBT **does not believe** a **supportive alliance alone is enough** (i.e., **necessary but not sufficient**) to make marked change. However, like in all group models, constructive interactions among group members, ranging from support to questioning and even confrontation, are considered essential.

CBGT typically entails **highly structured** and **time limited** formats with **homogeneous** populations employing such interventions as:

- Welcoming the group members.
- Reviewing the previous group session and homework assignments.
- Reviewing the current session plans or agenda.
- Highlighting central points of a new topic.
- *In vivo* practice of new skills, often through role-playing.
- Discussion.

Because of its value on empirical validation, CBT group treatment has amassed considerable evidence of its effectiveness for a very wide range of challenges including: depression, anxiety spectrum disorders (including generalized anxiety, panic disorders, obsessive compulsive disorders, and social phobia), and posttraumatic stress disorder. Promising results have also been obtained for psychotic disorders, eating disorders, and some personality disorders. CBT group models have been adapted to work with adolescents and children (Haen & Aronson, 2017).

Generally, outcome research has shown that CBT groups are as effective as individual CBT (Sochting, 2014) and more cost effective. The group format has the benefits of members' learning from each other's experiences, successes and setbacks, increased hope with the progress of others, a lessening of stigma, and opportunities to practice skills and exercises in the group. As in all forms of group, sometimes the most beneficial events may occur through members' interactions with each other.

Recommended Resources

Beck, A. T. (1979). *Cognitive therapy and the emotional disorders*. London: Penguin.

Bieling, P. J., McCabe, R. E., & Antony, M. M. (2013). *Cognitive-behavioral therapy in groups*. New York: Guilford Press.

Free, M. (2007). *Cognitive therapy in groups: Guidelines and resources for practice* (2nd ed.). Chichester: John Wiley & Sons.

Haen, C., & Aronson, S. (Eds.). (2017). *Handbook of child and adolescent group therapy: A practitioner's reference*. New York: Routledge.

Sochting, I. (2014). *Cognitive behavioral group therapy: Challenges and opportunities*. New York: Wiley.

Contemporary Psychodynamic Approaches

Psychodynamic approaches began with Freud's psychoanalytic work characterized by its focus on:

- Unconscious mental processes such as wishes, fears, motivations.
- Biological innate drives.
- Repetition compulsion.
- Defense mechanisms.
- An emphasis on early development and experience.
- Transference.

Group therapy continues to be influenced by the psychodynamic traditions to this day; however in contemporary practice most group leaders incorporate multiple aspects of different theories, approaches and styles. Few leaders hold fast to strict theories and methods from only one school.

Object Relational Group Psychotherapy

Object relations theory, originating with the work of Melanie Klein, is deeply embedded into our psychotherapy culture. Many prominent foundational group therapists have either worked directly with Klein (Bion, 1961) or are deeply impacted by her work. Essential tenets of object relations theory that inform group therapy include:

- Belief that human beings have an innate desire to connect with each other and the **primacy of relationship**.
- Early relationships form the foundation for one's internal experiences and **enduring views or templates of the self and others**.
- The group provides opportunities for the **re-enactment** in the here-and-now of these early self-other experiences to be observed, identified and reworked.

Object relations oriented groups are typically **less structured**, and members are encouraged to share their feelings and experiences about relationships in the here-and-now group, as well as both historical relationships and relationships outside of the group. The work of the group entails the enactment, observation, exploration and modification of **problematic or conflictual relational patterns** reflecting such themes as reluctance and fear, competition and aggression, care-taking and co-dependency, and a variety of other interpersonal issues. The goal is to help clients become more aware of their problematic relational patterns with opportunities to change them in order to increase relational effectiveness and satisfaction.

Ego Psychology Group Psychotherapy

Ego psychology and self psychology both focus on the development of more effective and **adaptive coping and defense strategies** as well as a **more resilient and competent self**. Ego psychology grew out of Freud's tripartite conceptualization of id (innate biological drives), ego (self system mediator), and super ego (critical and moralizing voice developed from societal and early authority figures). Freud's daughter, Anna Freud, and more recently George Valliant (1986), further elaborated on the concept of ego defenses and constructed a **developmental hierarchy of ego defenses:**

- Level I – pathological defenses (psychotic denial, delusional projection).
- Level II – immature defenses (fantasy, projection, passive aggression, acting out).
- Level III – neurotic defenses (intellectualization, reaction formation, dissociation, displacement, repression).
- Level IV – mature defenses (humor, sublimation, suppression, altruism, anticipation).

Group psychotherapy is an ideal setting for clients to learn about their **patterned responses to stress, threat, confusion, anxiety, and intimacy**, to witness the impact of their **current coping strategies and defense styles**, to learn from other members' approaches, and to practice new strategies. For instance, through ongoing participation in group, someone could move from a pattern of passive aggressive communication to becoming more clearly assertive in expressing one's feelings and needs.

Self Psychology and Group Psychotherapy

Heinz Kohut is generally regarded as the founder of self psychology, though some historians point out that Heinz Hartman proposed some similar ideas decades earlier. Self psychology focuses on the development of the emotional self and the recognition of **varied "self states"** that occur within oneself. Emphasis is placed upon identity, meaning, ideals, and self-expression. Being empathically responsive is regarded as a core part of the therapist's role, in contrast to a more traditionally neutral and opaque style.

Self psychology group approaches focus on the manifestations of maladaptive self-states and provide opportunities to increase awareness of and effect changes in **self-esteem** and **self-agency**. The **development of a cohesive self**, a primary therapeutic aim, is conceptualized along three axes:

- **Grandiosity axis** refers to the capacity to develop and maintain a positive and stable sense of self worth, assertiveness, ambition, and aliveness. Therapeutic work aims to become free from one's own internalized overly critical and punitive elements that drive defensive and compensatory needs to unrealistically idealize self.
- **Idealization axis** refers to the ability to form and maintain healthy and strongly held goals, ideals, and values.
- **Alter ego-connectedness axis** refers to the capability to empathize and communicate with others, leading to a satisfying sense of belonging.

Modern Psychoanalytic

Modern group psycho analysis was developed by Hyman Spotnitz and Louis Ormont, among others. The modern group approach embraces many classical Freudian conceptualizations including Eros (the life instinct), Thanatos (the death drive), repetition compulsion, cathartic discharge, and defense mechanisms. Similar to self psychology, a modern psycho analytic approach also examine narcissism or self-concept to help individuals develop (or maintain) accurate and adaptive self-perceptions and constructive relationships. **Examining resistances and particularly, compliance, defiance, and cooperation with the set of agreements known as the group contract** (cf. Chapter 6) are seen as important windows into the members' inner worlds.

Techniques and therapeutic processes associated with Modern Analytic group theory include:

- **Progressive communication:** constructive building upon interpersonal messages and not getting stuck in repetitive relational patterns or impasses.
- **Bridging:** encouraging members to talk directly to each other.
- Focus on **immediacy** of relationships between members with a full range of feelings.
- **Emotional insulation** helps members not get overly wounded in the lively exchanges in the group.

Interpersonal Group Psychotherapy

Drawing on the work of Harry Stack Sullivan, the interpersonal approach is among the most prominent in psychodynamic group work. While the traditional ideas of the unconscious, transference, **parataxic distortions**, repetitions, and relationship styles are at the forefront, Sullivan also placed emphasis on the innate desire to be close with others and have their approval. For Sullivan, the self was created in and exists primarily in the relational sphere. Irvin Yalom extended many of these ideas in his widely utilized editions of *The Theory and Practice of Group Psychotherapy*, hallmarks of which include:

- Here-and-now focus.
- Group as a social microcosm.
- Adoption and application of the framework of Interpersonal psychotherapy to the group, with primary foci on interpersonal disputes (such as unmet expectations), role transitions (entailing changes in primary roles), grief (emotional reactions to loss), and interpersonal deficits (such as poor communication skills).

Yalom's approach of exploring processes that emerge in the here-and-now of the group has become deeply ingrained within the contemporary practice of group psychotherapy. Also relying upon an interpersonal perspective but using more highly structured methods and focusing more on symptom reduction and skill building are the Interpersonal Group Psychotherapy (IGP) approaches developed by Myrna Weissman, Roy Mackenzie, and others that have amassed a substantial positive empirical record for depression, grief, anxiety, and eating disorders. (Burlingame, Strauss, & Joyce, 2013). Often this approach focuses on:

- grief
- interpersonal or role disputes
- role transitions
- and interpersonal sensitivity or deficits.

Relational Group Psychotherapy

In the early part of the last century, Sabrina Spielrein laid the groundwork for what was to become relational psychoanalysis as elucidated by Stephen Mitchell, Nancy Chodorow, and others. In actual practice many contemporary group leaders utilize some relational ideas and techniques in their work. Central tenets include:

- The impact of early relational experiences on personality and development.
- The inevitable subjectivity of therapist and group members.
- The value of authenticity in interpersonal relationships.
- The impact of the therapist's personality and behavior on the group; the therapist is not regarded as a "blank screen."
- Behavior can be understood from many invariably incomplete paradigms.
- An unfolding, less structured approach.
- Personal phenomenological examinations are valued.
- Curiosity is fostered within the group by focusing on: what is occurring; why is it occurring; and its impact on everyone.

Group members are seen as enacting early life patterns, regarded as both transference dynamics, but also as real relationship dynamics. As such, relational leaders also see themselves as real people with strengths and limitations who are seeking to know, understand and help clients. Both the leader and members are encouraged to be authentic, and the leader at times is encouraged to share personal experience in a direct and clear manner without the artifice of being overly technique oriented. The leader is not seen as the sole generator of wisdom and will often ask the group for their views and input into what is occurring.

Summary of the Psychodynamic Group Models

All psychodynamic groups work from a framework of unconscious beliefs, conflicts and motivations, transference enactments, dynamic relational patterns and defense strategies. Many schools place emphasis on different areas, and may use different techniques. In current practice, few leaders adhere strictly to even their own foundational theory,

and most psychodynamic group therapists will use a variety of approaches, an eclectic approach, to meet the needs of their clients.

While CBT groups have a very strong empirical lineage that shows significant changes in symptoms through their varied protocols, psychodynamic approaches have focused more on theory development, technical interventions, and clinical work, although empirical evidence is beginning to emerge (cf. Lorentzen et al., 2015).

Recommended Resources

Bion, W. (1961). *Experiences in groups and other papers*. London: Tavistock.

Rutan, J. S., Stone, W. N., & Shay, J. J. (2014). *Psychodynamic group psychotherapy*. New York: Guilford Press.

Klein, R. H., Bernard, H. S. & Singer, D. L. (Eds.) (1992). *Handbook of contemporary group psychotherapy: Contributions from object relations, self psychology, and social systems theories*, 27–54. Madison, CT: International University Press.

Kleinberg, J. L. (2015). *The Wiley-Blackwell handbook of group psychotherapy*. New York: Wiley.

Lorentzen, S., Fjeldstad, A., Ruud, T., Marble, A., Klungsøyr, O., Ulberg, R., & Høglend, P. A. (2015). The effectiveness of short-and long-term psychodynamic group psychotherapy on self-concept: Three years follow-up of a randomized clinical trial. *International Journal of Group Psychotherapy*, 65(3), 362–385.

Vaillant, G. E., Bond, M., & Vaillant, C. O. (1986). An empirically validated hierarchy of defense mechanisms. *Archives of General Psychiatry*, 43(8), 786–794.

Humanistic/Existential/Transpersonal Group Psychotherapy

Humanistic, existential, and transpersonal approaches to group work are distinct from either psychoanalytic or CBT traditions, primarily in their views about human nature, case conceptualization, and treatment goals. These traditions value the qualities of group leader presence and warmth, the importance of a client-focused agenda, the need for understanding clients holistically beyond symptoms, and working towards their personal growth and potential.

For the humanistic tradition, the **principles of unconditional positive regard, personal growth, and authenticity**, associated with the work of Carl Rogers are valued.

Yalom (1980) built upon existential philosophy to develop a therapy that addresses such themes as the inevitability of death, limitedness, existential isolation or solitude, meaning versus meaninglessness, and freedom and its consequent responsibility. Through deeply exploring these realms one can move towards the "good life" of choice, self-mastery, meaning, and connectedness.

The transpersonal tradition associated with Abraham Maslow focuses on human potential and spirituality in the group process. Some transpersonal group therapists draw from spiritual healing traditions in a manner that can been seen as a tribute to the wisdom in communal healing practices by some, but criticized as cultural appropriation by others.

Psychoeducational Groups

Starting with Pratt's initial group classes, psychoeduational approaches have a long and rich history as a group modality. While all therapy groups entail new learning as an important therapeutic goal, psychoeducation groups place significant emphasis on an educational component. As such, thousands of psychoeducation groups are conducted every day, not just in mental health settings, but also in government agencies, businesses, universities, military, and non-profit sectors. Psychoeducational groups focus on:

- New learning, often about new coping strategies.
- Providing support, fostering connections and reducing isolation.
- Expressing emotions in a safe place.
- Enhancing self agency.
- Increasing hope and reduction in symptoms (i.e., anxiety, depression, substance abuse).
- Providing support and education for family members and significant others.

Psychoeducational groups are currently employed in innumerable clinical situations, including:

- Medical illness education and support (cancer, HIV, ALS, and other diseases).
- Psychiatric disorders including anxiety, depression, bipolar disorder, schizophrenia, eating disorders, and relapse prevention.
- Quality of life improvement, including stress reduction, vocation exploration, anger management, life transitions such as retirement and divorce.
- Substance use disorders and addictions, including smoking cessation, overeating and dieting, and pathological gambling. Currently this approach is widely utilized in prevention programs of all types.

Nina Brown (2011) organized the **competencies** for leading such groups in her **KASST** model:

- **Knowledge** includes all the group leadership competencies of understanding group dynamics, stages of group development, ethics, instructional methods, learning theories and a **high level of expertise about the topics** being examined.
- **Art** comes from the leader's self knowledge, presence, warmth, and attunement to members.
- **Science** refers to the ability to plan, structure and organize the curriculum with clarity, accuracy and objectivity, as well as to evaluate clients' strengths, needs, and progress.
- **Skills** refer to proficiencies both in **group leadership** and in **teaching.**

  - Group leadership skills are comprised of monitoring tension levels, group pacing, conflict management and resolution, and the use of process commentary.
  - Teaching entails using a variety of educational approaches that match members' learning styles and clear communication skills.

- **Techniques** include leading exercises, role-plays, and group discussions and the effective use of teaching materials such as hand-outs, video and homework.

While psychoeducational approaches often stand on their own, they are also often incorporated into other group treatment models. Many cognitive behavioral groups utilize the strategies of psychoeducation at the beginning of the group and throughout the treatment.

Research into psychoeducational groups has generally been very positive across populations.

Recommended Resources

Brown, N. W., (2011). *Psychoeducational groups: Process and practice*. London: Routledge Taylor & Francis Group.

Yalom, I. D. (1980). *Existential psychotherapy* (Vol. 1). New York: Basic Books.

Systems-Centered Groups

Developed by Yvonne Agazarian, systems-centered work is a multifaceted integrative approach to group psychotherapy, based in the theory of living human systems. Postulates include:

- Human systems develop progressively from simple to increasingly complex organizations through the integration of information.
- Human systems can be as small as one individual or couple and as large as a group or an organization and theoretical and therapeutic principles apply equally to all systems.
- Psychotherapy groups, like all human systems, are energy organizing, self correcting, and goal oriented.
- Communications and information exchange within systems can contain the "noise" of contradiction, ambiguities, and redundancies that impede development and jeopardize survival.
- Isomorphy refers to the idea of a hierarchy of interrelated systems (from subsystem to system to suprasystem) that share similar structural and functional properties; changes that occur at one level induce similar changes at other levels in the hierarchy.

Functional subgrouping is a core systems-centered technique that helps members explore similarities and differences among themselves beyond the obvious or stereotypical. The **group's work is to explore, identify and integrate differences of attitudes, beliefs, needs and feelings within the group,** as opposed to ignoring, avoiding, or attempting to directly change the views of others.

Systems-centered group therapy is an integrative approach that addresses common emotional experiences (sadness, anger, masochism), coping strategies and relational patterns. The combination of thinking and reflection, emotional awareness and experiences, and trying new skills promotes a thorough examination and reworking of its group members' patterns. The leader is often fairly directive and the initial group meetings have higher levels of structure.

Exercise

As a group leader, what dimension of therapeutic change do you most focus on:
Uncovering and gaining of insight and understanding (Psychodynamic)
Changing behavior (Behavioral)
Modifying thinking patterns (Cognitive)
Learning new concepts and coping strategies (Psychoeducation)
Other change mechanisms?

Exercise

What approach do you think fits best with your current populations?
Do you think certain approaches fit your personality and leadership style better than others?

Recommended Resources

Agazarian, Y. (2004). *System-centered therapy for groups* (2nd ed.). New York: Guilford Press.
Gantt, S. P., & Agazarian, Y. M. (2010). Developing the group mind through functional subgrouping: Linking systems-centered training (SCT) and Interpersonal Neurobiology. *International Journal of Group Psychotherapy*, 60(4), 515–544.

Recent Developments in Contemporary Groups

Social Justice

Social Justice is an emerging movement that promotes (or advocates for) fair distribution of resources and opportunities across diverse populations within a community or a nation and throughout the world. With its roots in political theory and social movements, including **civil rights, feminism, and multicultural and diversity perspectives,** social justice groups take a societal view to help its members see the multifaceted reasons for their struggles including oppression and marginalization (Ribeiro & Turner, 2017). **Advocacy and empowerment** are part of the group treatment goals actualized through connecting members with resources and supporting the members in taking proactive steps (Singh, Merchant, Skudrzyk, & Ingene, 2012). Social justice group leaders are often skeptical of diagnosis as this locates the challenge strictly within the individual as opposed to destructive and inequitable forces in society. In this tradition, group leaders are often involved in making changes in community and national issues toward more justice and greater opportunity for all. Therapists are increasingly encouraged to adopt the active role of clinician/advocate to best serve their clients, and to create a world of more understanding and justice.

Recommended Resources

Chen, E. C., Budianto, L., & Wong, K. (2010). Professional school counselors as social justice advocates for undocumented immigrant students in group work. *The Journal for Specialists in Group Work, 35*(3), 255–261.

MacNair-Semands, R. R. (2007). Attending to the spirit of social justice as an ethical approach in group therapy. *International Journal of Group Psychotherapy, 57*(1), 61–66.

Ribeiro, M. D., & Turner, M. M. (2017). Racial and social justice implications on the practice of group psychotherapy. In M. D. Ribeiro, J. Gross, & M. M. Turner (Eds.), *The college counselor's guide to group psychotherapy, 36–55.* New York: Routledge.

Singh, A. A., Merchant, N., Skudrzyk, B., & Ingene, D. (2012). Association for Specialists in Group Work: Multicultural and Social Justice Competence Principles for Group Workers. *The Journal for Specialists in Group Work, 37*(4), 312–325.

Sullivan, N., Mitchell, L., Goodman, D., Lang, N. C., & Mesbur, E. S. (2013). *Social work with groups: Social justice through personal, community, and societal change.* London: Routledge.

Harm Reduction Groups

While groups are the most widely utilized form of therapy for substance abuse, many clients show minimal change with existing models. Based on the client driven models of needle exchange programs in Europe in the 1980s, substance abuse severity and harm are seen on a continuum. While sobriety may be an ultimate goal, decreasing the risks involved in substance use may be an initial goal. Any treatment model that does not require complete abstinence could fall under the harm reduction umbrella. Some basic principles of the harm reduction group culture include:

- Acceptance of where individuals are on the path to recovery and change.
- Respect for diversity in all its forms.
- Client driven topics.
- Influenced by Motivational Interviewing and other client centered approaches.
- Research oriented.

Recommended Resource

Little, J., Hodari, K., Lavender, J., & Berg, A. (2008). Come as you are: Harm reduction drop-in groups for multi-diagnosed drug users. *Journal of Groups in Addiction and Recovery, 3*(3–4), 161–192.

Spirituality Informed Group Psychotherapy

A tension can exist between spirituality and psychological science. For clinicians, spirituality can be seen as either inextricably woven into the fabric of one's life or outside the focus of psychotherapy and better addressed by clergy. In addition to spiritual study groups, many faiths use groups to address matters ranging from couple and family counseling to bereavement. All group leaders and members carry with them beliefs about life purpose, ethical behavior, and cosmology often derived from their spiritual backgrounds. For many individuals, spirituality and mental distress are seen as deeply interrelated. Group leaders need to be familiar with many orientations and stay cognizant of how their beliefs could impact their groups, as well as of their group members' views about healing and life meaning. Some contemporary clinicians who focus on topics of compassion, empathy, hope, forgiveness and transformation increasingly incorporate spiritual elements into their work.

Recommended Resource

Abernethy, A. D. (2012). A spiritually informed approach to group psychotherapy. In J. L. Kleinberg (Ed.), *The Wiley-Blackwell handbook of group psychotherapy*, 681–705. Chichester: John Wiley & Sons.

Mindfulness Based Group Therapies

Over the last twenty years mindfulness based therapy and group therapies have exploded in theory and practice. By incorporating principles of Eastern philosophies, particularly Buddhism, the popularity and empirical support for these modalities continues to grow. Kabat-Zinn (1994) provided an initial popular definition of the essential work as "**paying attention in a particular way: on purpose, in the present moment and non-judgmentally**" (p. 4).

Dialectical Behavioral Therapy (DBT)

Dialectical Behavioral Therapy (DBT) has become one of the most diligently researched and empirically supported treatments for an increasing number of psychological challenges, particularly self-harming behaviors, suicidal and para-suicidal ideation, self-regulation, and Borderline Personality Disorder. DBT focuses on four primary skills:

- **Mindfulness**: practicing becoming fully aware in the present moment.
- **Distress Tolerance**: developing increasing tolerance for stress and anxiety.
- **Interpersonal Effectiveness**: maintaining self-respect and respect for others in relationship while asking for what you want.
- **Emotional Regulation**: adaptively modulating emotions.

In DBT groups there is a hierarchy of treatment targets.

- **Life-threatening behaviors**: including self-injury, suicidal ideation or plans.
- **Therapy-interfering behaviors**: including irregular attendance and not collaborating in working towards goals.
- **Quality of life behaviors**: include behaviors that interfere with having improved psychological functioning (e.g. substance abuse, poor self care), relationship difficulties (e.g. cut-offs, fighting), and financial or housing crises.

- **Skills acquisition:** learning and practicing new behaviors that will help clients attain their goals.

The DBT group typically includes elements of:

- A brief mindfulness exercise, a check in, and review of the last session.
- Teaching and practicing a new coping skill (such as effective communication).
- Group discussion and/or practice of a new skill and how it may be used in the coming week.

Recommended Resources

Kabat-Zinn, J. (1994). *Wherever you go, there you are: Mindfulness meditation in everyday life*. New York: Hyperion.

Linehan, M. M., & Wilks, C. R. (2015). The course and evolution of dialectical behavior therapy. *American Journal of Psychotherapy, 69*(2), 97–110.

Linehan, M. (2012). Back from the Edge. Available at www.youtube.com/watch?v=967Ckat7f98

Mindfulness Based Stress Reduction

Mindfulness based stress reduction (MBSR), usually conducted in groups, is not designed to treat any specific psychiatric disorders, but rather to increase skills related to stress management. **MBSR** utilizes such techniques as mindfulness meditation, body scanning and simple yoga postures. There is also group discussion, homework, and daily practice outside the group. Members build cohesion through shared activities and sharing of stressful experiences and through support of each other in changing unhelpful coping behaviors. The research has been very positive towards the goal of decreased stress, and is also promising for other issues including improved health, relational satisfaction and sense of self and meaning.

Recommended Resources

Kabat-Zinn, J. (2011). Some reflections on the origins of MBSR, skillful means, and the trouble with maps. *Contemporary Buddhism, 12*(1), 281–306.

Imel, Z., Baldwin, S., Bonus, K., & MacCoon, D. (2008). Beyond the individual: Group effects in mindfulness-based stress reduction. *Psychotherapy Research, 18*(6), 735–742.

Mindfulness Based Cognitive Therapy (MBCT)

MBCT, a promising evidence-based approach (cf. Piet & Hougaard, 2011) uses the group format to address anxiety and depressive symptoms. This time-limited, structured program encourages group members' increasing awareness of and focus on the present moment through the use of mindfulness exercises, from yoga to mindful eating. This is combined with protocols from CBT groups, such as recognizing and challenging distorted beliefs, and behavioral approaches such as increasing exercise, proper nutrition, and increased sleep hygiene.

Recommended Resource

Piet, J. & Hougaard, E. (2011). The effect of mindfulness-based cognitive therapy for prevention of relapse in recurrent major depressive disorder: A systematic review and meta-analysis. *Clinical Psychology Review*, *31*, 1032–1040.

Mindfulness Based Relapse Prevention

This group treatment uses exercises and discussion to increase awareness of potential triggers that could lead to substance use, destructive patterns that may lead to relapse, and automatic cognitive and behavioral responses. Goals include:

- Learning to pause before reacting to create more behavioral choice.
- Increasing ability to work with emotional and physical discomfort.
- Increasing self-compassion.
- Creating an ongoing healthy and satisfying lifestyle.

Initial studies have shown diminished cravings and sustained sobriety when compared to traditional treatments of support groups and psychoeducation (Bowen, Vieten, Witkiewitz, & Carroll, 2015).

Recommended Resource

Bowen, S., Vieten, C., Witkiewitz, K., & Carroll, H. (2015). A mindfulness-based approach to addiction. In: K.W. Brown, J. D. Creswell, & R. M. Ryan (Eds.), *Handbook of mindfulness: Theory, research, and practice*, 387–404. New York: Guilford Press.

Acceptance and Commitment Therapy (ACT)

As applied in group format, ACT has its roots in mindfulness awareness training, combined with several psychological philosophies including clinical behavioral analysis and functional contextualism. The underpinnings include:

- Developing acceptance of unwanted private experiences which are out of personal control.
- Clarifying one's values in life.
- Highlighting moments of choice to allow clients to choose new behaviors akin to their values; making a commitment towards living a valued life.

Group members generally feel empowered through the process, as they work towards clarifying what is important to them, and begin to make changes that they endorse.

Mindfulness-Informed Group Psychotherapy

Mindfulness-based therapy groups typically integrate mindfulness practices and perspectives into another therapeutic orientation (e.g. psychodynamic). What mindfulness approaches have in common is the value on group members' attending to and reporting such transient experiences as a fleeting thought, a nascent feeling, or a subtle bodily sensation. In general the mindfulness-informed group leader promotes a slowing down and paying close attention to one's phenomenological experiences and bringing them into group for further understanding and exploration.

Recommended Resources

Baer, R. A. (Ed.) (2015). *Mindfulness-based treatment approaches: Clinician's guide to evidence base and applications.* New York: Academic Press.

Chang, C., Ciliberti, A., & Kaklauskas, F. J. (2017). Mindfulness approaches for groups in college counseling centers. In M. D. Ribeiro, J. Gross, & M. M. Turner (Eds.), *The college counselor's guide to group psychotherapy,* 218–238. New York: Routledge.

Walser, R. D., & Pistorello, J. (2005). ACT in group format. In S. Hayes & K. Strosahl (Eds.), *A practical guide to acceptance and commitment therapy,* 347–372. New York: Springer Science.

Concluding Thoughts

This chapter has reviewed many currently popular and historically relevant group models. However, this or any history cannot cover every group theory. Some theories that have grown less popular over time were not covered, for example the encounter group movement of the 1960s. Others were covered only briefly to allow the student to pursue those of interest.

Upon reading this review, newer group clinicians may feel overwhelmed with the variety of choices available to them when it comes to theoretical paradigms and approaches. For many clinicians, often the agency where they work will provide the frame and training to help them become proficient in at least one style. Many clinicians will have opportunities to conduct a variety of groups ranging from psychoeducation to interpersonal process throughout their careers. **Finding a paradigm that balances personal strengths and interests with your setting and clients' needs will allow you to do your best work.**

A significant movement in group psychotherapy is integration of group models, as purely utilizing only one system may not resonate with all therapists or best serve the needs of all clients (Van Wagoner, 2012). In actual practice, many group clinicians utilize multiple models. The important innovations in recent years of multiculturalism, neuroscience, attachment theory, mindfulness, and other discoveries continue to be assimilated into various group approaches.

Another vital contemporary trend to maximize effectiveness is the marriage of research and theory. Many of the modern research based manualized treatments have already produced positive findings, but the successful administration of these treatments is enhanced with a broader clinical understanding of managing group processes and dynamics (Paquin, 2017). **Contemporary best practice approaches combine empirically supported treatment, practice guidelines, and practice-based evidence with group specific training, clinical group experience, technical flexibility, and functional skills** (Barlow, 2013; Leszcz, 2018 Miles & Paquin, 2014).

Unfortunately, tension and apprehension between clinicians and researchers has limited the cross fertilization of ideas and approaches. Fortunately, the call for more collaboration between group researchers and clinicians continues to be increasingly answered. Greene (2012) highlights that every group clinician is in fact a social scientist who needs to continuously examine and track what is working and why. While clinical observations may not be formal quantitative research, this accumulative wisdom and the hypotheses generated by them are valued and acknowledged empirical evidence (American Psychological Association, 2006). Research and practice can be mutually enhancing; substantive group research is often conceived from clinical experiences and, conversely, clinical skills can be enriched through knowledge of psychotherapy research, especially process research.

Clinical practice and research need not be divided. By familiarizing and experiencing both domains, a unique depth of knowledge and understanding can be achieved (Berman, Chapman, Nash, Kivilghan, & Paquin, 2017). In reality both enterprises share many understandings of the complexity of group work including the therapeutic value of (Bernard et al., 2008; Leszcz, 2018:

- Empathic attunement.
- Interpersonal verbal interaction and appropriate use of feedback.
- Cohesion.

The contemporary group therapist should embrace both the enduring and emerging canon of group psychotherapy theory with the growing catalog of vital group psychotherapy and group dynamics research. While most individuals will focus in one area, sharing and integrating the wisdom of each domain will bring forth the most effective treatment (Berman, Chapman, Nash, Kivlighan, & Paquin, 2017). Luckily, for most of us, our careers will provide connections with a variety of peers, supervisors, and on-going trainings that will expand and inform our work, and likely ourselves.

Recommended Resources

American Psychological Association Presidential Task Force on Evidence Based-Practice in Psychology. (2006). Evidence-based practice in psychology. *American Psychologist*, 61, 271–285.

Barlow, S. (2013). *Specialty competencies in group psychology*. Oxford: Oxford University Press.

Barlow, S., Burlingame, G. M., Greene, L. R., Joyce, A., Kaklauskas, F., Kinley, J., Klein, R. H., Kobos, J. C., Leszcz, M., MacNair-Semands, R., Paquin, J. D., Tasca, G. A., Whittingham, M., & Feirman, D. (2015). Evidence-based practice in group psychotherapy [American Group Psychotherapy Association Science to Service Task Force web document]. Available at www.agpa.org/home/practice-resources/evidence-based-practice-in-group-psychotherapy.

Berman, M. I., Chapman, N., Nash, B., Kivlighan, D. M., & Paquin, J. D. (2017). Sharing wisdom: Challenges, benefits, and developmental path to becoming a successful therapist-researcher. *Counselling Psychology Quarterly*, *30*(3): 1–21.

Bernard, H., Burlingame, G., Flores, P., Greene, L., Joyce, A., Kobos, J. C., Leszcz, M., MacNair-Semands, R. R., Piper, W., Slocum McEneaney, A. M., Feirman, D. (2008). Clinical practice guidelines for group psychotherapy. *International Journal of Group Psychotherapy*, *58*, 455–542.

Greene, L. R. (2012). Group therapist as social scientist, with special reference to the psychodynamically oriented psychotherapist. *American Psychologist*, *67* (6), 477.

Miles, J. R., & Paquin, J. D. (2014). Best practices in group counseling and psychotherapy research. In J. L. DeLucia-Waack, C. R. Kalodner, & M. T. Riva, (Eds.), *The handbook of group counseling and psychotherapy 2nd Edition*, [178–192]. Thousand Oaks, CA: Sage.

Leszcz, M. (2017). A relational approach to evidence-based group psychotherapy (audio recording), *Louis R. Ormont lecture*. American Group Psychotherapy Association, New York.

Leszcz, M. (2018). The evidence-based group psychotherapist. *Psychoanalytic Inquiry*, *38*, 285–298.

Leszcz, M., & Kobos, J. C. (2008). Evidence based group psychotherapy: Using AGPA's practice guidelines to enhance clinical effectiveness. *Journal of Clinical Psychology*, *64*(11), 1238–1260.

Paquin, J. D. (2017). Delivering the treatment so that the therapy occurs: Enhancing the effectiveness of time-limited, manualized group treatments. *International Journal of Group Psychotherapy*, *67* (sup1), S141–S153.

Van Wagoner, S. L. (2012). From empathically immersed inquiry to discrete intervention: Are there limits to theoretical purity?. In J. L. Kleinberg (Ed.), *The Wiley-Blackwell handbook of group psychotherapy* [249–270]. New York: Wiley.

2 Towards Multicultural and Diversity Proficiency as a Group Psychotherapist

Francis J. Kaklauskas and Reginald Nettles

Regardless of how we compose our group membership (diagnosis, cultural backgrounds, age, etc.) inevitably our members will **share some similarities** and also mirror some **important differences. The ability for group therapists to effectively, inclusively, and empathically work with individuals from diverse backgrounds is requisite for our field.** This chapter aims to introduce many foundational ideas regarding diversity and multicultural approaches in group psychotherapy.

Historical Bias and Concerns

Collective healing practices to address the emotional needs of community members can be found across cultures and across time, such as African and Native American spiritual ceremonies and rituals, Taoist and Buddhist group practices in Asia, and early Greek theater. While some have proposed that the roots of contemporary group psychotherapy hark back to these traditions, most see its development as having been influenced primarily by the Judeo-Christian, White–European, heterocentric, gender binary, and patriarchal traditions of the Western world. To the extent this latter argument is valid, the **awareness and acknowledgment of these powerful though often unacknowledged Western influences and their potential biases are essential for developing group psychotherapy models that encompass and serve our diverse world citizenship** (Cone-Uemura & Bentley, 2017; Ribeiro & Turner, 2017).

Solomon (2013), in his conversations with Rwandan people, offers a clinical vignette illustrating how insensitivity to cultural differences on the part of mental health providers adversely affects the work:

> We had a lot of trouble with western mental health workers who came here immediately after the genocide . . . They came and their practice did not involve being outside in the sun where you begin to feel better, there was no music or drumming to get your blood flowing again, there was no sense that everyone had taken the day off so that the entire community could come together to try to lift you up and bring you back to joy, there was no acknowledgement of the depression as something invasive and external that could actually be cast out again. Instead they would take people one at a time into these dingy little rooms and have them sit around for an hour or so and talk about bad things that had happened to them. We had to ask them to leave.

In our increasingly globalized world, some have criticized traditional forms of counseling as an attempt to continue colonization power by applying the norms and values of European heritage onto culturally different and marginalized groups (Gorski & Goodman, 2015). While the group psychotherapy model has been enthusiastically adopted by some health practitioners in other cultures, it remains important that we **question whether it has universal application** or whether **significant culture-specific adaptations** need to be made.

These questions are particularly salient as certain populations, such as ethnic minorities, rural residents, and lower socioeconomic classes may underutilize psychotherapy services because of feeling misunderstood; **enhancing the multicultural competence of providers may increase utilization by disadvantaged populations** (Leong, Comas-Díaz, Nagayama Hall, McLoyd, & Trimble, 2014; Leong & Kalibatseva, 2011; Sue, Gallardo, & Neville, 2013).

Recommended Resources

Cone-Uemura, K., & Bentley, E. S. (2017). Multicultural/diversity issues in groups. In M. D. Ribeiro, J. Gross, & M. M. Turner (Eds.) *The college counselor's guide to group psychotherapy* (pp. 21–35). New York: Routledge.

Gorski, P. C., & Goodman, R. D. (2015). Introduction: Toward a decolonized multicultural counseling and psychology. In R. Goodman & P. C. Gorski (Eds.) *Decolonizing "multicultural" counseling through social justice* (pp. 1–10). New York: Springer.

Leong, F. T. L., Comas-Díaz, L. E., Nagayama Hall, G. C., McLoyd, V. C., & Trimble, J. E. (2014). *APA handbook of multicultural psychology*. Washington, DC: American Psychological Association.

Leong, F. T., & Kalibatseva, Z. (2011). Cross-cultural barriers to mental health services in the United States. *Cerebrum, 5*, 2011.

Ribeiro, M. D., & Turner, M. M. (2017). Racial and social justice implications on the practice of group psychotherapy. In M. D. Ribeiro, J. Gross, & M. M. Turner (Eds.) *The college counselor's guide to group psychotherapy* (pp. 36–55). New York: Routledge.

Solomon, A. (2013). *Depression: The secret we share*. [Video file] Retrieved from: https://www.ted.com/talks/andrew_solomon_depression_the_secret_we_share

Sue, D. W., Gallardo, M. E., & Neville, H. A. (2013). *Case studies in multicultural counseling and therapy*. Hoboken, NJ: Wiley.

Defining Culture and Multiculturalism

Our thoughts, feelings, and behaviors are shaped and reinforced by our embedding culture, a concept that encompasses (American Psychological Association, 2003) "belief systems and value orientations that influence customs, norms, practices, and social institutions, including psychological processes (language, care taking practices, media, educational systems) and organizations."

While there is no universal agreement regarding the definitions of diversity and multiculturalism, the American Psychological Association (2003) provides one useful listing that encompasses most of the dimensions along which cultures create perceived differences among people:

- Race.
- Ethnicity.
- Language.
- Sexual Orientation.
- Gender.
- Age.
- Disability.
- Class Status.
- Education.
- Religious/Spiritual Orientation.

Just as each group member brings ingrained experiences of childhood and family into the group, each member also brings a unique cultural heritage. **Each member may have beliefs, values, and customs that may be very different from our own, from the other group members, and from the culture of the organization that embeds the group.**

In the early years, the need for multicultural awareness in psychotherapy usually meant raising the consciousness of psychotherapists from the dominant cultural backgrounds to be more sensitive and effective when working with marginalized or minority individuals (Nettles & Balter, 2012). Recent efforts by the international and indigenous psychological movements are working towards more **globalization of psychological experiences** and not just importing of Western psychological ideas into other cultures or viewing other cultures through Western perspectives (Bullock, 2012). Alternative images and paradigms need to be represented if psychotherapy is to truly be an inclusive and diverse enterprise. Clinicians from both dominant and non-dominant cultures need to acquire skills in working with cultural differences and the potential conflicts they can stir (Chang-Caffaro & Caffaro, 2018). As leaders we cannot allow our groups to ignore or miss opportunities to explore and understand differences for the sake of psychotherapy effectiveness and our members' dignity and growth.

Exercise

In what ways might you feel like or be treated like an "other" in this field of group psychotherapy?

Recommended Resources

American Psychological Association (2003). Guidelines on multicultural education, training, research, practice and organizational change for psychologists. *American Psychologist, 58*, 377–402.

American Psychological Association (2015). Guidelines for psychological practice with transgender and gender nonconforming people. Retrieved from www.apa.org/practice/guidelines/transgender.pdf

American Psychological Association (2017). Multicultural guidelines: An ecological approach to context, identity, and intersectionality, 2017. Retrieved from http://www.apa.org/about/policy/multicultural-guidelines.pdf

Bullock, M. (2012). International psychology. In D. K. Freedheim & B. Weiner (Eds.) *Handbook of psychology: History of psychology (2nd ed.)* (pp. 562–596). Hoboken, NJ: Wiley.

Chang-Caffaro, S., & Caffaro, J. (2018). Differences that make a difference: Diversity and the process group leader. *International Journal of Group Psychotherapy, 68*, 483–497.

Nettles, R., & Balter, R. (Eds.). (2012). *Multiple minority identities: Applications for practice, research, and training.* New York: Springer.

Stereotypes

Stereotypes are social constructions that entail the oversimplification and overgeneralization of individuals based on specific attributes and can lead to stigmatization, disenfranchisement, prejudice and discrimination. Group participation can stir the enactment of these stereotypes giving rise to a range of emotional, even traumatic, reactions (cf. Haen & Thomas, 2018; Zaharopoulos & Chen, 2018). At the same time, however, the group can provide unique opportunities to deconstruct and rework these cultural stereotypes (Stevens & Abernethy, 2018).

The most common form of stereotyping is based on race and **the impact of race dynamics, racial inequalities, and racial stereotyping needs to be of central awareness for the multiculturally proficient group therapist.** Minimizing or avoiding the exploration of the impact of race on clients' experience will **limit connections, collaboration, understanding, and growth.** Exploration of race and its impact is essential in psychotherapy given our racially divided society and world (Holmes, 2012).

Gender identity and expression are also subject to discrimination and prejudice. The subjugation of women and transgender individuals throughout history continues currently, as seen in many dimensions including differential earnings and positions of leadership. While the earliest psychological theorists, including Freud and Jung, felt that all individuals had both masculine and feminine elements, the experiences of women, transgender, queer, intersex, and individuals who do not fit traditional binary gender roles or appearance have been marked by marginalization, prejudice, and disenfranchisement. Sensitivity to these issues is required for diversity proficiency as group psychotherapists (American Psychological Association, 2015; Haldeman, 2012).

In addition to race and gender, a stereotyping of the "other" can occur with such visible differences as age, appearance (height, weight, hair, etc.), religious garments, accents, but also concerning differences not so readily apparent such as:

- Sexual orientation.
- Disability.
- Acculturation.
- Social class.
- Medical conditions.
- Social support networks.
- Education level and cognitive ability.

Recently, the emerging movement of neurodiversity is gaining more attention. Neurodiversity respects and appreciates differences in neurological functioning and promotes the fair and just treatment of those who learn, communicate, and experience the world differently from the majority in the dominant culture. While this term originated in the autism rights movement, neurodiversity has expanded to include those with major mental illness diagnosis, learning challenges, and other neurological differences. Like all marginalized individuals, neurodiverse individuals can experience prejudice, devaluing of their potential contributions and infringement of their rights and freedom.

The multicultural group therapist works to become familiar with and sensitive to a broad range of **experiences of difference** that impact our clients. **Mental health and wellness cannot be assessed outside of a social context and clients must be understood within the fabric of their person-specific cultural experiences.**

One of the unique challenges of group therapy leadership is that group members will also present stereotypes and biases in their reactions to each other. **Exploring biases, privilege, unconscious assumptions and stereotypes pro-actively, regularly, and in the moment as they manifest will help all members feel more secure in this already challenging environment of group therapy.** The group leader works to create an environment where group members understand that all thoughts, feelings, and reactions can be talked about safely if members avoid attacking each other and are invested in the understanding of the other members' experiences. If a group member feels harmed by another group member or leader's comments, the group needs to find a way to work through the rupture constructively with the hope that harm can be repaired.

Berg-Cross and So (2011) suggest that therapists ask themselves two questions:

- Do I understand my own cultural baggage?
- Do I understand my clients' cultural baggage?

The answers should not be seen as static, but rather as an unfolding in the group as we and the members develop deeper and more encompassing understandings. Lou Ormont was known to say that a vital part of the work in group is the sharing of life stories. These narratives should focus on the impact of **cultural heritage as much as family, relational or vocational history.** But **exploring the role of culture and cultural diversity on one's identity needs to unfold in a climate of trust and safety** (Halderman, 2011. **Often, our members' cultural wounds, biases and defensive reactions have evoked relational discord and shame, and the group therapist needs to strike a delicate balance between maintaining group trust and safety and encouraging the addressing of sensitive and painful issues.** The goal is an unpacking and providing of support for members' deepening understanding and appreciating of their cultural histories, while avoiding re-wounding, re-traumatization, and overwhelming feelings of shame. Often the leader will need to be the primary regulating and containing force, drawing on established skills of moderating tension, protecting a scapegoat, expanding subgroup exploration, and providing psychoeducation information as needed.

Group leaders can also create a culture in which the spirit of being an *ally* is valued. The role of an ally is to assist, support, and advocate for another person who is being misunderstood, mistreated, or marginalized. Mizock and Page (2016) suggest allies can be helpful through having:

- Privilege awareness.
- Providing support and resourses.
- Power sensitivity.

In groups, an ally can make a misunderstood member or subgroup be more accurately known and feel protected. For instance, a male member can support a transgender individual by simply being aware of the privilege of his gender identity and helping a group move beyond binary gender terminology and concepts. Or when white members confront racial stereotyping by talking about the impact their skin privilege has had on their racial identity. **As leaders, we want to promote a group culture where members are invested in serving as allies to one another, where the topic of cultural identity is valued and safely explored, and where group events can be understood or interpreted in more than one way and not just from the dominant cultural paradigm.**

Exercise

How do you foster constructive and safe-enough multicultural exploration in your groups?

Recommended Resources

American Psychological Association. (2003). Guidelines on multicultural education, training, research, practice, and organizational change for psychologists. *American Psychologist, 58,* 377–402.

American Psychological Association. (2015). Guidelines for psychological practice with transgender and gender nonconforming people. *American Psychologist, 70* (9), 832–864.

Berg-Cross, L., & So, D. (2011). The start of a new era: Evidence-based multicultural therapies. *The Register Report, 37,* 8–15. [Web page]. Retrieved from www.nationalregister.org/pub/the-national-register-report-pub/the-register-report-fall-2011/evidence-based-multicultural-therapies-the-start-of-a-new-era

Haen, C., & Thomas, N. K. (2018). Holding history: Undoing racial unconsciousness in groups. *International Journal of Group Psychotherapy, 68,* 498–520.

Haldeman, D. (2011). Diversity training: Multiple minority awareness. In Nettles, R. & Balter, R. (Eds.): *Multiple Minority Identities: Applications for Research, Practice and Training,* p. 231–247, New York: Springer.

Haldeman, D. (2012). Guidelines for psychological practice with lesbian, gay, and bisexual clients. *American Psychologist, 67*(1), 10–42.

Holmes, D. E. (2012). Multicultural competence: A practitioner-scholar's reflections on its reality and its stubborn and longstanding elusiveness. *Register Report* 1–18. Retrieved from www.nationalregister.org/pub/the-national-register-report-pub/spring-2012-issue/multicultural-competence-a-practitioner-scholars-reflections-on-its-reality-and-its-stubborn-and-longstanding-elusiveness/

Mizock, L., & Page, K. V. (2016). Evaluating the ally role: Contributions, limitations, and the activist position in counseling and psychology. *Journal for Social Action in Counseling & Psychology, 8*(1), 17–33.

Stevens F. L., & Abernethy, A. D. (2018). Neuroscience and racism: The power of groups for overcoming implicit bias, *International Journal of Group Psychotherapy*, 68, 561–584.

Zaharopoulos, M., & Chen, E. C. (2018). Racial-cultural events in group therapy as perceived by group therapists, *International Journal of Group Psychotherapy*, 68(4), 629–653.

Tripartite Multicultural Model

The tripartite multicultural model (Sue et al., 1982) of awareness, knowledge, and skills has become a focal point of advancement endorsed by many professional organizations and training institutions (Chu, Leino, Pflum, & Sue, 2016; Jun, 2018; Sue, Arredondo, & McDavis, 1992).

- **Awareness** stresses the essential need for psychotherapists to explore their own worldviews and biases, and to recognize that these are deeply embedded in our **thinking, feelings, and clinical work**.
- **Knowledge** highlights the various cultural factors that influence the counseling process and therapist-client interactions including **cultural identity, cultural roles, power differentials, and norms of communication**.
- **Skills** refer to therapists' ability to develop meaningful therapeutic relationships with clients from different backgrounds and provide interventions that are **culturally sensitive and effective**.

Recommended Resources

Chu, J., Leino, A., Pflum, S., & Sue, S. (2016). A model for the theoretical basis of cultural competency to guide psychotherapy. *Professional Psychology: Research and Practice*, 47(1), 18–29.

Jun, H. (2018). *Social justice, multicultural counseling, and practice: Beyond a conventional approach*. New York: Springer.

Sue, D. W., Arredondo, P., & McDavis, R. J. (1992). Multicultural counseling competencies and standards: A call to the profession. *Journal of Counseling and Development*, 70, 477–486.

Sue, D. W., Bernier, J. E., Durran, A., Feinberg, L., Pedersen, P., Smith, E. J., & Vasquez-Nuttall, E. (1982). Position paper: Cross-cultural counseling competencies. *The Counseling Psychologist*, 10, 45–52.

Knowledge about Specific Cultures

Over the last few decades there have been many published suggestions regarding how to counsel psychotherapy clients from diverse backgrounds. Generally speaking, these works outline some central elements of values, beliefs, and communication styles of specific cultures. While such guides can provide some potential insights into understanding our clients, as clinicians, we must be careful to avoid overly reductionistic, stereotypical, and universal suggestions. **Within any cultural grouping many individual differences exist, and group leaders need to be vigilant to avoid allowing group members to be stereotyped or tokenized by other members as a representative and voice for a particular experience, issue, or diversity group.**

And, to add to the complexity, individuals may identify with more than one minority group (**multiple minority identity**) and consequently can be suffering from increased and cumulative marginalization (Nettles & Balter, 2012). For instance, a Muslim, African American woman may be treated differently and experience the world differently than other non-African American women, African American men, or individuals of other faiths, as well as individuals with just two of these three marginalized identities. No one identity developmental model may fit well with the individual's experience; each individual's identity development needs to be seen as unique.

Intersectionality describes the intersecting of social identities related to oppression, domination, and discrimination. Identity is the interplay of all identities towards the whole person's unique **standpoint** of perspectives and experiences. For instance, a clinician may have familiarity working with a gay, lesbian, or transgender population but may have little awareness of how to proceed when those identities intersect with racial minority or physical disability identities. Even if one has experience or training, listening to the clients' experience remains the best way to proceed.

In the therapy group, it is best to allow our clients to identify their own ethnocultural affiliations, gender and sexual orientations, etc., using the labels that they believe fit for them. Allowing our group members to **self identify** supports their **autonomy and choice**.

Understanding and Appreciating Differences

The history of ideas, including religion, philosophy, science, and psychology, provides countless examples of **quests towards universal, nomothetic, or reductionist concepts**. Much like the search for a unified theory of physics, psychotherapists have often sought unifying principles of personality and behavior (e.g. Freud's structural theory, Skinner's operant conditioning). This perspective, however, has long been challenged by such writings as White's seminal articles *Guidelines for Black Psychologists* (1969) and *Towards a Black Psychology* (1970). In addition, the decades of influential research and theory from feminist and ethnic studies, social psychology, anthropology, and post-modernism have provided a greater appreciation and acceptance of the idea that all individuals are bound within both **personal and cultural subjectivities** (Gough & Madill, 2012). While certain aspects of human experience appear to cut across cultural and historical lines, such as strong feelings surrounding love or grief, in actuality **the specifics of our internal worlds may be as varied as there are people.**

Carol Gilligan (1977) was one of many pioneers in the **move from universal principles to greater appreciation of differences between groups of people.** She found the prevailing views of moral development to be male-dominated and created a more gender inclusive model. Since that time there have been many important **culturally specific developmental models** such as racial and bi-racial identity development, gender and sexual orientation identity development, and immigration, colonization, and acculturation processes (D'Andrea, 2014).

One of the most popular and influential **multicultural developmental models** was developed by Sue and Sue (2012). They propose that **racial and cultural identity** develops through five phases. While this model **will not fit everyone** from every group, it provides a model that may be helpful in thinking about a client's identity development:

- The **conformity** phase: identification with the dominant group often with accompanying negative feelings about one's own cultural heritage and in the ways that it differs.
- The **dissonance** stage: a challenge to this conformity belief system through experiences that lead one to question the superiority of the dominant group often through being exposed to individuals who feel pride about their non-dominant identity.
- The **resistance and immersion** stage: an increasing pulling away from the dominant view, often accompanied by anger, guilt or shame, and the developing of a predominant identification with one's own heritage.
- The **introspection** stage: an investment in trying to deeply understand what it means to be part of a specific cultural or alternative group, as defined, for example by race, social economic class, religion, gender or sexual orientation, or other aspect of diversity.
- The **integrative awareness** stage: a growing appreciation of the positive aspects of one's own culture, of the dominant culture, and of other cultures.

Recommended Resources

D'Andrea, M. (2014). Understanding racial/cultural identity development theories to promote effective multicultural group counseling. In J. L. DeLucia-Waack, C. R. Kalodner, & M. T. Riva. *Handbook of group counseling and psychotherapy (2nd ed.)* (pp. 196–208). Thousand Oaks, CA: Sage.

Gilligan, C. (1977). In a different voice: Women's conceptions of self and of morality. *Harvard Educational Review*, 47(4), 481–517.

Gough, B., & Madill, A. (2012). Subjectivity in psychological science: From problem to prospect. *Psychological Methods*, 17(3), 374–384.

Sue, D. W., & Sue, D. (2012). *Counseling the culturally diverse: Theory and practice*. Chichester: John Wiley & Sons.

White, J. L. (1969). Guidelines for Black psychologists. *The Black Scholar*, 1, 52–57.

White, J. L. (1970, August). Toward a Black psychology. *Ebony*, 25, 44–45, 48–50, 52.

Bias

Despite our best attempts to educate ourselves, we are all prone to hold **unconscious assumptions** about people from diverse cultures and may inevitably "**other**" people who are different from ourselves. These unconscious assumptions can be developed through personal experience, societal influences, mass media depictions and training orientation.

At times, we may believe that we accurately and empathically understand another's experiences based on similar experiences of our own, but in fact our understandings may be markedly **incomplete or inaccurate**. Further, behaviors that seem unusual or even pathological from the therapist's cultural experiences may have **traditional meanings** that are supported in clients' communities. Western clinicians have at times misdiagnosed individuals through lack of awareness of their cultural norms and experiences. For example, we may determine that a native American girl who experiences the ghost of her deceased father is suffering from psychosis rather than having a culturally normative spiritual experience.

While in a field where we are often relied upon to be competent, regarding multicultural competence, the best course of action is to practice with **sustained awareness, openness to feedback, and humility** (Kivlighan & Chapman, 2018).

Recommended Resource

Kivlighan, D. M. III, & Chapman, N. A. (2018). Extending the multicultural orientation (MCO) framework to group psychotherapy: A clinical illustration. *Psychotherapy, 55,* 39–44

Understanding Our Biases

Generally, the first recommended course for addressing the challenge of bias is to look deeply at our own history, values, and beliefs, including what was modeled in terms of:

- Relationships.
- Communication styles.
- Cultural roles.
- Individual versus community focus.
- Values and beliefs, including what constitutes healthy and acceptable versus pathological and unacceptable.

Often, these are so **deeply ingrained** in our thinking and reactions that we do not notice the subtleties in our biases. Honestly considering our **own cultural indoctrination** and beginning to see the strengths, limitations, and assumptions of our experiences can make room for appreciating other cultures. **Prejudicial ideas about others and ourselves form very early in life and become procedural and unconscious.**

The first step in uncovering our biases is **accepting** that we have **biases about others who are different.** Generally speaking, people feel most comfortable with individuals they identify as similar to themselves.

Several models have been created to help clinicians work to understand their views, feelings, and identities. Among the most well-known is Hays' (2016) model, as reflected in Table 2.1.

Hays (2016) recommends that clinicians deeply explore their own histories to understand the ways in which they come from a position of privilege or disadvantage. Recognizing and accepting one's **privileged or marginalized** experiences, as well as the influences of other difficult experiences (past traumas, family of origin dynamics, health or mental health challenges) and positive life circumstance (stable relationships, education, never a victim of a crime, etc.) is vital work.

Exercises

Complete the Hays' Addressing model for yourself. In what ways do you experience yourself as privileged? In what ways marginalized?

Complete this model for a client in your groups or someone else who you know. In what ways does this help you understand your own and the other person's strengths and challenges, areas of privilege and of marginalization?

Think of a behavior that may be controversial, such as using recreational drugs, marriage infidelity or carrying a concealed weapon. What is your view of this behavior – acceptable or unacceptable, normal or abnormal? Can you identify early life influences that shaped your opinion?

Table 2.1. ADDRESSING: A model of cultural influences and their relationship to the social construct of power

Cultural Characteristic	*More Power*	*Less power*
• Age and Generational Influences	• Adults	• Children, adolescents, elders
• Disability at birth (may have impacted development)	• Able-bodied, cognitive functioning intact, no sensory impairments, healthy	• Individuals with limitations or disabilities
• Disability, acquired after birth and later in life	• Able-bodied, cognitive and sensory functioning intact	• Individuals with limitations or disabilities, psychiatric conditions
• Religion	• Christian or Secular	• Muslim, Jewish, Hindu, Buddhists, Indigenous, and other minority religions
• Ethnic and Racial Identity	• Euro-American	• People of Color(Asian, Latino, African, African-American, Middle Eastern, Indigenous, other non-white or European ethnicity)
• Socioeconomic Status	• Upper Class & Middle Class (professional, educated, safe living environment with access to and ability to pay for essentials and services)	• Poor & Working Class (occupations, access to accurate information, rural or inner city)
• Sexual Orientation	• Heterosexuals	• Gay, Lesbians, Bisexuals, Transgendered, Asexual Individuals
• Indigenous Heritage	• Non-native	• Native
• Native (or national) Origin	• U.S. born	• Immigrants & Refugees
• Gender	• Men	• Women, Queer, Transgendered, Intersex, other non-male identities

---

Recommended Resource

Hays, P. A. (2016). *Addressing cultural complexities in practice: Assessment, diagnosis, and therapy (3rd ed.)*. Washington, DC: American Psychological Association.

Unpacking Privilege

Despite recent changes, people of color and other non-dominantly oriented or marginalized individuals remain underrepresented in our field (Kohout, Pate, & Maton, 2014). MacIntosh's (1989) seminal paper, *White Privilege: Unpacking the Invisible Knapsack* delineates the many societal, legal, and economic inequalities accruing from privilege. Given our typical **position of power as therapists**, clients will have feelings about what they may see as our privilege and **our awareness of our privilege**.

Therapists who are able to **acknowledge the fortunate circumstances** that allowed them to succeed into a position of prestige and power will likely be **more successful** connecting with and assisting clients from marginalized groups (Minieri, Reese, Miserocchi, & Pascale-Hague, 2015). When issues of privilege come up in the group setting, it is important for the leader to have **humility, curiosity, and non-defensive open-mindedness**. While these interactions can be emotionally charged, through such conversations group members communicate vital information about their histories and identities, the life needs that were met and missed, an understanding of their external and internal worlds, and their desires and fears in the group.

Recommended Resources

Kohout, J. L., Pate, W. E. II, & Maton, K. I. (2014). An updated profile of ethnic minority psychology: A pipeline perspective. In F. T. L. Leong, L. Comas-Díaz, G. C. Nagayama Hall, V. C. McLoyd, & J. E. Trimble (Eds.), *APA handbook of multicultural psychology, Vol. 1. Theory and research*, pp. 19–42. Washington, DC: American Psychological Association.

MacIntosh, P. (1989). White privilege: Unpacking the invisible knapsack. *Peace and Freedom*, July/August, 10–12.

Minieri, A. M., Reese, R. J., Miserocchi, K. M., & Pascale-Hague, D. (2015). Using client feedback in training of future counseling psychologists: An evidence-based and social justice practice. *Counselling Psychology Quarterly*, 28(3), 305–323.

Microaggression

Microaggressions are subtle forms of stereotyping, discrimination, and **othering** that are commonplace when individuals from different cultures interact (Sue, 2013). Pierce (1974) conceived of this term when he witnessed non-African Americans often discounting, dismissing, and subtlety insulting African Americans. Mary Rowe (1974) extended this concept to discrimination of women and currently it is used with regard to all marginalized groups. Sue (2010) has created a useful taxonomy for these types of interactions.

- **Microassault** is an obvious derogation such as ignoring, verbal slurs, and resolute discriminatory behavior. An example may be allowing group members to use racial slurs in group or to stereotype group members due to their race or sexual orientations. An example would be if two new group members joined in the same week, and the one who was of a different race than that of the other group members was ignored, while the other one of a similar race to other members was welcomed.
- **Microinsults** are exchanges that are inconsiderate and degrade a person's ethnic heritage or group identity. An example would be group members asking a Russian immigrant if they like vodka as an introduction or initially trying to engage a new tall African American male about basketball in the first communication with him and not being interested in what he may want to share about his life.
- **Microinvalidations** are interactions that minimize or negate the psychological experience of a person of another group. An example would be a group member telling a transgender person that it is great she can express herself and minimizes the struggles that she had to face because of society's binary gender orientation. Another example would be to say to a paralyzed person how great it must be to move around in their fancy fast wheelchair.

Microaggressions are often not purposeful or necessarily conscious, but that does not minimize their impact. The effects of repeated microaggressions **negatively impact physical and mental health**. Microaggressions are so common and subtle that the person delivering them is often unaware of the ways that they are hurting, insulting, and distancing the other person. Unfortunately, the receiver also sometimes has become so **desensitized** as to accept the message without comment.

The recommendation is for the therapist to address these incidents **in the moment,** asking the target of the microaggression about its **impact** (Owen, Tao, Imel, Wampold, & Rodolfa, 2014). This will create a group culture in which individuals learn to be more sensitive over time. While it is possible the person being aggressed against or aggressing will minimize the effect of the statement, the group leader needs to stay diligent about uncovering the true impact and the true intent. Part of our work as leaders is for group members to better understand how their behavior affects others.

Exercise

In what ways have you witnessed microaggressions in the groups you run?
How did you work with them in the moment?
How did you encourage the group to understand their impact?
In what other ways might you have approached these situations?

Recommended Resources

Owen, J., Tao, K. W., Imel, Z. E., Wampold, B. E., & Rodolfa, E. (2014). Addressing racial and ethnic microaggressions in therapy. *Professional Psychology: Research and Practice*, 45(4), 283–290.
Pierce, C. M. (1974). Psychiatric problems of the black minority. In S. Arieti (Ed.), *American Handbook of Psychiatry*, pp. 512–523. New York: Basic Books.

Rowe, M. (1974). Saturn's Rings: A study of the minutiae of sexism which maintain discrimination and inhibit affirmative action results in corporations and non-profit institutions. In *Graduate and Professional Education of Women*, pp. 1–9. Washington, DC: American Association of University Women.

Sue, D. W. (Ed.) (2010). *Microaggressions and marginality: Manifestation, dynamics, and impact.* New York: Wiley.

Sue, D. W. (2013). Race talk: The psychology of racial dialogues. *American Psychologist, 68*(8), 663–672.

Difficult Dialogues

Group conversations about the impact of race, gender, and other differences are often difficult dialogues (Sue, 2016; Sue & Constantine, 2007). **Diversity discussions rarely resolve quickly and completely and often can leave people feeling attacked, abandoned, misunderstood and avoidant of future contact.**

To conspire to silence with this discourse is extremely limiting and damaging. Sue (2016) found that

> successful race talk must allow for the free expression of nested and impacted feelings, acknowledge their legitimacy and importance in dialogues, and be deconstructed so their meanings are made clear.
>
> (p. 145)

Exercise

An example of cultural bias is the situation where a heterosexual East Indian woman, Ananda, who comes to the United States for college and falls in love with an American woman, but her family has already arranged for her to marry a man in India when she completes her education. She enters a graduate student support group. The group of Western-based, American students pressures her to follow what she wants and to disregard her cultural tradition and family's wishes. What difficulties do you see potentially arising in this situation? What might you do as the leader?

Recommended Resources

Sue, D. W. (2016). *Race talk and the conspiracy of silence: Understanding and facilitating difficult dialogues on race.* New York: John Wiley.

Sue, D. W. & Constantine, M.G. (2007). Racial microaggressions as instigators of difficult dialogues on race: Implications for student affairs educators and students. *College Student Affairs Journal, 26*(2), 136–143.

Cultural Humility

Cultural humility is a **process-oriented approach** to multicultural competency (Chávez, 2012; Waters & Asbill, 2013). This refers to a client-centered, relational stance as we learn about the aspects of another's culture and the ways that it impacts identity, life choices, and inner processes (Hook, Davis, Owen, Worthington, & Utsey, 2013). Tervalon and Murray-Garcia (1998) outline three aspects of this work.

- A **lifelong commitment** to **self-evaluation** and **self-critique** through acknowledging that we always have more to learn. This means that curiosity, humility, and flexibility propel us to learn about others more thoroughly.
- The second aspect is to **fix power imbalances** that are unjust and detrimental. Clients are the experts on their lives, the impact of their cultural experiences, their symptoms, and strengths. This does not minimize or discount our expertise or experience, but rather levels the field so truer collaboration can exist.
- The third factor is **growing partnerships** through **advocating** with individuals and groups that can help create positive changes. As we reach across differences to learn, improve, and change systems, we change all of our lives.

Recommended Resources

Chávez, V. (2012). *Cultural humility: People, principles, and practices.* [Video file] Retrieved from https://www.youtube.com/watch?v=SaSHLbS1V4w

Hook, J. N., Davis, D. E., Owen, J., Worthington Jr, E. L., & Utsey, S. O. (2013). Cultural humility: Measuring openness to culturally diverse clients. *Journal of Counseling Psychology, 60(3),* 353.

Tervalon, M., & Murray-Garcia, J. (1998). Cultural humility versus cultural competence: A critical distinction in defining physician training outcomes in multicultural education. *Journal of Health Care for the Poor and Underserved, 9(2),* 117–125.

Waters, A., & Asbill, L. (2013). *Reflections on cultural humility.* Washington, DC: American Psychological Association.

Increasing Sensitivity

Bennett (1986) outlined a six-stage model of increasing multicultural/intercultural sensitivity, which has been applied to the work of therapists (Arredondo & Tovar-Blank, 2014):

- **Denial**
  In this stage, the therapist essentially denies that cultural differences are present and/or may construct homogeneous groups so as to avoid connections with individuals from diverse cultural backgrounds, reflecting the ultimate form of ethnocentrism that precludes empathic connection to the "other."
- **Defense against difference and perceived threats to the centrality of one's worldview**
  In this stage, therapists might acknowledge that some differences exist between cultures, but try to ignore this truth and/or see **their culture as superior.** In group this could be shown by having a client follow a treatment protocol that is in marked conflict with their cultural beliefs and current needs, for instance, using a depth

psychoanalytic approach when the client is in crisis and not having daily living needs met. Another example would be presenting a totally secular approach to someone with a highly spiritual orientation. Dismissing the concerns and beliefs of our clients and believing ours are superior will inevitably lead to early termination, poor outcomes, and potential injury.

- **Minimization**
  In this stage, the therapist minimizes cultural differences and believes that human similarities counterbalance cultural difference. Group leaders may overly emphasize underlying universal themes, while minimizing the impact of the members' cultural experiences on their development, challenges, behavior, strengths, and skills.
- **Acceptance**
  In this stage the group therapist shifts towards ethnorelativism, increasingly receptive to the idea that all cultures are valuable, valid, complex and meaningful and beginning to see all cultural perspectives as important without judgment. When working with a diverse heterogeneous group membership, this attitude is important to foster in the membership.
- **Adaptation to difference**
  In this stage, the therapist attempts to gain increased empathic ability to more deeply understand the perspective of other cultures, humble to the idea that full understanding may not be achieved. The group therapist gains more skill and comfort moving between cultural views and discussing these with the group members. Group members benefit from an expansion of perspective and possibilities.
- **Integration**
  In this final stage, therapists' views of themselves expand through inclusion of worldviews of other cultures in their work and likely in their personal lives. In this paradigm, it is the therapist's personal work that promotes increased capacity and effectiveness when working with individuals different from them.

Most multicultural therapists and researchers endorse the need for technical flexibility when working across diversity situations (Hays, 2016; Paniagua, 2013). Both **the goals and the process of therapy** need to be discussed and agreed upon between therapist and client. Certain empirically supported models need to be **adjusted** for clients to benefit the most from treatment. For instance, a group protocol for stress reduction that primarily uses examples and metaphors relevant for white upper middle class heterosexuals would need to be either replaced or expanded for a more diverse group membership. The integration of **culturally specific healing activities** should be considered and endorsed when possible.

While avoiding attacks and scapegoating is essential, focusing too intensely on group safety can limit exploration of these vital diversity topics. Eventually, **a group needs to move from *safe space* to *brave space* for deeper cross cultural understanding and dialogue** (Steffen, 2015). **Group members can be encouraged to face uncomfortable topics as part of the growth supported by a group leader who is fair, consistent, moderates tension levels, and protects all of the members.**

Recommended Resources

Arredondo, P., & Tovar-Blank, Z. G. (2014). Multicultural competencies: A dynamic paradigm for the 21st century. In F. T. L. Leong (Ed.), *APA handbook of multicultural psychology Vol. 2: Applications and training* (pp. 19–34) Washington, DC: American Psychological Association.

Bennett, M. J. (1986). A developmental approach to training for intercultural sensitivity. *International Journal of Intercultural Relations, 10*(2), 179–196.

Paniagua, F. A. (2013). *Assessing and treating culturally diverse clients: A practical guide.* Thousand Oaks, CA: Sage.

Steffen, J. (2015). A paradigm shift from safe space to brave space: Dialogues in multicultural group therapy. *The Group Psychologist, 25*(1), 6–8.

Multicultural Information in the Pre-Group Meeting

Understanding that clients are culturally rooted is essential for empathizing with their experiences and the totality of their being. Therapists must be diligent not to assume that they understand the client from what they may know about their culture or overly assume similarities between cultures. McAuliffe and Eriksen (2010) suggest **gathering information from clients about how one's gender, sexual orientation, social class, and ethnicity impacted their lives and how their families view these topics.** Sue, Gallardo, and Neville (2013) suggest **asking if clients and/ or their families have been subjected to discrimination, and if so, how it has impacted them, and how they understand such dynamics.** It is also important to ask about elements of a client's cultural experiences that they feel proud of or feel are strengths. Other questions could include whether their views about their culture have changed over time and how that has impacted them. When a member is joining a group, understanding the member's cross cultural experiences, both the constructive and damaging aspects, can help us stay alert for potential curative emotional experiences and avoid traumatizing encounters. Asking how clients identify themselves and how they would like their identity to be referred to in the group is useful in developing a positive bond and respecting their autonomy.

By exploring these issues in the intake process, the clinician sets a foundation that emphasizes the importance of these issues and openness to discuss them freely in the group. This will most likely lead to fruitful discussions of cultural impact and identities in groups. Understanding the client's experiences in this way allows the clinician to understand the client beyond presenting problem or diagnosis, but rather as whole individuals living within cultural context.

Recommended Resources

McAuliffe, G., & Eriksen, K. (2010). *Handbook of counselor preparation: Constructivist, developmental, and experiential approaches.* Thousand Oaks, CA: Sage.

Sue, D. W., Gallardo, M. E., & Neville, H. A. (2013). *Case studies in multicultural counseling and therapy.* Hoboken, NJ: Wiley.

Empirical Support for Multicultural Competence in Counseling

It is only over the last few decades that multicultural variables such as race, gender, and sexual orientation in therapy have been increasingly addressed, and the research on the impact of these variables and effective processes in multiculturally-informed group psychotherapy are rapidly expanding. Currently, **the research evidence points towards the positive impact of the therapist's sensitivity to cultural issues in treatment in terms of outcome and client's experience** (Chu & Leino, 2017; Tao, Owen, Pace, & Imel, 2015).

A recent movement in multicultural group therapy is adapting existing empirically supported treatment protocols to specific multicultural groups by including culturally informed values, language, rituals, and healing traditions into the curriculum. Generally this culturally informed empirical treatment has shown success across multiple diversity groups. In recent studies, culturally adapted therapy has demonstrated moderate to very significant effectiveness (Barrera, Castro, Strycker, & Toobert, 2013; Benish, Quintana, & Wampold, 2011; Domenech Rodríguez, & Bernal, 2012; Shehadeh, Heim, Chowdhary, Maercker, & Albanese, 2016; Tao, Owen, Pace, & Imel, 2015; Quintana, & Wampold, 2011). **Integrating culturally sensitive approaches into proven models of therapy is considered a best contemporary practice.** The group therapist faces choices in terms of:

- Utilizing a previous culturally adapted empirically supported protocol (if one is available).
- Working with others to bring increasing cultural sensitivity into an existing evidence-based treatment protocol.
- Creating new culturally sensitive protocols that may be efficacious, despite not being thoroughly researched at this time.

Regardless of the choice, the multicultural-informed therapist needs to be responsive, open and sensitive to the responses and feedback of the group members (i.e., cultural humility).

Many groups are conducted for specific diversity or minority populations such as refugees, those with specific chronic illness, or younger LGBTQQIP2SAA individuals (lesbian, gay, bisexual, transgender, questioning, queer, intersex, pansexual, two-spirit, androgynous, and asexual). However, in many settings, group membership is comprised of individuals with differing ethnicities, identities, and social orientations. While this is an area that needs to be further researched, the literature supports the view that therapists trained in multicultural approaches are more successful in navigating such situations (Chu, Leino, Pflum, & Sue, 2016; Constantine, 2002)

Recommended Resources

Barrera, M., Jr., Castro, F. G., Strycker, L. A., & Toobert, D. J. (2013). Cultural adaptations of behavioral health interventions: A progress report. *Journal of Consulting and Clinical Psychology, 81*(2), 196–205.

Benish, S. G., Quintana, S., & Wampold, B. E. (2011). Culturally adapted psychotherapy and the legitimacy of myth: a direct-comparison meta-analysis. *Journal of Counseling Psychology, 58*(3), 279–289.

Bernal, G., & Domenech Rodríguez, M. M. (2013). Tailoring treatment to the patient's race and ethnicity. In G. Koocher, J. Norcross, & B. Greene (Eds.)

Psychologists' desk reference (3rd ed.) (pp. 310–313). Oxford: Oxford University Press.

Chu, J., Leino, A., Pflum, S., & Sue, S. (2016). A model for the theoretical basis of cultural competency to guide psychotherapy. *Professional Psychology: Research and Practice, 47*(1), 18–29.

Chu, J., & Leino, A. (2017). Advancement in the maturing science of cultural adaptations of evidence-based interventions. *Journal of Consulting and Clinical Psychology, 85*(1), 45–57.

Constantine, M. G. (2002). Predictors of satisfaction with counseling: Racial and ethnic minority clients' attitudes toward counseling and ratings of their counselors' general and multicultural counseling competence. *Journal of Counseling Psychology, 49*(2), 255–263.

Domenech Rodríguez, M. M., & Bernal, G. (2012). Bridging the gap between research and practice in a multicultural world. In G. Bernal & M. Domenech Rodríguez (Eds.) *Cultural adaptations: Tools for evidence-based practice with diverse populations*, pp. 265–287. Washington, DC: American Psychological Association.

Hays, D. G., Arredondo, P., Gladding, S. T., & Toporek, R. L. (2010). Integrating social justice in group work: The new decade. *The Journal for Specialists in Group Work, 35*(2), 177–206.

Shehadeh, M. H., Heim, E., Chowdhary, N., Maercker, A., & Albanese, E. (2016). Cultural adaptation of minimally guided interventions for common mental disorders: A systematic review and meta-analysis. *JMIR Mental Health, 3*(3), e44.

Tao, K. W., Owen, J., Pace, B. T., & Imel, Z. E. (2015). A meta-analysis of multicultural competencies and psychotherapy process and outcome. *Journal of Counseling Psychology 62*(3), 337–350.

Training Issues

Defining what is and who has multicultural competence remains elusive (Holmes, 2012), although methods for conceptualizing, operationalizing, and assessing multicultural proficiency or competence continue to be refined and broadened. But it remains difficult to say what exactly is multicultural proficiency and where one is on such a spectrum. **Multicultural proficiency, much like clinical proficiency, is an ongoing process not a static end point from which one no longer needs support, training, and supervision.**

The effective teaching and training of multiculturalism to psychotherapists is a burgeoning area; with a variety of approaches and perspectives (Bemak & Chung, 2004). While historically most training programs have been didactic in nature, increasingly experiential group formats are being applied and strongly recommended. To the extent that the diversity training processes encourage open sharing, balance safety and confrontation, minimize scapegoating, and integrate new cognitions, affects and understandings, these trainings can help participants become increasingly aware of their own discomfort, anxiety, awkwardness, and defensiveness. Deeply held assumptions and biases often need relational experiences and some challenges in order to be discovered and modified. Such trainings often contain difficult dialogues and heated discussions, which can help attendees increase their comfort in dealing with similar dynamics in their own groups.

Conducting such groups is challenging, and the leader often must deal with overt hostility (Helms et al., 2003). However, further sharing of pedagogical approaches and additional research should continue to stir effective training efforts.

Recommended Resources

Bemak, F., & Chung, R. C. Y. (2004). Teaching multicultural group counseling: Perspectives for a new era. *The Journal for Specialists in Group Work*, *29*, 31–41.

Helms, J.E., Malone, L.S., Henze, K., Satiani, K., Perry, J., & Warren, A. (2003). First annual diversity challenge: How to survive teaching courses on race and culture. *Journal of Multicultural Counseling and Development*, *31*, 3–11.

Holmes, D. E. (2012). Multicultural competence: A practitioner-scholar's reflections on its reality and its stubborn and longstanding elusiveness. *Register Report* 1–18. Retrieved from www.nationalregister.org/pub/the-national-register-report-pub/spring-2012-issue/multicultural-competence-a-practitioner-scholars-reflections-on-its-reality-and-its-stubborn-and-longstanding-elusiveness/

Concluding Thoughts

Multicultural proficiency is a life long journey for a clinician, and perhaps even for nations and the world. As therapists, we have our areas of comfort, our sense of privilege, and our power, but also our own cultural wounds, limited and limiting experiences, and biases outside of our awareness. **Working with individuals markedly different from ourselves can be deeply rewarding as it introduces us to ideas, language, rituals, traditions, beliefs that are different from our own, encourages us to grow, and challenges us to expand our empathy and worldview.** This is also true for our group members; as their worldviews expand, they may feel increased self-acceptance and connection, increased flexibility in navigating varied and complex relational and social dynamics, and, also importantly, less symptomology.

In the group room, the impact of the complexity of identities and the deep histories of privilege, marginality and prejudice are prime to be explored and understood. Subgroups will form around various identities, and at times these subgroups will inevitably "other" different members and subgroups. Such subgrouping, scapegoating, or tokenizing actions are defensive attempts at enhancing safety. While these subgroup categories are real, they are also reductionistic and simplifying; **no one category captures the complexity of anyone**. Ideally over time members find various subgroup affiliations with all members. For example, two gay group members may identify with a gay group leader as being in a homosexual subgroup, however other identities (i.e., race, education, social class, interests, values, symptoms) may open up opportunities to align with other group members.

Often within multicultural conversations our members' coping, defensive, relational, and regulating strategies will be highlighted. As always, our **support, validation, and exploration** will deepen the work and encourage the group members to increase their support and understanding of one another's experience. And it is important for us as the leaders to model sensitivity, skills, and the desire for increasing our own knowledge and understanding.

As leaders we will often face challenges from our members in engaging in this type of work, such as their subtle testing of our ability to understand their experience to hostile revolt. As always, we need to monitor the emotional climate of the group, assessing the emotional bonds and therapeutic alliances in the group, exploring how we are handling such work, lest silently held ruptures and hurts undermine therapeutic process and progress.

As the topics of diversity, privilege, power, and marginalization become deeply integrated into our work, our comfort level and skills will increase. Starting in the pre-screening interview and continuing with the consistent, and sometimes challenging, discussions in the group process, members will often become invested in engaging in these topics of identity and culture.

While multiculturalism and diversity have been the focus of this chapter, the recommendation is not to make this the sole focus of your groups, but an important piece in understanding and helping your clients in vital and meaningful ways. While no single recommendation can address the complexity of moving towards cultural proficiency, perhaps **no other skill is as vital as listening with an open mind and open heart to our clients; to understand their histories, struggles, and successes within the context of their lives, to find their uniqueness beyond similar symptom clusters or identity demographics, and to reach across any obstacles that divide us and to work towards true collaboration and shared expertise. We need to allow ourselves to become increasingly open, curious, educated, flexible, and courageous in our methods and goals to meet the needs of those we serve.**

Module 2

Group Structure and Group Dynamics

3   Group Structure and Levels of Analysis

Les R. Greene

Introduction

What occurs in any moment can be regarded as the product of many factors acting independently and interactively, including:

- The members' and leader's personalities, agendas, and needs.
- The roles – both task oriented and emotion-oriented -that the members and leaders are taking.
- The tasks and goals of the group.
- The group's current social-emotional state or climate.
- The embedding context of the group including:
  - the constraints, resources, and values of the specific setting in which the group is located (e.g., outpatient agency or clinic).
  - the culture or mix of cultures within and surrounding the group.
  - the unique history and trajectory of this group.
  - historical and current dynamics within the larger societal and sociopolitical contexts.

All of these factors operate to create a **unique group ecology**, and in this way each group has its own distinctive journey. At the same time, **many commonalities and regularities** exist across groups. Group events and interchanges unfold at times in idiosyncratic and unforeseen ways, and at other times in predictable ways consistent with our theories or past experiences. This chapter focuses on structural perspectives of groups, including the boundaries and internal components that define the group. This conceptual framework helps us understand what occurs not only in psychotherapy groups, but also in other groups such as work groups or other task groups.

The Structural Perspective

Figures 3.1 and 3.2 depict the small psychotherapy group from a structural perspective. The simpler view on the left depicts the group merely as a collection of individuals, one designated as the therapist. From this vantage point what occurs is seen as emanating from the individual personalities of the participants, their unique histories and internalized experiences. While some group therapy models (cf. Wolf & Schwartz, 1962) have actually conceptualized therapeutic group work in this way, focusing on the

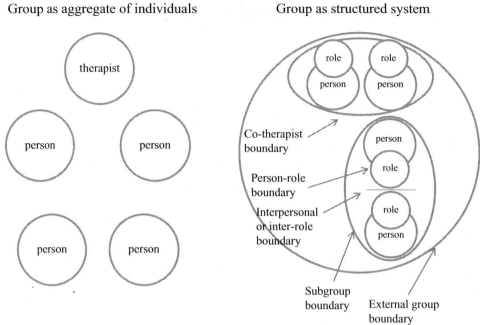

Figure 3.1 Structural perspectives of the small group

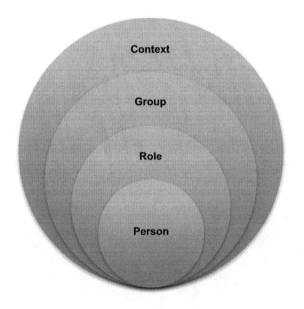

Figure 3.2 Systems view of groups

intrapsychic world of the individuals in the group and eschewing the exploration of group processes, today most group therapists would agree that such a model is too reductionistic and unnecessarily narrowing of the scope of inquiry.

Most experienced group therapists today would agree that the structural model shown on the right (adapted from Bernard & MacKenzie, 1994) is much more clinically useful in trying to sort out and understand the events and processes occurring in the group.

This diagram depicts the group as a bounded entity differentiated from the embedding environment by virtue of its task, time and space, and internally structured into differentiated components, such as roles and subgroups, as discussed in detail below. Conceptualizing the **group therapist as a manager of these boundaries** helps in many ways, especially:

- by highlighting key considerations and decisions that must be addressed when forming a group such as where, when and why the group meets and what work roles are assigned (see Chapter 7).
- and by monitoring and addressing processes that aim at obscuring, rigidifying or distorting the various group boundaries (see Chapter 5).

Levels of Analysis

Clearly, not everything can be attended to at the same time in the buzzing array of sensory and experiential data that is the psychotherapy group. The group therapist needs to choose what will be a primary focus at any moment and, further, needs to be able to shift attention and to consider phenomena from multiple perspectives. A group therapist who thinks about the group solely in terms of individual personalities misses many important kinds of information. Similarly, attending only to the internal workings of the group without consideration of external contextual influences is also limiting.

The general consensus in the literature and among clinicians is that the therapy group can and should be viewed from multiple levels of analysis (cf. Forsyth, 2010). Typically, and most simply, three levels of analysis need to be considered:

- The **personality of the individual patient,** and more particularly the internal world of needs, wishes, motives, anxieties, and "working models" of self and significant others.
- The **interpersonal relationship patterns and processes** occurring in the group.
- The collective or shared dynamics within the **group-as-a-whole,** such as the "**basic assumptions**" of the group (see Chapter 5).

Consider a clinical vignette of a group member who is noticeably silent and tight-lipped. From the perspective of **personality**, the therapist might hypothesize, explore and intervene in terms of the kinds of early scripts, internalized prohibitions and inhibitions, core conflictual relationships and pathogenic beliefs that drive this individual's behavior and that lead to social isolation. Taking a broader perspective, the therapist might observe a second, boisterous group member who is teasing the quieter member, trying to provoke the inhibited member to speak. From this vantage point of **interpersonal dynamics**, the group therapist might wonder about the interactive dance between these two, their entanglement and enactment, how each one is perceived by the other and what each one serves for the other. But stepping back even further to the level of the **group-as-a-whole,** the group therapist might notice that the rest of the group is intently watching this pair with some amusement and relief. Here the questions the therapist might pose are "What does this pair represent for the group-as-a-whole?" "How is the group using the pair to contain, compartmentalize and dramatize some internal conflict within the entire group?"

Another example of **flexibly viewing group life from these three perspectives** is provided by Tasca, Francis, and Balfour (2014) who provide the rationale for having multiple lenses to view group phenomena:

> Although there is an isomorphism between these three levels of group functioning, they each contain unique properties and dynamics that if left unattended can have consequences for the effectiveness of a group's functioning. Flexibly attending to and working within each group level will inform interventions that optimize the effectiveness of this very rich and effective treatment modality.
>
> (p. 28)

The necessity and utility of the group therapist holding multiple perspectives have been repeatedly endorsed (Rutan, Stone, & Shay, 2014; Yalom & Leszcz, 2005).

Systems View of Groups

More complex conceptualizations of levels of analysis derive from systems theory in which group phenomena are viewed and depicted as a series of concentric circles (Agazarian, 1982; Agazarian & Peters, 1981; Miller, 1976; Miller & Rice, 1967; Rice, 1969). Each circle represents a unique system that interacts with, influences and is influenced by the other systems.

A. **Person system** consists of the entirety of the individual's personality, including coping, defense, cognitive and character styles, tolerances for stress and anxiety, intellectual capacities, and such group-relevant capacities as psychological mind-edness, empathy and the repertoire of social skills. The internal world of the individual member, alternately referred to as internalized **"self and object representations"**, **"social cognitive templates,"** **"working models of self and others,"** or **"person schemas,"** is typically viewed as the subsystem of the person system.

B. **Role system.** The construct of role is a core structural concept that links the individual to the group. There are three kinds of roles that are useful to consider:

   1. **Formal work role.** This structural component refers to the **official work position** that explicates the expectations, responsibilities and authority for doing the work in this role. The formal work role is the description found in an organizational flow chart that details what is expected in that position. **In group psychotherapy there are two differentiated formal work roles: therapist and member.** In orientation sessions with prospective members (see Chapter 6), the therapist needs to spell out what the work expectations (or "agreements" or "contract") are for these two roles.

   2. **Member role.** These are roles and behavior that a member may assume, such as a provocateur, a rescuer, or silent invisible member. As opposed to being explicitly delegated, members **assume** these roles based on past roles that members have held or witnessed within their families and early life. The concept

of member role can be considered as a **transference enactment** where perceptions of and behavior in the current group are influenced by earlier life experiences.

3. **Group role.** The concept refers to the member's serving as a "voice" or "spokesperson" or "container" for a particular emotional issue or need that is being disavowed by the group-as-a-whole and is being projected on to an individual. The concept of **valency** reflects the idea that individuals have specific preferences to voice specific group needs and enact specific group roles, such as:

- Scapegoat.
- Member in crisis or need; the "identified patient."
- Fight leader or rebel.
- The voice of emotion.
- The voice of rationality.

C. The **subgroup system** is a temporary system of one or more members that may or may not be present at any particular moment. It is useful to differentiate:

- Dysfunctional subgroups are defensive structures of "us versus them" polarities and exaggerated differences, formed through processes of splitting and projection. They serve to keep anxiety-arousing material at arm's length by externalizing and locating it into the "other" and thus can restrain the work of the group.
- **Functional subgroups** are therapeutically formed camps composed of group members identified as sharing similar feelings and thoughts and distinguished from other subgroups with different feelings, designed to help the group discover differences in the apparently similar and similarities in the apparently different (Agazarian, 1982).

D. **The embedding context of the group includes:**

1. The **immediate organizational context** (particularly its primary task, values, needs and concerns). For ensuring the viability of the group embedded in a larger treatment environment, such as a clinic or hospital, it is crucial that the boundary between the group and its immediate environment be flexible and permeable, allowing information to cross in both directions. **The therapist needs to consider the "fit" or "match" between the group and its environment.** Does the group support or conflict with the general goals and values of the larger organization? **Are the administrators and colleagues within the larger organizational context cognizant of, comfortable with and supportive of the aims and processes of this specific therapy group?** (Bernard et al., 2008; Brabender & Fallon, 2019). These questions are important for the therapist to address for as Nitsun (2000) warns

   groups in organizations are often feared, mistrusted, disenfranchised, and sabotaged.

   (p. 465)

2. The **larger societal context** reflecting economic, sociopolitical, and cultural issues, tensions and values.

Concluding Thoughts

It is always difficult for the group therapist to decide what to focus on at any moment in the group: the noisiest? most visible? the most recent? the most painful? Theory can help. For example, there are "top-down" models that suggest the therapist's primary attention be on the group-wide themes and tensions that emerge in the here-and-now. There are other models, such as that by Horwitz (2014), that are inductive or bottom up, suggesting that the initial focus be on individual issues before turning to group-as-a-whole themes. But, as Kernberg (1975) argues, theory is not enough. Ultimately the therapist's personal resources need to be mustered to decide what level of abstraction to focus on. **Hovering and free-floating attention, accessing one's own internal world, experiencing here-and-now emotions and sensory information, thinking about what is not apparent – all are useful capacities in determining at any moment what becomes the primary focus and what, for the moment, is part of the background.**

Exercises

1) Can you identify a characteristic member role that you take in groups? Do you tend to become a spokesperson or voice for a particular theme or issue in the group?
   Do your roles in groups parallel or reflect roles you have had in your early life? How do you understand this phenomenon?
2) Think of a member you have observed in a group and consider processes at various levels of analysis.

   a) Who is the individual member, in terms of history, values, goals, and agendas?
   b) What group role is the member taking? Why?
   c) What subgroups has the member joined in the group?
   d) What cultural factors may be affecting this member's behavior in the group?

3) In the previous example, what might you say as the group leader to address

   a) the individual member's history, symptoms, or character style
   b) The group role this member is taking.
   c) The subgroup this member is a part of.
   d) the overall dynamic in the group.

Recommended Resources

Agazarian, Y.M. (1982). Role as a bridge construct in understanding the relationship between the individual and the group. In M. Pines & L. Rafaelson (Eds.),

The individual and the group, boundaries and interrelations, Vol. I, Theory, pp. 182-192. New York: Plenum Press.

Agazarian, Y.M., & Peters, R. (1981). *The visible and invisible group.* London: Routledge & Kegan Paul.

Bernard, H., Burlingame, G., Flores, P., Greene, L., Joyce, A., Kobos, J., Leszcz, M., MacNair-Semands, R.R., Piper, W.E., Slocum McEneaney, A.M., & Feirman, D. (2008). Clinical practice guidelines for group psychotherapy. *International Journal of Group Psychotherapy, 58,* 455–542.

Bernard, H.S. & MacKenzie, K.R. (1994). *Basics of group psychotherapy.* New York: Guilford.

Brabender, V.M. & Fallon, A. (2019). *Group psychotherapy in context. Inpatient, partial hospital and residential care.* Washington, DC: American Psychological Association.

Forsyth, D. R. (2010). "The nature and significance of groups." In R. K. Conyne (Ed.), *The Oxford handbook of group counseling,* pp. 19–35. New York: Oxford University Press.

Horwitz, L. (2014). *Listening with the fourth ear: Unconscious dynamics in analytic group psychotherapy.* London: Karnac Books.

Kernberg, O. (1975). Systems approach to priority setting of interventions in groups. *International Journal of Group Psychotherapy, 25,* 251–275.

Miller, E. J., & Rice, A. K. (1967). *Systems of organization.* London: Tavistock Publications.

Miller, E. (Ed.) (1976). *Task and organization.* New York: Wiley.

Nitsun, M. (2000). The future of the group. *International Journal of Group Psychotherapy, 50,* 455–472.

Rice, A. K. (1969). Individual, group and intergroup processes. *Human Relations, 22,* 565–584.

Rutan, J. S., Stone, W., & Shay J. (2014*). Psychodynamic group psychotherapy* (5th ed.) New York: Guilford.

Tasca, G. A.; Francis, K., Balfour, L. (2014). Group psychotherapy levels of interventions: A clinical process commentary. *Psychotherapy, 51,* 25–29.

Wolf, A. & Schwartz, E. (1962). *Psychoanalysis in groups.* New York: Grune & Stratton.

Yalom, I.D. & Leszcz, M. (2005). *The theory and practice of group psychotherapy.* New York: Basic Books.

4 Therapeutic Factors

Les R. Greene, Sally Barlow, and Francis J. Kaklauskas

Introduction

Group psychotherapy works! The ever increasing body of **outcome studies** provides strong empirical support for the therapeutic effectiveness of group psychotherapy, across settings, diagnoses, and cultures (Barlow et al. 2015; Burlingame, Strauss, & Joyce, 2013). However, psychotherapy **process research**, those studies that explore mechanisms by which therapeutic change occurs, is less robust. Methodologically, it is much easier to empirically document that therapeutic change has occurred (essentially by comparing relevant measures before treatment and at the end of treatment) than to explore the mediators, processes or mechanisms of that change (i.e., how the change came about). Much of our current thinking and understandings of therapeutic process has developed from decades of keen clinical observation. This chapter explores and explains what is known about the **"how"** and **"why"** of group therapy effectiveness.

Recommended resources

Burlingame, G., Strauss, B., & Joyce, A. (2013). Change mechanisms and effectiveness of small group treatments. In M. J. Lambert (Ed.), *Bergin & Garfield's handbook of psychotherapy and behavior change*, 6th Ed. (pp. 640–689). New York: Wiley & Sons.

Barlow, S., Burlingame, G.M., Greene, L.R., Joyce, A., Kaklauskas, F., Kinley, J., Klein, R.H., Kobos, J.C., Leszcz, M., MacNair-Semands, R., Paquin, J.D., Tasca, G.A., Whittingham, M., & Feirman, D. (2015). Evidence-based practice in group psychotherapy [American Group Psychotherapy Association Science to Service Task Force web document]. Retrieved from www.agpa.org/home/practice-resources/evidence-based-practice-in-group-psychotherapy.

Yalom and Leszcz' (2005) Therapeutic Factors

The term "Therapeutic Factors" is a complex construct referring to those

- **Conditions** (such as reinforcing a sense of safety).
- **Processes** (such as inviting members to be curious and open).
- **Mediators** (such as gaining understanding of the impact of one's behavior on others).

that **underlie or facilitate therapeutic change. Knowledge of these factors and how and when to promote them** are core competencies for the group psychotherapist (Barlow, 2013).

There are two kinds of therapeutic factors:

- **Specific** or **technical** factors that are tied to a particular school of therapy (such as "transference analysis" in psychodynamic therapy, the identification of pathogenic beliefs in cognitive behavioral group therapy, or the imparting of information in psychoeducational groups).
- **Common** or **nonspecific** factors, that are not tied to a specific school of psychotherapy.

Review

The best known list of therapeutic factors is by Yalom and Leszcz (2005), who developed this work over several decades, drawing on earlier conceptualizations by Corsini and Rosenberg (1955), Powdermaker and Frank (1953), and others:

- **Universality:** Opportunities to recognize that other members in the group share similar feelings, thoughts, and problems ("We're all in the same boat.").
- **Altruism:** Extending help to other group members with support, understanding, or guidance. This can enhance one's self esteem through the experience of being helpful to others and feeling connected to them.
- **Instillation of hope:** Enhanced optimism for one's own improvement by witnessing others' successes in the group and developing a deeper commitment to therapeutic change.
- **Imparting information:** Receiving new understandings, education, or advice from the therapist or other members.
- **Corrective recapitulation of primary family experience:** Opportunities to reenact critical and problematic early life dynamics with other group members and to rework these experiences. One may discover that the anticipated feared outcome (e.g., feeling shamed, guilty or blamed) does not occur, that one's views and opinions are valued, and that having a range of emotions is acceptable and valued.
- **Development of socializing techniques:** The group provides members with an environment and therapeutic norms that foster adaptive, flexible, and effective communication. Members practice and receive feedback on their communication and relational styles.
- **Imitative behavior:** Members expand their personal knowledge and skills through the observation of other members' self-exploration, working through, and personal development.
- **Cohesiveness:** Feelings of trust, belonging, and acceptance, a sense that the member is part of something unique or special, a feeling of "we."
- **Existential factors:** Coming to terms with and accepting responsibility for one's life decisions, as well as exploring a range of existential themes.
- **Catharsis:** Venting of strong feelings about past or present experiences.
- **Interpersonal learning-input:** Opportunities to gain personal insight about one's impact on others in the group through feedback provided by other members.

- **Interpersonal learning-output**: opportunities to learn how to offer interpersonal feedback in adaptive and constructive ways.
- **Self-understanding**: Gaining of insight into the psychological motivations underlying one's behavior and emotional reactions.

Recommended Resources

Barlow, S. H. (2013). *Specialty competencies in group psychology.* New York: Oxford University Press.

Corsini, R. J., & Rosenberg, B. (1955). Mechanisms of group psychotherapy: Processes and dynamics. *Journal of Abnormal and Social Psychology,* 51, 406–411.

Yalom, I. D., & Leszcz, M. (2005). *The theory and practice of group therapy* (5th ed.). New York, NY: Basic Books.

Over 50 studies have been conducted asking group therapy members to rank order the importance of Yalom's therapeutic factors as they are experienced in their groups. These studies reveal that members' rankings of what factors are important for therapeutic change depend upon:

- The specific kind of group being conducted, such as structured psychoeducation versus process-oriented groups.
- The specific clinical population being treated, including whether it is homogeneous versus heterogeneous with regard to some specific pathology, psychological issue, or life issue.
- The specific setting in which the group is conducted such as inpatient, outpatient or day treatment.
- **The only substantive conclusion that can be drawn from these studies is that there is no universal hierarchy of perceived therapeutic importance that applies to all groups; that is, different groups endorse different priorities of therapeutic factors.**

Recent Developments

Yalom's therapeutic factors have been critiqued for not being a systematic or integrated theory of therapeutic change, given that the factors are presented as a mere listing of discrete entities with no articulation as to how they might overlap and interact with each other in different ways at different times in different groups. Similarly, the research that explores perceived importance of Yalom's therapeutic factors has been critiqued as being too methodologically and conceptually limited (Kivlighan, Miles, & Paquin, 2010). Recently two significant efforts have attempted to bring greater **conceptual clarity to Yalom's therapeutic factors by identifying a smaller number of superordinate or higher-order concepts.**

Therapeutic Factors Group Typology

One effort is by Kivlighan et al. (2004), who have argued that creating yet another ranking of therapeutic factors is not going to be a beneficial strategy for enhancing our knowledge about the role of therapeutic factors in group treatment.

(p. 32)

Using data from many of the studies on Yalom's therapeutic factors they identified **four-clusters of groups**, based on the relative ranking of perceived therapeutic factors:

a. **Affective insight groups** where acceptance, catharsis, interpersonal learning and self-understanding are viewed as most important (e.g., psychodynamic therapy group).
b. **Affective support groups** where acceptance, instillation of hope, and universality are perceived as most important (e.g., trauma group).
c. **Cognitive support groups** where vicarious learning and guidance are ranked most important, (e.g., Twelve-step support groups).
d. **Cognitive insight groups** where interpersonal learning, self-understanding and vicarious learning are most important (e.g., CBT group).

Exercise

In one of your groups (as leader or member), what therapeutic factors do you consider to be most important?

Can you place this group within one of the four clusters listed above?

Have the relative value or importance of the therapeutic factors in this group changed over time as a function of group development?

Higher-Order Therapeutic Factors from the Therapeutic Factors Inventory

Another major effort to find more abstract and superordinate therapeutic factors is the ongoing development of the Therapeutic Factors Inventory. Originally designed to capture all of Yalom's therapeutic factors (Lese & MacNair-Semands, 2000), subsequent research (Joyce, MacNair-Semands, Tasca, & Ogrodniczuk, 2011; MacNair-Semands, Ogrodniczuk, & Joyce, 2010; Tasca et al., 2016) has aimed at identifying a smaller number of higher-order therapeutic factors. Joyce, MacNair-Semands, Tasca, and Ogrodniczuk (2011) have recently suggested that **the research on therapeutic factors is better served by trying to identify fewer, more global therapeutic factors that may provide greater clarity about the underlying mechanisms of therapeutic change.** These studies have suggested **four higher-order group therapeutic factors**, shown with factor names, descriptions and representative items from the Therapeutic Factors Inventory

a. **Social Learning** emphasizes skills learned through exploring and communicating one's thoughts and feelings in the here and now with the goal of increasing the ability to put insight into productive action.

My group is kind of like a little piece of the larger world I live in: I see the same patterns, and working them out in group helps me work them out in my outside life.

Because I've got a lot in common with other group members, I'm starting to think that I may have something in common with people outside group too.

b. **Secure emotional expression** reflects the open, honest, and vulnerable communication and sense of connection between members and within the group culture

Even though we have differences, our group feels secure to me.

I feel a sense of belonging in this group.

c. **Instillation of hope** reflects renewed optimism about the future.

This group inspires me about the future.

In group I've learned that I have more similarities with others than I would have guessed.

d. **Awareness of Relational Impact** endorses the cognitive-affective learning and insight that emerges from the within group relationships.

By getting honest feedback from members and facilitators, I've learned a lot about my impact on other people.

I pay attention to how others handle difficult situations in my group so I can apply these strategies in my own life.

Tasca et al. (2016) have suggested that these four therapeutic factors can be reduced into just one global factor (measured by just 8 items): They conceptualize this factor as

feeling hopeful about the processes of emotional expression and relational awareness, which then translate into and promotes social learning.

(p. 140)

They urge that training highlight these more global factors to improve therapist skills and create better patient retention and outcome.

Exercise

As a developing group therapist, do these conceptualizations of four or just one global therapeutic factor seem helpful or limiting to you as means of tracking therapeutic progress?

Recommended Resources

Joyce, A. S., MacNair-Semands, R., Tasca, G. A., & Ogrodniczuk, J. S. (2011). Factor structure and validity of the Therapeutic Factors Inventory–Short Form. *Group Dynamics: Theory, Research, and Practice, 15*, 201–219.

Kivlighan, D. M., Jr., & Holmes, S. E. (2004). The importance of therapeutic factors: A typology of therapeutic factors studies. In J. L. DeLucia-Waack, D. A. Gerrity, C. R. Kalodner, & M. T. Riva (Eds.), *Handbook of group counseling and psychotherapy* (pp. 23–36). Thousand Oaks, CA: Sage.

Kivlighan, D. C. M. & Kivlighan, D. M. (2014). Therapeutic factors. In J. L. DeLucia-Waack, D. A. Kalodner, & M. T. Riva (Eds.), *Handbook of group counseling and psychotherapy* (2nd ed.) (pp. 46). Thousand Oaks, CA: Sage.

Kivlighan, D. M., Miles, J. R. & Paquin, J. D. (2010). Therapeutic factors in group counseling: Asking new questions. In R. Conyne (Ed.), *Oxford handbook of group counseling* (pp. 121–136). New York: Oxford University Press.

Lese, K. P., & MacNair-Semands, R. R. (2000). The therapeutic factors inventory: Development of a scale. *Group, 24,* 303–317.

MacNair-Semands, R. R., Ogrodniczuk, J. S., & Joyce, A. S. (2010). Structure and initial validation of a short form of the Therapeutic Factors Inventory. *International Journal of Group Psychotherapy, 60,* 245–281.

Tasca, G. A. Cabrera, C., Kristjansson, E., MacNair-Semands, R., Joyce, A. S.,& Ogrodniczuk, J. S. (2016). The Therapeutic Factors Inventory-8: Using item response theory to create a brief scale for continuous process monitoring for group psychotherapy. *Psychotherapy Research, 26,* 131–145.

The Role of Cohesion

Introduction

While all of the therapeutic factors are theorized to be positively related to outcome, **cohesion has garnered the most substantial empirical support in relationship to positive therapeutic outcome** (Burlingame, McClendon, & Alonso, 2011). There is general consensus in both the clinical and research literatures that cohesion is a good thing (Bernard et al., 2008). **Especially in the early stages of group formation (see Chapter 6),** therapists want to be particularly sensitive to helping the group develop a sense of "us" or "we" such that each member feels intricately connected to or bonded with the group as an entity. Moreover, cohesion needs to be in place before other therapeutic factors can unfold (Burlingame, Fuhriman, & Johnson, 2002).

Importantly, **therapists also need to monitor and help restore group cohesion when the group is experiencing some threat to its integrity from either inside or outside the group.** For example, the cohesive bonds may lessen when a new member joins the group, when a member abruptly leaves or is a no-show, or when there is some dysregulated expression of anger. By exploring and validating members' experience, and re-clarifying the group boundaries, this sense of cohesion or "groupness" can be restored.

There is no consensually agreed upon operational definition of the term *cohesion,* and this has created a database intractable to empirical and theoretical synthesis (Greene, 2016). It has been defined and measured in many ways, as a:

- **Sociological** construct – the aggregate of members' interpersonal feelings for each other
- **Sociopsychological construct** – the individual member's connection to the group as a whole.
- **Psychological** construct – the sense of immersion in or fusion with the group entity.

Unfortunately, the relationships among these many disparate measures have not been explored; still cohesion remains a primary principle for developing effective groups.

Exercise

As a group therapist how do you define cohesion? If you were a research scientist, how would you measure it?

Exercise

Hornsey, Olsen, Barlow, and Oei (2012) have designed an interesting non-verbal **one item measure of cohesion.** This consists simply of a series of six diagrams with five circles in each, with one circle in the middle surrounded by the other circles. The middle circle represents the self, and the surrounding circles represent the other group members. In each successive diagram, the circles are located closer to one another and to the middle circle. The group member is asked to indicate which of the six diagrams best represents the sense of interconnectedness and closeness among the group members. The rationale is that the various spatial distances among the circles are designed to reflect different degrees of cohesion in the group. Do you think this is a meaningful measure of group cohesion? Why or why not?

The relationship of cohesion (and all of the other therapeutic factors) to outcome is complex. And much is yet to be learned about cohesion, such as when too much cohesion can be an obstacle to psychological growth or can arouse anxieties over loss of differentiation and individuality (Barlow & Burlingame, 2006). Further, individuals may have **differential needs for and sensitivities to cohesion,** some craving a sense of closeness while others feeling threatened by too much closeness. For example, some research evidence suggests that anxiously attached patients respond positively to efforts to increase group cohesion while those with avoidant attachment styles may either be threatened by or less sensitive to group cohesion (cf. Gallagher, Tasca, Ritchie, Balfour, & Bissada, 2014). While, in general, there is a **universal tension between the need to belong and bond,** on one hand, *and* to possess a **sense of an individuated self,** on the other hand, it is important to remember that among the members of any specific group, **individual differences in preferences for closeness and distance likely exist** (Kivlighan, Lo Coco, Gullo, Pazzagli, & Mazzeschi, 2017).

Effective cohesion is that which appropriately binds the group members together while still allowing for a sense of the individual self, so that coercion, scapegoating, fear of psychic merger and other damaging group processes do not occur and every member's unique needs are kept in mind.

The relationship between the individual's experience of group cohesion and therapeutic outcome is further complicated by that member's positive bonds to the group leader and to other members. Research suggests that the greater the **intrapersonal discrepancies** between these experiences (e.g., feeling bonded with the group but not liking the leader) the less the positive outcome for that member. Similarly, the greater the discrepancy between the individual member's experience of group cohesion and the experiences of cohesion held by the other members (**interpersonal discrepancies**) the less positive the outcome for that individual. (Kivlighan, Li, & Gillis, 2015; Kivlighan et al., 2017).

Therapeutic Principles and Tasks to Promote Cohesion

Burlingame, Fuhriman, and Johnson (2002) offer some important guiding principles that serve to enhance group cohesion in most kinds of groups:

1. **Use of Structure.** These three principles emphasize the importance of the therapist taking an active and proactive stance in orienting the new patient and the new group.

   - **Principle One:** Conduct pre-group preparation that sets treatment expectations, defines group rules, and instructs members in appropriate roles and skills needed for effective group participation and group cohesion.
   - **Principle Two:** The group therapist should actively establish clarity regarding group processes and norms in early sessions given the typical initial levels of anxiety.
   - **Principle Three:** Composition requires clinical judgment to balance intrapersonal (individual member) and intragroup (amongst group members) considerations asking both whether the group will be beneficial for this particular individual and whether this individual will be good for this group.

2. **Verbal Interaction.** These two principles emphasize the importance of timing and tact in giving feedback to members.

   - **Principle Four:** The therapist can serve as a model for the process of offering effective interpersonal feedback.
   - **Principle Five:** The timing and delivery of feedback should be guided by the aim of facilitating relationship building.

3. **Establishing and Maintaining an Emotional Climate.** These principles emphasize the importance of trying to strike the right balance between anxiety level and emotional expressiveness so that optimal psychological exploration and growth can occur.

   - **Principle Six:** The therapist's management of his or her own emotional presence is critically important and can provide a powerful positive model for the group-as-a-whole.
   - **Principle Seven:** A primary focus of the group therapist should be on facilitating group members' emotional expression, the responsiveness of others to that expression, and the shared meaning derived from such expression.

Research Developments

There is growing consensus that more empirical and theoretical work is needed, not by constructing still other measures of cohesion, but through efforts to either:

- **Deconstruct** the term into constituent components. **Are there differing specific facets of cohesion?**
- **Embed** it within higher order terms. **Is cohesion part of more global therapeutic processes?**
- **Distill** the essential ingredients within all of its extant definitions and measures. **What are the essential features of cohesion?** (Barlow, 2013; Greene, 2016).

Some recent studies have focused on exploring whether cohesion and other familiar constructs could be combined into more **global therapeutic factors** (Johnson, Burlingame, Olsen, Davies, & Gleave, 2005; Krogel et al., 2013). These promising works suggest **three superordinate factors:**

- The **positive bonding relationship** (combining measures of cohesion, engagement, and emotional bond), as represented by the item "the other members were warm and friendly towards me."
- The **positive working relationship**, reflecting a shared agreement on therapeutic tasks and goals, as represented by the item "The leader and I agree on what is important to work on."
- The **negative relationship** that combines measures of conflict, avoidance and empathic failure, as represented by the item "The other group members did not always understand the way I felt inside."

Recommended Resources

Barlow, S. H. & Burlingame, G. M. (2006). Essential theory, processes, and procedures for successful group psychotherapy: Group cohesion as exemplar. *Journal of Contemporary Psychotherapy*, 36, 107–112.

Bernard, H., Burlingame, G., Flores, P., Greene, L., Joyce, A., Kobos, J. C., Leszcz, M., MacNair-Semands, R. R., Piper, W., Slocum McEneaney, A. M., & Feirman, D. (2008). Clinical practice guidelines for group psychotherapy. *International Journal of Group Psychotherapy*, 58, 455–542.

Burlingame, G., Fuhriman, A., & Johnson, J. (2002). Cohesion in group psychotherapy. In J. Norcross (Ed.), *Psychotherapy relationships that work: Therapist contributions and responsiveness to patients.* (pp. 71–87). New York: Oxford University Press.

Burlingame, G. M., McClendon, D. T., & Alonso, J. (2011). Cohesion in group therapy. *Psychotherapy*, 48, 34–42.

Burlingame, G. M., McClendon, T., & Yang, C. (2018). Cohesion in group therapy: A meta-analysis. *Psychotherapy*, 55, 384–398.

Corsini, R. J., & Rosenberg, B. (1955). Mechanisms of group psychotherapy: Processes and dynamics. *Journal of Abnormal and Social Psychology*, 51(3), 406.

Gallagher, M. E., Tasca, G. A., Ritchie, K., Balfour, L., & Bissada, H. (2014). Attachment anxiety moderates the relationship between growth in group cohesion and treatment outcomes in group psychodynamic interpersonal psychotherapy for women with binge eating disorder. *Group Dynamics*, 18, 38–52.

Greene, L. R. (2016) Group psychotherapy research studies that therapists might actually read: My top 10 list. *International Journal of Group Psychotherapy*, 67, 1–26.

Hornsey, M., Olsen, S., Barlow, F. K., & Oei, T. P. S. (2012). Testing a single-item visual analogue scale as a proxy for cohesiveness in group psychotherapy. *Group Dynamics*, 16, 80–90.

Johnson, J., Burlingame, G. M., Olsen, D., Davies, R., & Gleave, R. L. (2005). Group climate, cohesion, alliance, and empathy in group psychotherapy: Multi-level structural equation models. *Journal of Counseling Psychology*, 52, 310–321.

Kivlighan, D. M. Jr., Li, X., & Gillis, L. (2015). Do I fit with my group? Within-member and within-group fit with the group in engaged group climate and group members feeling involved and valued. *Group Dynamics*, 19, 106–121.

Kivlighan, D. M. Jr., Lo Coco, G., Gullo, S., Pazzagli, C., & Mazzeschi, C. (2017). Attachment anxiety and attachment avoidance: Members' attachment fit with their group and group relationships. *International Journal of Group Psychotherapy*, 67(2), 223–239.

Kivlighan, D. M. Jr., Lo Coco, G., Oieni, V., Gullo, S., Pazzagli, C., & Mazzeschi, C. (2017). All bonds are not the same: A response surface analysis of the perceptions of positive bonding relationships in therapy groups. *Group Dynamics*, 21, 159–177.

Krogel, J., Burlingame, G., Chapman, C., Renshaw, T., Gleave, R., Beecher, M., & MacNair-Semands, R. (2013). The Group Questionnaire: A clinical and empirically derived measure of group relationship. *Psychotherapy Research*, 23, 344–354.

Powdermaker, F. B., & Frank, J. D. (1953). Group psychotherapy; studies in methodology of research and therapy. Report of a group psychotherapy research project of the US Veterans Administration.

Wampold, B. E., & Imel, Z. E. (2015). *The great psychotherapy debate: The evidence for what makes psychotherapy work*. New York: Routledge.

Other Concepts of Therapeutic Factors in Group Psychotherapy

Different schools of group psychotherapy emphasize different therapeutic processes and factors, although there is also considerable overlap.

Therapeutic Factors from an Attachment Perspective

The following seven processes from an **attachment** perspective are considered essential in enhancing a sense of security and stability from which psychological growth can occur (Marmarosh, Markin, & Spiegel, 2013):

1. **Empathic attunement.** This refers to efforts at resonating with a group member's experience, not just expressed surface emotions, but underlying or defensively hidden feelings or needs. These attempts at joining empathically to a group patient ideally are made not only by the group therapist, but by other patients. Accurate empathic attunement can contribute vitally to the continual forward movement of the group especially during times of ambivalence and stagnation (Westra & Norouzian, 2018). When connection fails, when a patient feels misunderstood or misperceived, efforts to "repair the rupture" have a corrective emotional experience that can be very therapeutic.

2. **Facilitating mentalization via group process and feedback.** These processes, similar to empathy, are those efforts to truly understand another's perspective and experience rather than relying on assumptions or projections (Fonagy, Campbell, & Bateman, 2017). Asking **"do I have it right?"** is one way of assessing whether one's understanding of another group member fits that member's own understanding.

3. **Identification of transference and parataxic distortions.** These processes entail exploring how one's **"internal working models"** or **"social cognitive templates"** or

"**internalized representational world**" can distort one's perceptions of the actual here-and-now social field. The identification and interpretation of such distortions provide each group member with opportunities to re-examine and reappraise current social perceptions. This process is much more salient in groups guided by psychodynamic theories of change than other kinds of groups, and in fact, the interpretation and analysis of transference patterns in the group are considered core processes in psychodynamically oriented groups (Piper, Ogrodniczuk, Joyce, & Weideman, 2011).

4. **Emotional and cognitive insight.** There are **different levels of insight** (Yalom & Leszcz, 2005), ranging from:

    o   basic experiencing about how one is perceived by others (e.g., "you often see me as being sarcastic and joking").

    o   to more complex learning about patterns of interactions with others (e.g., "I often respond with sarcasm and humor when someone tries to get close to me").

    o   to increasing awareness of the motivational aspects of these patterns (e.g., "I use sarcasm and humor as means of protecting myself from anticipated rejection by you").

    o   to a deeper understanding of the early childhood origins of these relational patterns (e.g., "I often felt betrayed or undermined in my relationships to my mother").

5. **Corrective emotional experience.** This process entails experiencing that not only the anticipated or expected unpleasant social interaction (e.g., feeling rejected or dismissed by the other) did not materialize in the group, but that the interaction evoked unanticipated positive reactions (e.g., you really seem interested in me).

6. **Internalization.** Often regarded as the most robust of therapeutic factors, this refers to the development of new representations of self and other or modification of existing representations with more benevolent and less malevolent attributes. This process is thought to be facilitated by encouraging the group members to step back from the immediate experience and reflect on its significance, a kind of highlighting or boldfacing of some immediate experience in the group.

7. **Group cohesion.** As suggested earlier, developing a sense of "we" and a commitment to the group is usually regarded as a therapeutic condition. However patients with particular personalities, such as avoidant attachment styles or introjective depression, where maintaining independence and self-reliance are of primary concern, the promoting of cohesion may be threatening. **It is important for the group therapist to sensitively assess the effects of developing cohesion on each patient in the group.**

Therapeutic Factors from an Interpersonal Psychotherapy Perspective

Three therapeutic processes considered critical to therapeutic change from an **interpersonal psychotherapy perspective** (Kivlighan, 2014):

1. **Bringing the discussion into the here-and-now.** This refers to efforts at moving stories about the there-and-then to exploration of immediate here-and-now feelings, reactions and perceptions, as well as discovering potential links between the past and the present.
2. **Making impact disclosures.** The therapist's disclosures of how a patient's or the group's participation is emotionally affecting the therapist can help increase understanding of one's interpersonal patterns and the kinds of emotional reactions they evoke in others.
3. **Creating a corrective emotional experience.** Presenting opportunities for the group members to discover, for example, that the **feared or dreaded anticipated responses from others do not materialize** and that others can be more benign than previously assumed. This entails having new forms of relatedness with others that can assist in changing internalized self and other representations.

Therapeutic Factors from a Cognitive Behavioral Perspective

Perhaps surprising, many clinicians argue that attention to and management of therapeutic group processes are important parts of the work in **cognitive-behavioral, psychoeducational, and skill building group approaches** which tend to be relatively structured in format.

> The group leader plays a pivotal role in determining whether the treatment proceeds essentially as individual therapy within a group setting or from the perspective of enhancing the CBT by recognizing and building on group processes.
> (Bieling, McCabe, & Antony, 2006)

Both clinical observation and some promising research suggest that attending to and promoting therapeutic group processes in structured CBT or psychoeducational groups can be therapeutically advantageous (Lawson, 2010; Rivera & Darke, 2012; Taube-Schiff, Suvak, Antony, Bieling, & McCabe, 2007).

Several group processes can facilitate the task of CBT groups (Bieling, McCabe, & Antony, 2006):

1. **Instillation of hopefulness and optimism,** in part generated by the therapist serving as a model for giving positive feedback.
2. **Inclusion** or **universality,** the sense that one is not alone in having particular symptoms or problems, a particularly robust therapeutic factor in homogeneous groups such as CBT groups.
3. **Group based learning,** referring not to the didactic psychoeducational material that is part of the leader's agenda, but to the interpersonal feedback and sharing of here-and-now experiences in the group.
4. A sense of **altruism** generated by giving effective feedback to others in the group.
5. The **modification of maladaptive relational patterns** in the here-and-now.
6. **Identifying and processing difficult or painful emotions** in the here-and-now that may otherwise be resistances to learning the psychoeducational material.
7. **Group cohesion.**

These factors are essentially the same as those identified in more process-oriented groups. Bieling, McCabe, and Antony (2006) urge that CBT therapists use the power inherent in the group process to facilitate the CBT tasks. For example, they advise that the therapist not merely review homework assignments by focusing on one isolated patient at a time, but rather encourage interactions among members during this review. Similarly they suggest that the CBT group not be structured merely as a classroom with lecturing teachers and passive students but rather as an interactive conversation focusing on the didactic material. They encourage CBT group leaders to invite group conversations about how the treatment is progressing for each patient and about how each is feeling about the group experience.

Other Therapeutic Factors, Conditions, and Processes

Safety

While the concepts reviewed above capture most of the therapeutic factors identified in the clinical literature, still a few others have been posited. Perhaps above all is the requirement, true for all forms of psychotherapy, that the therapeutic situation be experienced as a safe space. The members must come to experience a sense of safety in the group in order to risk:

- Moving from singleton status to participating group member.
- Giving and receiving feedback.
- Hearing, perhaps for the first time, psychological truths about self and one's relationship patterns.

Without some degree of security and assurance that one's sense of self and integrity will not be damaged, or that one will not be overwhelmed with intractable painful emotions such as shame and guilt, psychological exploration, curiosity and discovery will not be risked. **Managing boundaries, stressing confidentiality, professional communication with outside stakeholders when needed, and exploring individual member's needs around safety and trust will increase therapeutic effectiveness.**

Working Through

This concept refers to the **repeated processing or practicing** of new learning, understandings and skills. **Change is a slow, nonlinear process, hampered by resistances, restraining forces or defenses.** It is important for the group therapist and the group as a whole to develop a sense of timing and pacing of the work, to be patient about the tempo of psychological change, and to view resistances not with frustration but appreciation of the human tendency to avoid psychological truths.

In Vivo Practice

Related to the concept of working through, in vivo practice refers to the practice of new skills and behaviors during the group time. This may include addressing a difficult interpersonal or symptom- eliciting situation in a new way in the here-and-now group, such as a situation that heretofore has been avoided due to anticipated anxiety, shame or guilt, for example, encouraging or challenging an inhibited, quiet member to speak more or a fearful member to voice irritation to another group member. This in-group practice can result in new learning and expanded relational and behavioral patterns particularly when accompanied by empathy and support.

Emotional Regulation and Mindfulness

Spurred by advances in neuroscience (Chapter 11), structured exercises to enhance emotional regulation and mindfulness, often introduced at the beginning of a group session or as a homework assignment, are increasingly being incorporated into various group models, such as dialectical behavior therapy, acceptance and commitment therapy, and mindfulness-based cognitive-behavioral therapy for depression and anxiety, and mindfulness-informed group approaches (Chang, Ciliberti, & Kaklauskas, 2017). When individuals are regulated, they are better able to learn new information, interpret life events more accurately, and consider choices without becoming reactive. Similarly, mindfulness has been shown to increase focus, cognitive flexibility, and relational satisfaction, and to decrease stress and rumination (Davis & Hayes 2011).

Concluding Thoughts

Group psychotherapy provides numerous opportunities for healing growth and change, including

- New interpersonal experiences.
- New learning or truths about self and self-other relations.
- More adaptive coping skills.
- Increased self-reflection and understanding.

"Therapeutic factors" is the broad term that refers to those processes, conditions, and interventions that bring about change. **Most leaders draw on a variety of these therapeutic factors depending upon**

- The type of group.
- Stage of group development.
- Group composition.
- Setting or embedded context.

The effort to identify essential therapeutic factors is a work in progress. With few exceptions, the complexity of group psychotherapy **precludes** having any **lockstep formula** about what specific therapeutic factors need to be promoted at any specific phase in the development of the group.

Early in the formation of the group and in instances of **threat to its integrity, cohesion** needs to be monitored and reinforced.

In the **mature working phase** of the group, interpersonal learning, emotional and cognitive insights, and corrective emotional experiences might well be fostered.

In the **termination phase** of the group, the therapist would do well to encourage internalization so that what has been learned remains vivid, to emphasize existential factors such as accepting responsibility for one's life decisions, and encouragement to apply the learning and new experiences in broader range of situations. Beyond these generalities, much remains to be explored regarding therapeutic factors.

The search for parsimonious, higher-order dimensions that make a therapeutic difference is being pursued both empirically and clinically. In the absence of a more explicit and comprehensive set of guidelines regarding the implementation of therapeutic factors, **it is important to keep all of the therapeutic factors in mind and to ask in the moment, in the session, and throughout the entire group trajectory:**

> What can I do to promote a therapeutic environment and a group process that will facilitate therapeutic change?

Recommended Resources

Bieling, P. J., McCabe, R. E., & Antony, M. M. (2013). *Cognitive behavioral therapy in groups.* New York: Guilford.

Davis, D. M., & Hayes, J. A. (2011). What are the benefits of mindfulness? A practice review of psychotherapy-related research. *Psychotherapy, 48*(2), 198–208.

Fonagy, P., Campbell, C., & Bateman, A. (2017). Mentalizing, attachment, and epistemic trust in group therapy. *International Journal of Group Psychotherapy, 67*(2), 176–201.

Kivlighan, D. (2014). Three important clinical processes in individual and group interpersonal psychotherapy sessions. *Psychotherapy, 51,* 20–24.

Marmarosh, C. L.; Markin, R. D., & Spiegel, E. B. (2013). Processes that foster secure attachment in group psychotherapy. In C. L. Marmarosh, R. D. Markin, & E. B. Spiegel (Eds.) *Attachment in group psychotherapy* (pp. 97–122). Washington, DC: American Psychological Association.

Lawson, D. M. (2010). Comparing cognitive behavioral therapy and integrated cognitive behavioral therapy/psychodynamic therapy in group treatment for partner violent men. *Psychotherapy, 47,* 122–133.

Rivera, M. & Darke, J. L. (2012). Integrating empirically supported therapies for treating personality disorders: A synthesis of psychodynamic and cognitive-behavioral group treatments. *International Journal of Group Psychotherapy, 62,* 2012, 501–529.

Taube-Schiff, M., Suvak, M. K., Antony, M. M., Bieling, P. J., & McCabe, R. E., (2007). Group cohesion in cognitive-behavioral group therapy for social phobia. *Behaviour Research and Therapy, 45,* 687–698.

Westra, H. A., & Norouzian, N. (2018). Using motivational interviewing to manage process markers of ambivalence and resistance in cognitive behavioral therapy. *Cognitive Therapy and Research, 42*(2), 193–203.

5 Anti-Therapeutic, Defensive, Regressive, and Challenging Group Processes and Dynamics

Les R. Greene and Francis J. Kaklauskas

Introduction

As reflected in the previous chapter, there is a good deal of clinical writing and wisdom on therapeutic processes that contribute to positive outcomes. However, the literature also identifies many ubiquitous processes that lead to treatment failures, limited successes, and groups that have gone horribly off course. **An appreciation of those processes that can disrupt therapeutic aims and pose challenges for even the most experienced group therapist is essential for competent leadership.**

Grossmark (2015), Levine (2011) and Nitsun (2014) have each recently described these regressive (i.e., destructive, confusing, anti-therapeutic, restraining) forces and their complex, dialectic relationship with progressive (healing, helpful, productive, driving) forces in the group.

> Rather than communicate their thoughts and feelings directly, members may avoid, block, exclude, excite, arouse, dismiss, attack, scapegoat, monopolize/dominate, direct/instruct, judge, withdraw, isolate, care-take, and collude with others to keep themselves from addressing and containing uncomfortable feelings. Members can be intolerant of the intensity and the experience of primitive feelings. An inability to hold and contain feelings leads to an unbearable experience of helplessness. Internal self/object relationships are triggered and life histories are manifested in group re-enactments.
>
> (Levine, 2011, p. 637)

All types of groups can experience this flood of negativity. While these regressive processes may actually be encouraged in less-structured settings such as psychodynamic psychotherapy and Tavistock self-study groups, they can also readily arise in other types of groups, including more structured psychoeducational groups (Brown, 2011; Sochting, 2014). **The challenge of the group therapist is to "harness" these potentially disruptive forces in the service of the work of the group,** as Ettin (1992) asserts in his analysis of a psychoeducational group:

> Ongoing group processes or hidden agendas arise spontaneously, owing to the idiosyncratic character or circumstances of the members, the eliciting quality of the didactic material, evolving interactions among participants, and reactions (realistic and transferential) to the manner and sensitivity of the group leader's presentational style . . . No amount of careful planning or captivatingly colorful presentation can

prevent dynamic group processes from arising. **The leader's only choice is how and when to use group process to support psychoeducational aims.**

(p. 243)

To maximize learning opportunities, the psychoeducational group leader must be attuned to the stirrings within the group. Ongoing attention to group processes allows for proper presentational timing, selection of relevant informational points, and a sensitivity as to when it is advisable or even necessary to interrupt and punctuate the lesson plan in the service of ventilation, integration, and assimilation.

(Ettin, 1992, p. 243)

Exercises

1. Have you ever been part of or led a group that felt like it was being non-productive or out of control?
2. How do you understand what occurred?
3. Was it resolved? If not, what else might the leader have done to "harness" the disruption?

Recommended Resources

Brown, N. (2011). *Psychoeducational groups: Process and practice* (3rd ed.). New York: Brunner-Routledge.

Ettin, M. (1992). Managing group process in non process group: Working with structured theme-centered tasks. In M. Ettin, *Foundations and applications of group psychotherapy* (pp. 233–259). Boston, MA: Allyn & Bacon.

Grossmark, R. (2015). The edge of chaos: Enactment, disruption, and emergence in group psychotherapy. In R. Grossmark & F. Wright (Eds.), *The one and the many: Relational approaches to group psychotherapy* (pp. 57–74). London: Routledge/Taylor & Francis Group.

Levine, R. (2011). Progressing while regressing in relationships. *International Journal of Group Psychotherapy, 61*, 621–643.

Nitsun, M. (2014). *Beyond the anti-group: Survival and transformation*. London: Routledge.

Söchting, I. (2014). *Cognitive behavioral group therapy: Challenges and opportunities*. New York: Wiley.

Bion's Basic Assumptions: Fight-Flight; Dependency; Pairing

One of the earliest theorists to elucidate the challenging aspects of group life was the British analyst Wilfred Bion. His concept of the basic assumptions have been incorporated into the work of countless group therapists and theorists (Billow, 2015; Rioch, 1970).

- The **fight-flight basic assumption** refers to an "as if" mentality where the group members behave as if the task of the group were **to identify and then fight off or flee from an enemy**, whether it be

  - The leader.
  - The group as a whole.
  - An individual member in a role like scapegoat, rebel, or help-rejecting complainer.
  - Some external "bad object" which could be an individual, another group, an external situation or an abstract idea.

- In the **basic assumption dependency** group, which often manifests in the early stages of group formation, the group acts as if its goal is **to obtain total security for its members.** In this position, the group wishes to be looked after, protected and sustained by an idealized and omnipotent leader who will care for their every need. When frustrated by the leader's inability to gratify all dependency needs, the group may fall into a counter-dependency mode and become aggressive, dismissive, uncooperative, or disheartened.

- In the **basic assumption pairing** group members focus on two people while others take a more passive role. This identified couple could be two members, a member and a leader, or even two leaders. The group develops **a messianic fantasy that this couple will miraculously or magically save the group**, preserving its integrity and identity or help it move to a deeper level of healing. Even if the leader tries to broaden the dynamics, the group will continue to move the attention back to this pair.

Bion also described two interrelated and oscillating levels of group life:

- Rational task-oriented functioning of the **sophisticated work group** in which members are interdependent and autonomous individuals perceived and valued for their task-relevant skills and differentiated work roles. The group climate has a scientific quality where task-relevant hypotheses are generated and tested, and members learn about themselves, the material of the group, and make progress on the group task.

- The reductionistic and defensive functioning of the **basic assumption groups** where members lose their abilities to learn and remember, become "deskilled" in terms of task-relevant functioning, have no interest in predictions or consequences, and lose their sense of individuality and autonomy. As Turquet (1974) describes, in this mode the group has "little or no desire to know (or understand), since knowledge might be an embarrassment, might cause disturbance in the dysfunctional harmony of the group" (p. 358).

Recommended Resources

Billow, R.M. (2015). *Developing nuclear ideas: Relational group psychotherapy.* London: Karnac Books.

Rioch, M.J. (1970). The work of Wilfred Bion on groups. *Psychiatry, 33,* 56–66.

Turquet, P. (1974). Leadership: the individual and the group. In G.S. Gibbard, J.J. Hartman & R.D. Mann (Eds.), *Analysis of groups.* San Francisco, CA: Jossey-Bass.

Loss of Self as an Autonomous and Interdependent Individual Group Member

Groups can put members in a peculiar dialectic. On one hand they want to be a part of this wonderful joining together (a sense of "we"), and on the other hand, they desire to be apart, independent and individuated (a sense of "me"). Hartman and Gibbard (1974) posit:

> Group process can be viewed as an oscillation between a symbiotic relatedness with the group-as-a-whole and individuation. This symbiosis is desired in the form of inclusion in the group and is feared and defended against by the assertion of independence, individuality and uniqueness.
>
> (p. 175)

These formations are essentially **exaggerated or distorted forms of cohesion,** leading on one hand to **experiences of merger and loss of self and,** on the other hand, to **feelings of rupture and fragmentation.** The most theoretically developed of these concepts is Hopper's (2003) **basic assumption incohesion: aggregation/ massification.**

Massification refers to a group formation where the sense of differentiated self is lost in the experience of **merger** or **fusion** with the group-as-a-whole, an "oceanic" state where interpersonal or intragroup conflict, interpersonal difference, the "skin of thy neighbor" (Turquet, 1975) are neither perceived nor experienced, a kind of excessive cohesion.

Conceptually similar phenomena are:

- **basic assumption oneness** (Turquet, 1974),
- **deindividuation** (Deiner, 1979,
- **good mother group** (Scheidlinger, 1974),
- **group as utopia** (Gibbard & Hartman, 1973),
- **groupthink** (Janis, 1972).

At the other extreme, a sense of interpersonal connection and group identity are lost and only the sense of "me" exists as reflected in such concepts as:

- **aggregation** (Hopper, 2003),
- **fragmentation** (Springmann, 1976),
- **disarroy** (Turquet, 1975),
- **basic assumption me-ness** (Lawrence, Bain, & Gould, 1996).

The simple analogy of potatoes has been used to describe this oscillation between aggregation and massification. Sometimes a group and its members want or act like a collection of individual potatoes completely apart from one another, while at other times they desire to be and behave like a pot of mashed potatoes losing all sense of separateness and individuality. Back and forth swings the group.

Recommended Resources

Deiner, E. (1979). Deindividuation: The absence of self-awareness and self-regulation in group members. In P. Paulus (Ed.), *The psychology of group influence.* Hillsdale, NJ: Erlbaum.

Gibbard, G. S. & Hartman, J. J. (1973). The significance of utopian fantasies in small groups. *International Journal of Group Psychotherapy, 23*, 125–147.

Hartman, J. J. & Gibbard, G. S. (1974). Anxiety, boundary evolution and social change. In G.S. Gibbard, J. J. Hartman, & R. D. Mann (eds.) *Analysis of groups.* San Francisco, CA: Jossey Bass.

Hopper, E. (2003). *Traumatic experience in the unconscious life of groups: The fourth basic assumption: Incohesion: Aggregation/massification or (ba)I:A/M.* London: Jessica Kingsley.

Hopper, E. (2007). Moral Corruption and Ethical Dilemmas in Professional Life. Paper presented at the 64th Annual Meeting of the American Group Psychotherapy Association, Austin, TX.

Janis, I. L. (1972). *Victims of groupthink: A psychological study of foreign-policy decisions and fiascoes.* Boston, MA: Houghton Mifflin.

Lawrence, W. G., Bain, A., & Gould, L. (1996). The fifth basic assumption. *Free Associations, 6*, 28–55.

Scheidlinger, S. (1974). On the concept of the "Mother-Group". *International Journal of Group Psychotherapy, 24*, 417–428.

Springmann, R. (1976). Fragmentation in large groups. *Group Analysis, 9*, 185–188.

Turquet, P. (1974). Leadership: the individual and the group. In G.S. Gibbard, J. J. Hartman, & R.D. Mann (Eds.) *Analysis of groups.* San Francisco, CA: Jossey-Bass.

Turquet, P. (1975). Threats to identity in the large groups. In Kreeger, L. (Ed.), *The large group: Dynamics and therapy* (pp. 87–144). London: Constable.

Anti-Group

Several concepts, in addition to Bion's fight-flight basic assumption, have been developed to address the destructive potential in groups. Drawing on the works of Bion (1961), Foulkes and Anthony (1965), Kernberg (1980), and Ganzarain (1989), among others, Nitsun (1996, 2014) has developed the notion of the **anti-group, a** concept which refers to members' collective projective endowment of disowned "bad" inner content into and onto the group as a whole. The anti-group is thought to arise from members' frustrations at the inherent restrictions imposed by the group situation including:

- The desire for an exclusive relationship with the leader will necessarily be thwarted.
- Inevitable misattunements among the members and leader.
- The limitations on interpersonal connections and the need to share attention.
- The inevitable emerging of uncomfortable feelings.

Members will likely experience:

- Non-reality based wishes that cannot be gratified.
- Strong fears and desires.
- Feelings of aggression and competition.

- Impaired ability to think rationally.
- Reactivation of early, less functional coping strategies.

Hallmark characteristics of the anti-group are:

- **Regression** (to developmentally early, less functional, defensive and coping patterns and distorted views of self and other).
- **Survival anxiety** (fear of physical and/or psychic annihilation).
- **Failure of communication** (inability to communicate effectively).
- **Projective Identifications** (disowned and projected feelings without opportunities for reality testing and reclaiming of projections),
- **Envy** (negative self-judgments and the inability to tolerate what others have).
- **Interpersonal disturbance** (inherent chaos given the complexity of having numerous relationships in the group).
- **Aggression, hatred and the death instinct** (towards the group, the other members, or the leader given the frustrations inherent in group life).

Nitsun (2014) developed the notion of the anti-group to redress what he considered an overly and naively positive view of group process in the literature and he calls for leaders to be accepting of this aspect of group life. As with the notion of resistance, anti-group dynamics are not to be denied or eradicated, but rather acknowledged and contained in a dialectic relationship to progressive, life-affirming processes. For Nitsun, accepting the destructive elements as only a part of the overall configuration of group life can be reassuring, strengthening, and transforming for the group as a whole and its individual members.

Exercises

Have you ever been in a group that displayed any of these anti-group phenomena? How was it worked with? Did it resolve or remain unresolved? Why?

Recommended Resources

Bion, W. (1961). *Experiences in groups and other papers*. London: Tavistock.

Foulkes, S. H., & Anthony, E.J. (1965). *Group psychotherapy: The psycho-analytic approach*: London: Karnac Books.

Ganzarain, R. (1989). *Object relations group psychotherapy*. Madison, CT: International Universities Press.

Kernberg, O. (1980). Regression in groups. In O. Kernberg, *Internal world and external reality: Object relations theory applied*. New York: Jason Aronson.

Nitsun, M. (1996). *The Anti-Group: Destructive forces in the group and their creative potential*. London: Routledge.

Nitsun, M. (2000). The future of the group. *International Journal of Group Psychotherapy, 50*, 455–472.

Nitsun, M. (2014). *Beyond the anti-group: Survival and transformation*. London: Routledge.

Violations of the Therapeutic Frame

As described in Chapter 3, the therapy group can be thought of as a social system characterized by an **external boundary** that uniquely defines its

- space,
- time,
- and task,

and **internal boundaries** that define

- **divisions of authority** and labor,
- and **differentiated work roles** (cf. Cohn, 2014).

In this structural view of the group, the therapist is regarded as the **manager of these boundaries**, variously referred to as the **therapeutic frame**, the **group contract** (Ormont, 1992), or **group agreements** (Rutan, Stone, & Shay, 2014). Group life inevitably entails many processes that aim at distorting (either exaggerating or blurring) these various boundaries; for example, subtly changing the work of the group from psychological exploration and growth to mere complaining or small talk is known as **task or mission drift.** Other common boundary violations and distortions include:

- refusing or resisting the work of the group (Billow, 2006),
- refusing to pay or paying late (Ben-Noam, 2010),
- challenging the time and space boundaries as in coming late,
- secret meetings between group members that are not brought back to the group,
- attacking other group members,
- using ethnic, racial or gender slurs and microaggressions,
- refusing to speak or dominating the talking time.

As a leader, it is essential to confront boundary violations and, at times, to firmly intervene to maintain a sense of containment and safety (Billow, 2006; Ormont, 1992; Yalom & Leszcz, 2005). However, if possible, the leader and group can also work towards understanding the meaning of the behavior for the benefit of the member and the group. For instance, if a member is repeatedly coming late, the group could explore whether this behavior was a member's way of communicating dissatisfaction with the group or the leader, of gaining attention, of caring for other members by allowing them to choose their seats first, of repeating a non-healthy desire to be rejected, or of manifesting some other motive.

Recommended Resources

Ben-Noam, S. (2010). The fee: A clinical tool in group therapy. In S.S. Fehr (Ed), *101 interventions in group therapy* [Rev. ed.] (pp. 539–542). New York: Routledge.

Billow, R. M. (2006). The three R's of group: Resistance, rebellion, and refusal. *International Journal of Group Psychotherapy, 56*, 259–284.

Cohn, B. (2014). Creating the group envelope. In L. Motherwell & J. Shay, (Eds.), *Complex dilemmas in group therapy: Pathways to resolution* (2nd ed.). New York: Routledge/Taylor & Francis Group.

Ormont, L. (1992). *The group therapy experience: From theory to practice.* New York: St. Martins.

Rutan, J. S., Stone, W. N., & Shay, J. J. (2014). *Psychodynamic group psychotherapy* (5th ed.). New York: Guilford.

Yalom, I. D., & Leszcz, M. (2005). *The theory and practice of group psychotherapy.* New York: Basic Books.

Splitting and Dysfunctional Subgrouping

Splitting refers to the collective and collusive arrangements (often unconscious) among group participants to divide the group into us-versus-them polar opposite sides, each side containing warded off and projected content from the opposing camp, each side blaming the other. Without efforts to challenge dysfunctional splits in the group, group-as-a-whole cohesion is thwarted and group task achievement can be significantly curtailed.

Agazarian and Gantt (2012) differentiate **dysfunctional** subgrouping formed on the basis of defensive splitting from **functional subgrouping,** intentional and conscious therapeutic efforts to systematically identify psychological dissimilarities (i.e., attitudes, affects, wishes) among the group members in a contained manner that ultimately can lead to the containment and integration of such differences.

Recommended Resource

Agazarian, Y., & Gantt, S. (2012). "The Interpersonal Neurobiology of Building Mindful Systems through Functional Subgrouping" Available at: www.youtube.com/watch?v=p3UE3c_ndxw

Deviant Roles, Scapegoating, Countertransference Enactments, and the Process of Projective Identification

Deviant Roles

Members will assume roles during the group process, sometimes helpful and functional and, at other times, psychologically limiting for both the individual and the group (Gibbard, 1974; Horwitz, 1983; Shay, 2011; Weber, 2014). For example, the group might "invite" a member to serve as "fight leader" or provocateur towards the leader because of their fear of directly expressing frustration, disappointment, or anger. Or a member might serve as the "identified patient" by repeatedly presenting with a crisis, thus allowing others to avoid directly working on their own goals. The group might even select individuals, based on racial, ethnic or gender stereotypes, to enact specific emotional issues for the group as a whole (cf. Chapter 2 on stereotypes and tokenism). **The group creates these specialized group roles to serve its emotional and defensive**

needs. The dynamics of group roles that Gibbard (1974) identified and articulated more than 40 years ago continues to occur in contemporary groups.

> The most common response of a group faced with frustration, ambivalence or internal conflict is splitting and compartmentalization. Role differentiation, then, is in part defensive and restitutive; and the cost of such differentiation, to the individual and the group, is that splitting, projection and compartmentalization all entail some distortion and simplification of emotional life. On the other side of the coin, role differentiation may serve primarily adaptive functions for the individual and the group. Rather than becoming flooded with conflict, the group can make use of individuals to circumscribe, localize, and isolate conflict through projective identification a group is divided into actors and audience. Members are recruited to dramatize the central conflicts of the collectivity, and other members are able to participate vicariously in this dramatization. Compressed into a smaller arena, conflict can be worked through, which in turn makes possible a reintegration of the group.
>
> (p. 250)

Scapegoating

A common deviant role is that of the **group scapegoat** (Gemmill, 1989). In constructing this role, the group selects a member who is blamed for all of the current troubles in the group, reflected by the remark or thought **"if it weren't for you, this group would be great."** As with all such roles based on projective processes, the therapeutic task is not to banish the scapegoat but rather to explore what that role is serving for the group as a whole and, ultimately, how the members' disowned contents can be re-integrated into the group.

> There is always a collusion between the targeted member's character style on the one hand and the group's needs on the other. Groups quickly learn which members are best able to express anger, who can deal most comfortably with closeness and libidinal attraction, and who can experience dependency with a minimum of conflict.
>
> (Horwitz, 1983, p. 270–271)

Scheidlinger (1982) advises that in the emotionally charged climate of scapegoating, interpretations of the group process may not be heard and the therapist may need to employ other interventions – such as limit setting and support – to ensure optimal degrees of safety and levels of anxiety. Ormont (1992) suggests joining the scapegoat to direct frustration back towards the leader who is better able to tolerate and understand what is occurring in the group at that moment. Group therapists need to be aware of the potential part they can play in scapegoating dynamics including:

- not managing tension levels causing the group to regress and destructively discharge,
- allowing or promoting members to act on the leader's own countertransference feelings and wishes,
- avoiding conflict as a leader and allowing members to attack one another,

- not clarifying or enforcing group agreements around attacking other members or taking responsibilities for one's own feelings,
- acting out on the sadistic projective identification in the group.

When a member is scapegoated the entire group becomes less safe as members may worry if they will be next to be targeted. Remember that despite an individual member's behavior, **scapegoating is a group dynamic** which is different than providing feedback to another member that may be helpful.

Countertransference Enactments

By virtue of the centrality, prominence, and authority of the role, the leader is a frequent target of collective projections and wishes to fulfill certain roles by the members. Ultimately the **leader's work is to not accept the invitation to play the defensive emotionally charged role implicitly requested by the group but to help the group explore the underlying emotional needs** (Horwitz, 2014).

In the context of the small group where the therapist may be simultaneously projected upon by some or all of the members, there is always the problematic potential for the group leader to become transformed into the wished for "other," enacting some emotionally or defensively needed role that is not in the service of therapeutic work. These transformations, called **countertransference enactments,** can take a variety of forms such as failing to attend to boundary violations or collusively avoiding the therapeutic work of the group.

It is important for the leader to:

1) **appreciate and experience the projections,**
2) **not be transformed by them,**
3) **create a reflective space to foster psychological exploration and reality-testing,**
4) **help members re-own and reintegrate what they have projected.**

For instance, the group may perceive the leader as not taking the group seriously enough, as being over controlling, or perhaps as favoring a particular member. By fostering curiosity and exploration, the leader can help the group sort through what is actually occurring internally and externally, help members re-assimilate their projections, more effectively manage countertransference enactments, and help the group can move forward in new ways.

The Process of Projective Identification

A core mechanism by which these deviant roles emerge is the process of **projective identification.** (Horwitz, 1983; Ogden, 1979; Steinberg & Ogrodniczuk, 2010). Ogden (1979) summarizes:

> Projective identification . . . is a psychological process that is simultaneously a type of defense, a means of communication, a primitive form of object relationship, and a pathway for psychological change.

> - As a **defense,** projective identification serves to create a sense of psychological distance from unwanted (often frightening) aspects of the self,

- as a **mode of communication**, projective identification is a process by which feelings congruent with one's own are induced in another person, thereby creating a sense of being understood by or of being "at one with" the other person,
- as a type of **object relationship**, projective identification constitutes a way of being with and relating to a partially separate object,
- and finally, as a **pathway for psychological change**; projective identification is a process by which feelings that one is struggling with are psychologically processed by another person and made available for re-internalization in an altered form.

(p. 362)

The mechanism entails:

- a **splitting off or disowning** of some part of one's internal experience,
- **projection of that disowned content onto others** in the group, including the leader, a subgroup or the group as a whole,
- **identification** (keeping the disowned parts at arm's length by trying to induce the other to act in accord with that projected content).

The object or target of the projective identification process can feel possessed and pulled into thinking, acting, and feeling in ways unfamiliar. Segal (2006) describes the recipients' experience of projective identification as living like "a puppet in someone else's nightmare" (p. 53). When holding these disavowed experiences, recipients may be overwhelmed by strong emotional feelings, lose their familiar sense of self, and have strong somatic responses. Often, individuals on both sides of the projections have no or very limited insight into what is occurring.

In all types of groups projective identification processes have the potential to be very damaging and destructive. The projected feelings are often powerful, confusing, and uncomfortable. In dyadic therapy, the therapist becomes the regulator who can hold, organize, and help "metabolize" the disowned experience, making it more palatable to be re-integrated by the patient (Schore, 2002). In the group, the leader, a member, a subgroup, or the group-as-a-whole can become the holding, organizing, and metabolizing container towards re-integration.

It is important to understand that **the process of projective identification also has the potential for tremendous healing in the group context, as working through this primitive coping method and the reactions to it are likely to improve everyone's interpersonal functioning.** Underneath the turmoil, it can be seen as an attempt to share one's deep intrapsychic experience with others and thus as a way to connect and be closer. Through the group experience new ways of relating are practiced and projective identification processes lessen.

In some ways, the technical work has similarities to working with transferences. Common interventions include:

- Asking the group, "Why am I feeling sad?" (or whatever the projected feeling is).
- Asking "In what ways are members not feeling like themselves?"
- Helping members own all of the various aspects of their experiences.
- Maintaining the group's capacity for containing and safety by supporting members in not acting out in destructive ways with these powerful feelings.

Exercises

1) Have you ever gotten "swept away" in a group process only to later experience guilt, shame, or regret about your participation?
2) Have you ever experienced a scapegoating process in groups? In reflection what may have contributed to this dynamic?
3) What kind of leader countertransference enactments are you susceptible to? (e.g., joining the group in attacking a "difficult" patient, keeping the group superficial to avoid conflict, putting off discussing psychoeducational material and joining with a group resistance to the group's task)?
4) Have you ever felt like you experienced projective identification where you were implicitly invited to play some role for the group. What was it like and how did you resolve it?

Recommended Resources

Gemmill, G. (1989). The dynamics of scapegoating in small groups. *Small Group Behavior, 20*, 406–418.

Gibbard, G. S. (1974). Individuation, fusion and role specialization. In G. S. Gibbard, J. J. Hartman, & R. D. Mann (Eds.) *Analysis of groups*. San Francisco, CA: Jossey-Bass.

Horwitz, L. (1983). Projective identification in dyads and groups. *International Journal of Group Psychotherapy, 33*, 259–279.

Horwitz, L. (2014). *Listening with the fourth ear: Unconscious dynamics in analytic group psychotherapy*. London: Karnac Books.

Ogden, T. (1979). On projective identification. *International Journal of Psychoanalysis, 60*, 357–373.

Scheidlinger, S. (1982). Presidential address: On scapegoating in group psychotherapy, *International Journal of Group Psychotherapy, 32*, 131–143.

Schore, A. (2002). Clinical implications of a psychoneurobiological model of projective identification. In S. Alhanati (Ed.), *Primitive mental states, Vol. II: Psychobiological and Psychoanalytic Perspectives on Early Trauma and Personality Development* (pp. 1–65). London: Karnac, 2002.

Segal, H. (2006). *Dream, phantasy and art*. London: Routledge.

Shay, J. (2011). Projective identification simplified: Recruiting your shadow, *International Journal of Group Psychotherapy, 61*, 238–261.

Steinberg, P. I., & Ogrodniczuk, J. S. (2010). Hatred and fear: projective identification in group psychotherapy. *Psychodynamic Practice, 16*(2), 201–205.

Weber, R. (2014). Unraveling projective identification and enactment. In L. Motherwell & J. Shay, (Eds.), *Complex dilemmas in group therapy: Pathways to resolution* (2nd ed.). London: Routledge/Taylor & Francis Group.

Expanding Our Horizons: Social Psychology, Anthropology, Multicultural Perspectives, and the Cross Fertilization of Ideas

Group psychotherapy and group psychology offer important insights and understandings of human collective behavior, but these are not the only realms of knowledge about group behavior and group dynamics. Other disciplines and domains provide equally important conceptualizations about collective behavior, and the deepening of our understanding of the processes of group psychotherapy will be best served by striving to integrate these diverse schools of thought into our work.

- **Social psychology** has provided important understandings and theories of human behavior related to group functioning. While the intersection and integration of social psychological science into group psychotherapy remains partial, awareness of this literature can help leaders understand their groups more thoroughly (Forsyth, 2000, 2018; Kaklauskas & Olson, 2008). For example, the classic studies of Kurt Lewin (Experimental Studies in the Social Climate of Groups, 1953 (2013) on models of leadership as **authoritarian, democratic, or laissez-faire,** Milgram's (Pennsylvania State University, 2016) studies of **obedience to authority** and Asch's (Asch Conformity Experiment, 2007) experiments on **conformity** all have important implications for the exercise of authority by the group therapist and its influence on the group member.
- **Organizational and industrial psychology** are scientific disciplines that have implications for group psychotherapy, particularly in the areas of task performance, group decision-making, effective leadership, and cultural and environmental impacts on group behavior.
- Virtually all cultures utilize groups for healing, emotional support, and transformative experiences. Competence in group psychotherapy leadership increasingly entails an understanding and appreciation of the influence of culture on group life (cf. Chapter 2). A **multicultural perspective** helps us appreciate the complexity of our work (Mead, 1951). **Group leaders need to understand that group dynamics, roles, and required leadership styles need to be adjusted depending on the cultural context in which the group is embedded.** Leading groups in Beijing, Dar Es Salaam, or Caracas will each differ from leading a group in New York. Even leading groups in urban and suburban America may be different from leadership in rural America. Group leaders need to stay aware that our perspectives and interpretations are culturally bound. Leading groups with members with strong cultural identities may lead us to misinterpret the dynamics. For example, Asian culture and Indigenous cultures may entail more space between interactions and greater respect of and deference towards the leaders than groups with white millennial college students. We need to work collaboratively with our members and communities in which we are practicing as leadership roles, social norms, goals, and values may be very different and our styles will need adjustment depending on setting.

Recommended Resources

Asch Conformity Experiment. (2007). Available at www.youtube.com/watch?v=TYIh4MkcfJA

Experimental Studies in the Social Climate of Groups, 1953. (2013). Available at www.youtube.com/watch?v=J7FYGn2NS8M

Forsyth, D.R. (2000). The social psychology of groups and group psychotherapy: One view of the next century. *Group*, 24(2–3), 147–155.

Forsyth, D.R. (2018). *Group dynamics*. Boston, MA: Cengage Learning.

Kaklauskas, F.J., & Olson, E.A. (2008). Large group process: Grounding Buddhist and psychological theory in experience. In F.J. Kaklauskas, S. Nimanheminda, L. Hoffman, & M. S. Jack (Eds.), *Brilliant sanity: Buddhist approaches to psychotherapy* (pp. 133–160). Colorado Springs, CO: University of the Rockies Press.

Mead, M. (1951). Group psychotherapy in the light of social anthropology. *International Journal of Group Psychotherapy*, 1(3), 193–199.

Pennsylvania State University (producer). (2016). The Milgram experiment 1962 full documentary, Available at www.youtube.com/watch?v=wdUu3u9Web4

Concluding Thoughts

In this chapter, we reviewed some of the dynamics that can arise in various types of groups and in particular psychotherapy groups. The views of the early group psychology theorist Gustave Le Bon (1895) remain pertinent to this day.

> Whoever be the individuals that compose it, however like or unlike be their mode of life, their occupations, their character, or their intelligence, the fact that they have been transformed into a group puts them in possession of a sort of collective mind which makes them feel, think, and act in a manner quite different from that in which each individual of them would feel, think, and act in a state of isolation. There are certain ideas and feelings which do not come into being, or do not transform themselves into acts except in the case of individuals forming a group. The psychological group is a provisional being formed of heterogeneous elements, which for a moment are combined, exactly as the cells which constitute a living body form by their reunion a new being which displays characteristics very different from those possessed by each of the cells singly.
>
> (p. 29)

In group psychotherapy a myriad of forces intersect to create powerful and unique dynamics. While group members will inevitably enact their familiar communication patterns and their family of origin roles, the group also takes on an animation of its own. Below the visible exchanges between members, invisible forces pull and push members to act in unique and often uncharacteristic or unhelpful ways (Agazarian, 1983). Through experience, observation, and education, the group therapist can point out, steer, and address these undercurrents to the benefit of our members.

When stuck in what seems like less than ideal group dynamics, several suggestions can be made across settings.

- **Notice your own perceptions and reactions**, including needs, expectations, and anxieties, and ask if they are the same as the group members. For instance, as group therapists we may be used to high levels of intimacy but for our group members this may be new territory. Continually checking and studying our countertransference reactions will help us have more conscious choices and more accurately see what is occurring and meet the goals of the members.

- **Less may be more.** When a group is struggling with some emotional tension, often containment, safety, consistency, curiosity, and reflection, will help more than extravagant intellectual or affective interventions.
- **Patience and Hope.** Groups will inevitably struggle, go through lulls, become confused and confusing, but often find their way out of these periods and back into doing its work.
- Helping the members **explore and discuss the often unseen processes** in the group can change the homeostatic dynamic.
- **Consultation and Supervision.** Talking openly and honestly about your groups with an experienced group leader whom you trust is perhaps the best way to care for yourself and your groups, broaden your intervention options, and enjoy your work.

Module 3

Group Formation and Group Development

6 Preparing to Begin a New Group

J. Scott Rutan, Les R. Greene, and Francis J. Kaklauskas

Decisions, Decisions, Decisions

To ensure the establishment of successful therapy group, the therapist has many decisions to make – both clinical and administrative – that need careful and thoughtful attention (Turner, 2017). The following steps are needed in creating a successful therapy group enterprise. Supervision and consultation can be extremely valuable to explore the internal and external factors that inform the choices we make at this formative stage.

Recommended Resource

Turner, M. M. (2017). Nuts and bolts: The group screen. In M. D. Ribeiro, J. Gross, & M. M. Turner (Eds.), *The college counselor's guide to group psychotherapy* (pp. 145–155). New York: Routledge.

Assessing the Feasibility of Establishing a New Group

Needs Assessment

Regardless of orientation, many essential tasks must be initiated **prior to beginning a group**. First and foremost in designing a group, a prospective leader should determine whether there is a **need** for this specific group. A therapist may *want* to form a particular group based on personal or professional interest, but sufficient need or demand in the area might not be present. By asking colleagues and potential referral streams one can get a sense of the **feasibility** for establishing any particular group. Moreover, for groups to be implemented within an embedding treatment environment, such as a clinic or day treatment program, feasibility also entails assessing whether the group fits the values, needs and mission of the larger institution. In a clinic, for example, that primarily conducts structured, time-limited CBT oriented groups, in part based on economic considerations, an ongoing psychodynamic interpersonal process group may be a hard sell to the administration. As Berne (1966) said years ago, **the group therapist working in institutions has two roles: group therapist and organizational staff member**. In the latter role, the group leader must facilitate information flow between the group and its environment to ensure that the group is supported and appreciated and is serving the larger needs of the embedding organization.

Increasingly psychotherapy clinics and college counseling centers are employing **group coordinators** to oversee the development and implementation of group programming and positive group psychotherapy cultures (Gross, 2017). These individuals can be of vital help to the organization in educating consumers and staff alike about the role and benefits of group psychotherapy, in building effective group screening processes, in organizing group specific training for clinicians, and in analyzing program effectiveness.

Recommended Resources

Berne, E. (1966). *Principles of group treatment*. New York: Grove Press.
Gross, J. M. (2017). The group coordinator: Promoting group culture by managing stages of program development. In M. D. Ribeiro, J. Gross, & M. M. Turner (Eds.), *The college counselor's guide to group psychotherapy* (pp. 131–144). New York: Routledge.

Referral Stream

An adequate referral network is essential to ensure that the group can form and then sustain. Having five or so members is a good starting point. New groups typically experience higher numbers of dropouts than ongoing groups, so referral resources are particularly crucial to keep a fledgling group going until a sense of safety and trust can be established (Jensen, Mortensen, & Lotz, 2014; Kegel & Flückiger, 2015). And this work is made even more difficult because it is usually easier to get referrals for an established group that has acquired a good reputation than for one that is just being formed.

Recommended Resources

Kegel, A. F., & Flückiger, C. (2015). Predicting psychotherapy dropouts: A multilevel approach. *Clinical Psychology & Psychotherapy*, 22(5), 377–386.
Jensen, H. H., Mortensen, E. L., & Lotz, M. (2014). Drop-out from a psychodynamic group psychotherapy outpatient unit. *Nordic Journal of Psychiatry*, 68(8), 594–604.

Marketing

Making certain that one has a sufficient referral stream entails marketing. While many therapists are uncomfortable with this aspect of the work, the professional community needs to be informed of your proposed group. Within an agency or organization, some staff may lack knowledge or have misconceptions about group psychotherapy. Having empathic conversations that address staff's past experiences or concerns about group may help reduce the reluctance of an agency to expand their group psychotherapy program (Kaplan, 2017).

It is essential that marketing materials be clear and explicit about the rationale and potential benefits of the group, including the evidence that supports its effectiveness, who might be a good fit in terms of inclusionary and exclusionary criteria, fees, and structural arrangements such as time and place. In disseminating this information, group coordinators or clinicians must know their intended audiences and gear the information to them.

As marginalized groups often underutilize psychotherapy services, the use of inclusive language in marketing and application of multicultural methods can expand the group recruitment and participation. Individuals from specific groups, and often marginalized groups, may prefer a more homogeneous therapy group experience. Many clinics now offer groups for individuals with specific culturally-defined identities such as a group for exploring gender identities or for individuals who identify as a person of color.

Your valuing of the group is not enough; it is crucial for referral sources, whether they are fellow colleagues in the private practice community or co-workers in your agency or clinic, to understand and appreciate the value and need of your proposed group and the therapeutic benefits of enrolling.

Recommended Resource

Kaplan, S. A. (2017). The art of the sell: Marketing groups. In M. D. Ribeiro, J. Gross, & M. M. Turner (Eds.), *The college counselor's guide to group psychotherapy* (pp. 117–130). New York City: Routledge.

Designing the Group Structure

As reviewed in Chapter 1, there are many types of groups, each requiring a number of initial decisions about the following **structural parameters.**

Scheduling the Group

An initial challenge for the leader is scheduling a viable time for the group when all the members can meet. Often this might mean scheduling the group outside of a typical work day, such as early morning, late afternoon, evening, lunch hour, or even weekends. Leaders need to be careful when selecting a time because once a group time is established **changing that time is often very difficult or impossible** given the varied schedules of the members. You want to avoid the predicament of discovering that some, but not all, of the members want to change the time, a predicament that if handled poorly can negatively impact the trust and safety of the group and erode members' confidence in the leader. A general rule is to not to change the time of a group unless it has been talked about in depth and all members are fully willing to commit.

Group Size

Group size is determined by the confluence of many factors, including the supply of referrals and, for those groups within an agency, the needs, limitations and constraints of that organization. The nature of the group also influences its size, as **form follows function.** Traditionally, psychodynamic and process-oriented groups have a smaller membership of between 6 and 10 members designed to optimize interpersonal interactions while psychoeducational or CBT groups, structured more like a classroom, tend to accommodate larger memberships.

Group size matters. A comparatively small group is often thought to evoke familiar family-of-origin dynamics while groups with greater numbers have the potential to evoke regressive large group dynamics. Some members will feel more at ease and safer in a smaller group, but a smaller group will also put more responsibility on each member to participate actively. In larger groups, the leader needs to be alert to those members with tendencies to hide or remain withdrawn or passive to help them become engaged.

Logistics also plays a role in determining group size. Not every clinician or clinic has room for larger groups and cramming a group into too small a space can disturb the members' and even the therapist's personal space. On the other hand, sustaining a group with few members is also challenging particularly when there are absences. Inevitably members will miss a session, often affecting the optimally established size of the group. These absences should be explored in terms of their impact on group morale, specifically the quality of the group climate, level of member engagement, and commitment to the group's work (Paquin & Kivlighan, 2016).

Clearly one size does not fit all, and therapists need to consider the above factors in determining an optimal size for each of their groups with **sensitivity as to how the spatial arrangement and number of chairs might affect members' – and the therapist's own – personal and interpersonal reactions.**

Recommended Resource

Paquin, J. D., & Kivlighan Jr, D. M. (2016). All absences are not the same: What happens to the group climate when someone is absent from group? *International Journal of Group Psychotherapy*, 66(4), 506–525.

Closed or Open Group

The leader needs to make an initial decision about the **permeability of the external boundary** of the group, that is, whether the group is closed or open to the introduction of new members once it has begun. A closed group has membership that is set at the beginning. It is a **cohort** that collectively experiences the same beginning, middle phases, and ending of the group. This structure is usually preferred in a group with a curriculum so that everyone is, literally, on the same page.

In contrast, an open group with a more permeable boundary has comings and goings of members over time, characteristic of dynamic/relational/interactional approaches. In open ended groups it is crucial for the therapist to monitor the inevitable processes of **accommodation** (does the group readily let the new member into its midst?) and **assimilation** (is the newcomer sensitive to and curious about the way the group functions and its culture?) when someone joins the group. **Comings and goings provide opportunities for the group to review where it has been and where it is going;** on the downside, these boundary crossings may slow, or even temporarily reverse, the developmental progression of the group.

Dosage: Session Frequency, Spacing and Length

Another vital choice the leader must make at the start is the dosage of groups, the frequency, spacing and length of its sessions. Curriculum based groups often rely on a well-established format of about 12 sessions conducted weekly for 90 minutes each. Of course, many other dosages are possible. For example, some training groups, such as those practiced within the AGPA Institute, are conducted intensively with 12 or more hours of a group experience over two days. Research on the impact of group dosage is limited, but the leaders should have a theoretical rationale for their **choice of a dosage that matches the group goals and their theory of change.** For a group of individuals looking for support and encouragement to sustain long term sobriety, a schedule of once per month meetings may be sufficient to be an effective holding environment. On the other hand, individuals suffering from some acute stressor, such as a natural disaster or terrorist act, may need daily sessions to work through the traumatic experience and restore a sense of the familiar. While a psychoeducational format for anger management might require only 12 sessions to cover and process the basic material, the working through of characterological issues, as with a group of personality disordered individuals, realistically needs an extended time period to effect significant change. **Decisions about dosage need to be made not merely on the basis of practical and logistical considerations, but with an explicit hypothesis about the intensity of the treatment that optimizes the psychological work that is to be done.**

Homogeneous versus Heterogeneous Groups

Yet another initial decision for the therapist is whether the group is to be hom**ogeneous** or **heterogeneous**. In homogeneous groups, very prominent in clinic settings, members' experience a shared identification of a problem (such as anxiety) or theme (such as going through divorce), typically evoking an initial impression that "we are similar and it is so good to be with people who understand our situation." However, composition in homogeneous groups can still be quite varied in terms of members' personal resources, such as psychological mindedness, defense and character styles, and cultural backgrounds. Thus while homogeneous groups may have an advantage in the development of cohesion in the early phases of group formation, over time homogenous groups begin to note, "Despite our apparent similarities, we're not all the same after all."

In contrast, in heterogeneous groups (typically longer term, open-ended process-oriented groups run in private practice) more time is needed for the group to bond, with members often wondering, "Why did you place me in *this* group?" In time, however, as the group coalesces, members begin to sense, "Beneath all our apparent differences, we share many similarities."

Explicating the Work Roles

Clarifying the expectations of work for you and the members may seem obvious, but it is important that you have in mind an explicit understanding of what constitutes work in your group. Defining the work is invaluable in helping you distinguish the myriad of ways that non-work activities (such as resistances or refusals to work) can infiltrate the group process (see chapter 5) and in ensuring that the patients understand what they are signing up for. In some groups the work may entail completing homework and practicing skills, while in other groups the work may be articulating your relational experience in the present moment.

Selection and Composition

As elaborated in AGPA's Clinical Practice Guidelines (Bernard et al., 2008), decisions about who should be placed in your group, whether forming a new group or adding to an ongoing group, need to be considered from the **dual perspectives** of the individual candidate (**selection**) and the group-as-a-whole (**composition**). These two perspectives drive two questions, respectively, that need to be addressed:

- **Will this particular group benefit this patient?**

Knowing about the group you are creating or running, in terms of its goals, work roles assigned to the members, group norms and culture, you need to ask whether this candidate has the "right stuff", that is the psychological resources and attributes, to benefit from this particular group. Ideally, selection is based on careful and comprehensive evaluations of all potential members (Gans & Counselman, 2010) to learn whether they are capable of benefitting from the kind of feedback they will receive from any particular group. At the very least, the following **inclusion criteria** needed to be assessed for proper selection:

- The desire to be in a group, including assessments of ambivalence, anxiety, defensiveness, and commitment to attend reliably.
- Nature and severity of core self and/or interpersonal difficulties.
- Self-reflective capacity.
- Empathic ability.

The following **exclusion criteria** indicate that the candidate will likely not benefit from group feedback (MacNair-Semands, 2002):

- Acute substance abuse or withdrawal.
- Severely impaired cognitive functioning.
- Active psychosis.
- Angry hostility.
- Severe social inhibition.

Our clinical capacities to accurately judge and predict are limited and group selection measures can be administered to supplement our clinical judgement (Burlingame, Cox, Davies, Layne, & Gleave, 2011). Surprises can occur as when a new patient, assessed in a screening as being very well regulated emotionally, becomes verbally abusive in the group and unwilling to comply with group norms. Nevertheless, the question must be considered as to **whether this particular group can usefully offer something beneficial to this particular patient.**

Of course, administrative needs may outweigh clinical considerations in decisions about selection. For example, due to limited staff resources or financial considerations, agencies and clinics may pressure clinicians to place clients in groups even when clinically not indicated. And sometimes clinicians may put someone into a group primarily from a desire to fill up a group.

- **Will this patient fit well into this group?**

Here the question is whether the potential patient can add something to help the group in its therapeutic work and developmental tasks. **The question of fit entails considerations of salient differences between the candidate and the rest of the group. The general rule of thumb is that too much divergence or incompatibility between the prospective candidate and the group can be disruptive,** as in adding a highly dysregu- lated and impulsive person to a group of traumatized individuals (Cloitre & Koenen, 2001), a grandiose attention seeking patient to a newly forming group, or a withdrawn and dismissive patient to a higher functioning group (Kealy, Ogrodnic- zuk, Piper, & Sierra-Hernandez, 2016). The question of fit is complicated, however, because sometimes differences in psychological attributes between a candidate and the rest of the group can change the overall group functioning for the better. Piper, Ogrodniczuk, Joyce, and Weideman (2011) for example found that having a few patients with more mature levels of object relations can raise the overall functioning of the group. While the concept of fit is important for the therapist to carefully consider (Kivlighan, Li, & Gillis, 2015), it cannot be predicted with complete certainty that a candidate will be a good addition for the group, leaving clinical judgement necessary for deciding how to handle an emerging mismatch. **It is crucial for the therapist to monitor in an ongoing way the dual processes of assimilation and accommodation to assess the adjustment between the new patient and the group, in order to manage potentially disruptive processes such as scapegoating, ostracism or drop-out occur.**

Recommended Resources

Bernard, H., Burlingame, G., Flores, P., Greene, L., Joyce, A., Kobos, J., Leszcz, M., MacNair-Semands, R.R., Piper, W. E., Slocum McEneaney, A. M., & Feirman, D. (2008). Clinical practice guidelines for group psychotherapy. *International Jour- nal of Group Psychotherapy*, *58*, 455–542.

Burlingame, G. M., Cox, J. C., Davies, D. R., Layne, C. M., & Gleave, R. (2011). The Group Selection Questionnaire: Further refinements in group member selection. *Group Dynamics: Theory, Research, and Practice*, *15*(1), 60–74.

Cloitre, M., & Koenen, K.C. (2001). The impact of borderline personality disorder on process group outcome among women with posttraumatic stress disorder related to childhood abuse. *International Journal of Group Psychotherapy*, *51*, 379–398.

Gans, J. S., & Counselman, E. F. (2010). Patient selection for psychodynamic group psychotherapy: Practical and dynamic considerations. *International Journal of Group Psychotherapy*, *60*(2), 197–220.

Kealy, D., Ogrodniczuk, J. S., Piper, W. E., & Sierra-Hernandez, C. A. (2016). When it is not a good fit: Clinical errors in patient selection and group composition in group psychotherapy. *Psychotherapy*, *53(3)*, 308–313.

Kivlighan, D. M. Jr., Li, X., Gillis, L. (2015). Do I fit with my group? Within-member and within-group fit with the group in engaged group climate and group members feeling involved and valued. *Group Dynamics: Theory, Research, and Practice, 19(2)*, 106–121.

MacNair-Semands, R. R. (2002). Predicting attendance and expectations for group therapy. *Group Dynamics: Theory, Research, and Practice, 6(3)*, 219–228.

Piper, W., Ogrodniczuk, J., Joyce, A. & Weideman, R. (2011). *Short-term group therapies for complicated grief.* Washington, DC: American Psychological Association.

Pre-Group Preparation and Orientation

Pre-group meetings with prospective patients serve several important functions. One task is a **psychological assessment** that is particularly relevant for group therapy, entailing information about the individual's patterns of interpersonal relationships (including characteristic interpersonal needs and fears) and sense of identity. Recent papers (Hewitt, Mikail, Flett, & Dang, 2018; Whittingham, 2018) nicely illustrate the utility of developing formulations about the patient's problematic interpersonal patterns, based on assessments from formal standardized instruments and clinical observations, and sharing these impressions with the patient in this assessment phase in order to identify specific goals to be worked in in the group.

In addition, information should be collected about previous treatments, whether these treatments were perceived as helpful or not and why, the desire to be in group, and goals for this treatment. This information is crucial in considerations of whether this particular patient will fit with the group.

Additional goals of pre-group work are:

- Starting to build both a **positive emotional bond** and a **positive working alliance** with the patient.
- Informing the patient about the nature of the group, how it will work, the **patient's work role**, and, importantly, answering questions the patient may have.
- Reviewing the **group agreements**, discussed below, such as fee collections, appropriate terminations, extra-group contact, absence policies, norms, and expectations.
- Reviewing **logistic information** about the time and location of the group.
- Exploring and addressing **assumptions, anxieties, and resistances.**

It is particularly important in this pre-group work to provide opportunities to explore and clarify what may be **unrealistic expectations, assumptions, beliefs, anxieties and resistances** about being in the group. **Prerequisites for successful group treatment include adequate preparation and orientation of the patient to the group and the identifying and working through of potential barriers such as misassumptions, fears, and false expectations.** As articulated in the AGPA revised Core Battery (Burlingame et al., 2006), it is important to review common **myths about group therapy**, such as:

- group being a second-class form of treatment,
- groups are coercive or "forced confessionals,"

- everyone will actually get worse through a process of emotional contagion,
- the group will reject or ostracize the individual,
- the individual will lose personal identity and be swept away by the group.

Inevitably, members bring their personal histories into the group, and, even more importantly, bring their histories of groups, past and present, including their families, peer groups, and work groups. For most individuals, the experiences of the groups in their lives are mixed, evoking a range of positive and negative emotions about being a part of a collective. These experiences also are likely imbued with both unrealistic hopes and wishes of being unconditionally accepted, understood, and supported, as well as unrealistic fears and anticipations of being mistreated, misunderstood, and maybe eventually banished from the group. **It is important for incoming members to understand that while they are likely to have positive experiences of support and learning, there will also be times of challenge, confusion, and feedback that may be difficult to hear.** It is also important for the patient to understand that the psychotherapy group provides a unique opportunity to rework older interpersonal distortions and wounds that may require quite a bit of personal effort, courage and risk taking to be most effective.

Further, the identification of problematic interpersonal behaviors or patterns and understanding that such phenomena are likely to surface again in this new group are important tasks in this pre-group work. Many group leaders recommend that new group members sit back for a few sessions to get the lay of the land. Of course, this advice is not always heeded and some new members may be prone to jump in to try to dominate or direct the group, ignoring the established norms and culture and thus inviting themselves to be scapegoated. It is important to remember that as a leader you have the authority to direct members so they can remain in the group and benefit from the experience. While this can be done with compassion and gentleness, at times a stronger approach is needed.

Exercise

Do you remember any of your early preconceptions about group psychotherapy? How have your ideas changed?

Recommended Resources

Burlingame, G.M., Strauss, B., Joyce, A., MacNair-Semands, R., MacKenzie, K.R., Ogrodniczuk, J., & Taylor, S. (2006). *Core Battery – Revised: An Assessment Tool Kit for Promoting Optimal Group Selection, Process and Outcome*. Available through the AGPA store.

Hewitt, P. L., Mikail, S. F., Flett, G. L., & Dang, S. S. (2018). Specific formulation feedback in dynamic-relational group psychotherapy of perfectionism. *Psychotherapy, 55*, 179–185.

Whittingham, M. (2018). Innovations in group assessment: How focused brief group therapy integrates formal measures to enhance treatment preparation, process, and outcomes. *Psychotherapy, 55*, 186–190.

Initial Group Agreements

A discussion around the expectations and norms of behavior in the group is essential to provide a viable therapeutic environment. Whether referred to as "group agreements" (Rutan, Stone, & Shay, 2014), "treatment contract" (Ormont, 1992), or "responsibilities" (Burlingame et al., 2006), this listing of the roles and rules of the group help to create predictability and a safe working environment. Some group leaders have members sign an agreement form as a way of clarifying and explicating the expected participation. **Agreements help members know what to expect and what is expected of them.** As Singer, Astrachan, Gould, and Klein (1975) posit:

> It is through the contract that the leader derives his authority to work: to propose activities, to confront a member, to make interpretations. And it is by virtue of the contract that certain activities can be declared "out of bounds" . . . A clear contract provides valuable guidelines by which both leader and member can legitimately act or make demands in or on the group.
>
> (p. 147)

The group agreements should include:

- **Confidentiality** – a shared commitment to protect the names and identities of group members, a requisite for experiencing the group as safe enough to take risks.
- A **commitment to the therapeutic goals** of the group.
- A shared **understanding of the expected work roles** of the members (and leader) which will depend on the nature of the group. For instance, in a psychoeducational or cognitive-behavioral group, members might agree to learning the didactic material and completing all homework assignments, while in affect-oriented or process groups, members may be expected to put their here-and-now feelings and experiences into words. Members also need to understand what the work activities are within each session. For instance, some groups may start with reviewing the previous week's didactic information, the current week's homework, or a brief check in to see who wants time, and then have a time for the presentation of new material and open processing.
- An understanding of how **extra-group contacts or member-member socializing** will be handled, which also depends on the nature of the group. In ongoing psychodynamic groups, such encounters are often discouraged since they can lead to the keeping of secrets, contribute to implicit collusive relationships, or keep important feelings out of the group. In support groups for anxiety or sobriety, socializing may be supported as part of ongoing connection and support. When groups are conducted in closed environments, such as inpatient wards or day treatment programs, prisons, college campuses, or small towns, such extra group contact may be inevitable. In these groups, perhaps a group agreement could be, "If you have contact with a group member outside the group meetings and you have feelings about that meeting, you agree to talk about this in the group." What is important is that the leader have a dependable, overt, and therapeutically guided way of dealing with such encounters.
- A shared agreement about how **fees and payments** are to be handled, a topic that often makes therapists and patients uncomfortable. Many of us are uncomfortable about the

idea of "selling" our therapeutic relationship. Likewise, many patients find it easier to speak about sex or aggression than money. Nonetheless, as Gans (1992) has observed, understanding how our patients view and use money is an important window into their psyches. A maxim of most group therapy is that there are no secrets in the group, and to that end, it is important that fees and payment be part of the group discussions. This can be particularly dicey, and particularly important, when therapists use sliding fees, multiple funding sources, or add pro bono members into the group. The therapist's competent attention to money issues can demonstrate reliability, professionalism, and care around the seriousness and value of the work. Conversely, avoiding these issues can decrease the sense of safety as members may not know where the boundaries are or what boundaries can be violated next.

- The agreements should spell out what constitutes **unacceptable behavior**, particularly noting behaviors that could lead to termination, such as physical violence, breaking confidentiality, or coming to group intoxicated.
- Lastly, the agreements should spell out **expectations about leave-takings and terminations**. Termination can be an opportunity for departing members to receive feedback about therapeutic progress, try to address any unfinished business, gain additional support, and review what was learned. In time-limited groups, termination plans should built into the curriculum. In open-ended groups, this review can also be beneficial for the other members, especially new members, to hear and witness how the group has been impactful.

In both time-limited and open-ended groups, members may leave prematurely. The preferred way of leaving is to provide sufficient time to process the feelings that arise for both the leave-taking member and the rest of the group.

Group departures offer everyone an opportunity to learn more about how to appropriately say goodbye. The leader might facilitate the review by asking the group such questions as: 1) What will you miss about the departing member? 2) What changes have you noticed? 3) Are there any concerns or wishes that should be spoken?

Regardless of the accepted protocol for a proper ending, it is not unusual to have members drop out of group, sometimes announcing abruptly that the current session is their last one, and at other times simply stopping attending without any communication. **Dropout rates are particularly high in the initial stages of groups**. When a member leaves unexpectedly, unannounced or with short notice, it can be disruptive to the group. The remaining members may feel confused, rejected, and even betrayed and might experience doubts about the benefit of the group. Strong feelings can be directed at the leaving member (whether present of not) and at the leader for not keeping the group container intact. Therapeutically, it is crucial to explore the impact of the departure on the remaining members. This can be time when members critically review what has been working and what not working in the group. Sometimes the leaving member is acting out unstated feelings of others in the group. The leader and the group can also reflect on ways to prevent future unplanned leavings such as more actively and regularly checking members' experiences of and reactions to the group.

Finally, it is important to note that there is no one-size-fits-all set of group agreements. **Conditions and arrangements should be articulated to facilitate achieving group goals and to minimize hindrances to task accomplishment for your particular group**. Some group leaders may prefer to deal with these issues dynamically as they arise rather than explaining or prohibiting them pre-emptively. This is just one more of many decisions in starting a group. It is important to remember that despite the details of beginnings, new groups are launched regularly and successfully, and once a group is established it takes less work to sustain its functioning.

Recommended Resources

Gans, J. S. (1992). Money and psychodynamic group psychotherapy. *International Journal of Group Psychotherapy*, 42(1), 133–152.

Gans, J. S., & Counselman, E. F. (2000). Silence in group psychotherapy: A powerful communication. *International Journal of Group Psychotherapy*, 50 (1), 71–86.

Ogrodniczuk, J. S., Joyce, A. S., & Piper, W. E. (2005). Strategies for reducing patient-initiated premature termination of psychotherapy. *Harvard Review of Psychiatry*, 13(2), 57–70.

Ormont, L. R. (1992). *The group therapy experience: From theory to practice.* New York: St. Martin's.

Rutan, J. S., Stone, W. N., & Shay, J. J. (2014). *Psychodynamic group psychotherapy.* New York: Guilford.

Singer, D., Astrachan, B., Gould, L., & Klein, R. (1975). Boundary management in psychological work with groups. *Journal of Applied Behavioral Science*, 11, 137–176.

Concluding Thoughts

A spark of inspiration often ignites the beginning of any new group. However between that initial idea and the completion of the first session, there are:

- options to be considered,
- strategic choices to made,
- pre-group meetings to convene,
- forms to be completed,
- a room to reserve,
- and a myriad of other practical and logistical tasks to complete.

For new leaders, a range of anxieties – fear of failure, anticipated narcissistic bruises, dealing with so many unknowns – may accompany this journey while more experienced leaders likely have already experienced a multitude of setbacks and failed launches that help guide each new attempt. Beginning a new group is often a practice of hope and perseverance. Sometimes it all comes together easily, but more often than not it takes some endurance and grit. For leaders, members, and agencies starting a new group can bring forth a mix of feelings from hopefulness to dread. It is important to remember that regardless of inevitable obstacles, new groups do launch and the majority of members benefit from group attendance. Both in the creation and ongoing leadership of groups remaining realistic, attending to the details, and holding onto faith in the unfolding processes can allow one's best work to come forth.

7 Group Development

Les R. Greene and Francis J. Kaklauskas

Introduction

Groups change over time, both structurally and dynamically. Since the earliest psychotherapy groups, leaders have noted evolving dynamics in their groups. Pratt (1907), for example, noted that his patients became more open and forthcoming over time, while Bion noticed that over time, group members desired less involvement from the leader. The question in this chapter is whether these changes follow some invariant sequence across all groups. **Are there general consistencies and regularities in the ways groups change over time?** There is some agreement that groups do in fact normally follow a developmental progression. However a variety of models have been constructed regarding the nature of this developmental sequence, in large part because observations and model-building have occurred over a wide range of groups: closed- and open-ended, short- and long-term, psychotherapy groups and classroom self-study groups.

Knowledge of these developmental models helps the group leader formulate what kinds of interventions are most useful at any particular moment in the life of a group. For example in the initial, formative stage of group development, helping the group experience a sense of safety and cohesion are fundamental (see Chapters 4 and 6). In groups that have matured, interventions that further and deepen the therapeutic work are particularly beneficial. And in the termination or "adjourning" stage, helping the group members review and internalize new learnings and new discoveries ensure that positive gains will be maintained after the group ends (cf. Lo Coco, Gullo, Di Fratello, Giordano, & Kivlighan, 2016). Moreover, as Agazarian and Peters (1981) assert:

> The working through and mastering of group development phases induces the working-through and mastering of individual developmental phases.
>
> (p. 130)

Stages of Group Development

Gibbard, Hartman, and Mann (1974) provide an enduring and **useful three-category classification system** of most of the existing models of group development, derived from observations of psychotherapy groups, training and process groups and workplace organizations:

Progressive-Linear Models

These models view groups as **normally evolving through prescribed and invariant stages or phases of development**, each marked by specific cognitive-affective-dynamic themes and structural arrangements.

By far, the most well-known of these **progressive-linear models** is Tuckman's (1965) four stages of:

1. **Forming** (testing of and dependence on the leader),
2. **Storming** (intragroup conflict and emotional expression among the members),
3. **Norming** (developing group cohesion and increasing compliance to the rules of engagement),
4. **Performing** (functional role taking and relatedness in the service of work).

Tuckman and Jensen (1977) later added a fifth and final termination stage, **adjourning**, in which the process of disengagement occurs as well as a review of what has occurred and been achieved.

Agazarian and Gantt (2003), adapting Bennis and Shepard's (1956) classic progressive-linear model, have constructed a six phase linear-progressive model:

1. **Dependence-flight** (focusing on avoidance of the anxieties attending a new group and the implicit dependence on the group leader to keep things safe),
2. **Counterdependence-fight** (fighting between members as an implicit rebellion against the group leader),
3. **Power-authority** (reflecting the group's direct confrontation of the leader's control and authority and ultimate resolution of the power struggle between the group and leader by the group assuming its own authority for the work of the group),
4. **Overpersonal enchantment** (reflecting a euphoria over cohesiveness and closeness),
5. **Counterpersonal disenchantment** (entailing a shared demoralization that the closeness experienced in the previous stage doesn't last),
6. **Interdependence-work** (a mature working stage providing opportunities for ever-deepening levels of working through).

Life Cycle Models

Life cycle models view the group in terms of stages of normal human development, progressing from "infancy," through "adolescent rebellion," to "maturity." These models are similar to the linear-progressive models, but are also seen, discussed, and conceptualized along the lines of models of the human life cycle. One may hear clinicians discuss these phases using life cycle language such as the group is in its

- Infancy – seeing if the world is safe and trustworthy,
- Toddler exploration – getting to know each other and experimenting with interactions,
- Latency – a sense of ease and quiet but with underlying issues still needing to be explored,

- Teenage rebellion – dissatisfaction with the leader and the search for a unique identity,
- Mature functioning – comfort with the process and each other and working productively,
- End of life – coming to terms with the ending of the group.

Rutan, Stone, and Shay's (2014) four stage life cycle model follows:

1. **Formation** (with prominent issues of trust and safety),
2. **Reactive** stage (where competitive needs to maintain individual identity are prominent),
3. **Mature** stage (reflecting the functioning of a sophisticated work group),
4. **Termination** stage.

Comparably, MacKenzie's (1997) four stage life cycle model consists of:

1. **Engagement** (experience of group cohesion and universality),
2. **Differentiation** (marked by themes of self-definition and self-assertion, with resulting interpersonal conflict),
3. **Interpersonal work,**
4. **Termination.**

Wheelan's (2005) integrative model, applicable to both organizational work groups and psychotherapy groups, has received some empirical support:

1. **Dependency and Inclusion** (reliance on the leader for direction, inclusion, and safety issues),
2. **Counterdependency and Fight** (members disagree about group goals and procedures),
3. **Trust/Structure** (more openness, cooperation, and task orientation),
4. **Work/Productivity** (focused productivity towards goals),
5. **Termination** (with themes of separation and appreciation).

One of the more recent empirically informed models is Brabender and Fallon's (2009a) five stage model:

1. **Formation and engagement,**
2. **Conflict over authority and rebellion,**
3. **Unity and intimacy** (cohesiveness),
4. **Integration and work** (similar to a sophisticated work group with constructive exploration and productive role taking),
5. **Termination** (entailing a thorough review of oneself, others in the group, leadership and the group experience and of what work remains to be done.

Commonalities across Linear Progressive and Life Cycle Models

There is **considerable overlap and consensus** across the linear progressive and life cycle models, with respect to thematic, structural and dynamic changes over time:

1. All of these models propose an **initial formative stage** that typically reflects the **anxieties of joining a group**, concerns over submerging aspects of one's individuality for the sake of group cohesion, committing oneself to the task and values embodied by the group, and dependence upon the leader for providing safety and direction.
2. For groups with a clear ending point, there is usually a **termination** stage of reflection, integration and internalization of the experience as members evaluate their experiences and work on separating from the group as a whole.
3. Most of the models suggest that some form of **confrontation with and resolution of reactions to the leader's authority** is necessary for the group to progress to a more productive **work stage** that typically reflects comparatively mature role relatedness, a toning down of conflict of preceding phases, and an increase in work efficiency.

Pendular or Recurring-Cycle Models

These models envision groups not as following a linear path of development but rather a **cyclical or spiraling pattern, revisiting earlier themes and resuming earlier patterns of relationships, in a process of deepening and working through of ever present issues and tensions.** Examples of the **pendular** model are:

1. Bion's view of an ongoing interplay and oscillation between two group mentalities, the **sophisticated work group** marked by functional and rational role relatedness and the defense based structures and processes of the **basic assumption group (see Chapter 5).**
2. Hartman and Gibbard's (1974) model of an ongoing oscillation between the **existential anxieties** of group life and the emergence of temporary and partial **socially shared defensive structures and processes,** designed to contain tensions and permit productive work before anxieties reemerge that may require new defensive configurations.
3. Schutz's (1958) early and intuitively appealing model of cyclical needs for inclusion, control, and affection.
4. Levine's (2011) view of a continual oscillation between regressive and progressive forces toward growth.

Some authors have suggested that the two predominant models – **linear progressive** (including **life cycle** models) and **cyclical or pendular** models – could be conceptually integrated, whereby certain themes, tensions, or anxieties (such as the wish-fear dilemma of fusion and individuation) are revisited through successive stages of group life (Brabender & Fallon, 2009a; MacKenzie, 1997).

Additional Notes on Group Development

1. While linear progressive, life cycle, and pendular models have been the predominant models of group development, recent years have seen the rise of new models of stage development in groups, such as the application of chaos and complexity theories which attempt to model **nonlinear dynamic change** in all living systems (Brabender, 2016; Brabender & Fallon, 2009a; Rubenfeld, 2001; Schermer, 2012). The models look at the movement between order and chaos, as well as the tension between simple and increasingly complex ways of interaction

2. All of the models above define and describe **normal** development, where groups address and **resolve stage-specific conflicts and achieve stage-specific tasks** that allow them to progress to the next stage. However, most of the models also posit that group development, as with human development, can become **fixated** at various stages or **regress** to earlier stages when anxiety or threat is not adequately managed or contained.

3. **Structured groups and group development**: Although not often explicitly stated, most of the manualized treatment protocols for structured groups such as CBT and psychoeducational groups present an agenda that is in line with a model of group development (Bieling, Milosevic, & McCabe, 2014; Brown, 2018). Initial sessions are used to promote group processes of inclusion, cohesion, and universality, as well as to establish norms and a sense of safety (Bieling, McCabe, & Antony, 2006; Thorgeirsdottir, Bjornsson, & Arnkelsson, 2015). These groups also usually include a termination protocol that emphasizes concretizing new learning and behavioral patterns, and celebrating successes. The leaders of such groups need to be skilled not only in cognitive behavioral methods, but also in helping to manage the processes inherent in the various stages of group development.

4. **Open ended groups and group development**: While many of the models of group development have been constructed from observations of closed and time limited groups, stages of development also emerge in open groups. In these contexts it is particularly important for the leader to help a new member become included by clarifying the expectations and being sensitive to the current culture and developmental stage of the ongoing group. For instance, joining an ongoing group when a push against authority is occurring will likely evoke very different experiences and concerns for a new member than joining the group in a working phase.

5. **Development of groups within embedding treatment contexts**: Groups within treatment settings such as clinics, day programs, or hospitals are vulnerable to pressures from those settings that may impede optimal development and even lead to fixations and regressions. Administrative demands, for example, to keep existing groups filled by bringing in new patients may exceed the capacity of the group to adequately contain such changes and lead to feelings of anxiety and instability, threatening the normal and optimal trajectory of development. "Here we go again!" may be the cry of veteran group members faced again with the influx of new members and raising again early themes of safety and dependence on the leader. Similarly, the administratively-dictated, rapid turnover, and terminations of patients in some programs can arouse early concerns over the viability and trustworthiness of the group. However, it is important for the therapist to understand that the revisiting of earlier themes and dynamics is not necessarily merely a repetition of patterns once considered resolved but rather likely an ever deepening working through of old existential issues.

6. **Research evidence on group development**: There is a small but promising body of research that generally supports the models, especially the linear progressive models, of group development. Importantly, research findings also suggest a positive relationship between group development and outcome: the more developmentally advanced the group the greater the outcome or task achievement (Agazarian & Gantt, 2003; Brabender & Fallon, 2009a) While, the empirical question of whether there is an invariant sequence of stages that unfolds across groups remains open, the evidence points to the usefulness of group leadership being familiar with and incorporating a developmental perspective for the benefit of

the clients' productivity and outcomes (Lo Coco, Gullo, Di Fratello, Giordano, & Kivlighan, 2016).

Group development and culture. It is important to note that most models of development to daté have not adequately accounted for variations that may be based on different cultures, ethnicities, identities and contexts. Group leaders need to be sensitive to consider how these factors can influence expectations and needs among the group participants, which, in turn, can affect how the group evolves over time (Chen, Kakkad, & Balzano, 2008).

Exercises

1. Recall your first session in any kind of group (therapy group, team, committee, etc.) you have participated in. What were your feelings? How anxious were you and what were you worried about? How did you cope? What did you want from the leader, from other members, from yourself?
2. What similarities and differences did you experience in your first sessions in different kinds of groups? How do you understand these?
3. What model of group development appeals to you most and why?

Recommended Resources

Agazarian, Y., & Gantt, S. (2003). Phases of group development: Systems-centered hypotheses and their implications for research and practice. *Group Dynamics: Theory, Research, and Practice*, 7(3), 238–252.

Bennis, W. G., & Shepard, H. A. (1956). A theory of group development. *Human Relations*, 9, 415–457.

Bieling, P. McCabe, R. E. & Antony, M. M. (2006). *Cognitive-behavioral therapy in groups*. New York: Guilford.

Bieling, P., Milosevic, I., & McCabe, R. E. (2014). Groups for depression. In J. L. DeLucia-Waack, C.R. Kalodner, & M.T. Riva, (Eds.) *Handbook of group counseling and psychotherapy*, 2nd ed. (pp 367–380). Beverley, CA: Sage Publications.

Brabender, V. (2016). Chaos theory and group psychotherapy: 15 years later. *Group*, 40(1), 9–15.

Brabender, V., & Fallon, A. (2009). *Group development in practice: Guidance for clinicians and researchers on stages and dynamics of change*. Washington, DC: American Psychological Association.

Chen, E. C., Kakkad, D., & Balzano, J. (2008). Multicultural competence and evidence-based practice in group therapy. *Journal of Clinical Psychology*, 64(11), 1261–1278.

Gibbard, G. S., Hartman, J. J., & Mann, R. D. (1974). Group process and development. In G.S. Gibbard, J. J. Hartman, & R. D. Mann (Eds.), *Analysis of groups* (pp. 83–93). San Francisco, CA: Jossey-Bass.

Hartman, J.J., & Gibbard, G.S. (1974). Anxiety, boundary evolution and social change. In G.S. Gibbard, J.J. Hartman, & R.D. Mann (Eds.), *Analysis of groups* (pp. 154–176). San Francisco, CA: Jossey-Bass.

Levine, R. (2011). Progressing while regressing in relationships. *International Journal of Group Psychotherapy*, *61*, 621–643.

Lo Coco, G., Gullo, S., Di Fratello, C., Giordano, C., & Kivlighan D. M., Jr. (2016). Group relationships in early and late sessions and improvement in interpersonal problems. *Journal of Counseling Psychology*, *63*(4), 419.

MacKenzie, K. R. (1997). Clinical application of group development ideas. *Group Dynamics*, *1*, 275–287.

Rubenfeld, S. (2001). Group therapy and complexity theory. *International Journal of Group Psychotherapy*, *51*(4), 449–471.

Rutan, J., Stone, W., & Shay, J. (2014). *Psychodynamic group psychotherapy* (5th ed.). New York: Guilford.

Schermer, V. (2012). Group-as-a-whole and complexity theories: Areas of convergence. *Group Analysis*, *45*, 275–288.

Schutz, W. (1958). *FIRO: A three-dimensional theory of interpersonal behavior.* New York: Rinehart.

Thorgeirsdottir, M. T., Bjornsson, A. S., & Arnkelsson, G. B. (2015). Group climate development in brief group therapies: A comparison between cognitive-behavioral group therapy and group psychotherapy for social anxiety disorder. *Group Dynamics: Theory, Research, and Practice*, *19*(3), 200.

Tuckman, B. W. (1965). Development sequence in small groups. *Psychological Bulletin*, *63*, 384–399.

Tuckman, B. W., & Jensen, M. (1977). Stages of small-group development revisited. *Group and Organization Studies*, *2*, 419–427.

Wheelan, Susan A. (2005). *Group processes: A developmental perspective.* Auckland: Pearson Education New Zealand.

Concluding Thoughts

With the availability of many group development models, a clinician can feel over-whelmed as to which one may be best to utilize in any given situation. As covered above, considerable overlap exists between many models and no one model will likely fit all groups given the contextual elements ranging from the host organization to the cultural influences of the individual group members. Group development models provide maps that assist leaders in navigating each group towards mature productive functioning. For instance, if a group feels stagnant, from a developmental perspective the leader could explore whether

- introducing an earlier group task such as achieving greater cohesion might be useful,
- the group is enacting some reaction, such as defiance or avoidance, to the leader's authority,
- or whether the group is oscillating between a temporary period of "nonwork" before returning to mature productive work.

One of the ongoing tasks of group leadership is to help the group move towards ever increasing levels of productivity and maturity – the sophisticated work group. By means of a developmental perspective, the leader can explore, both in the mind and in the group, where the group is developmentally, what current obstacles, tasks yet to be achieved and group-wide conflicts are preventing progress, and what interventions, from a vast array of possible interventions, might help the group in moving forward.

Module 4

Group Leadership

Tasks and Skills

8 Basic Leadership Tasks

J. Scott Rutan, Les R. Greene, and Francis J. Kaklauskas

Introduction

Despite our best efforts at forecasting and prognosis, the multiple-person arena of a therapy group often unfolds in surprising ways. As leaders we are always confronted with what to do or what not to do at any given moment. As Kurt Lewin (1951) summarized, there is nothing so practical as a good theory and, indeed, **one's theoretical framework can help guide decision making about how, when, and why to intervene at any moment.** As presented earlier, there are many approaches towards understanding group dynamics and the therapeutic change process, and one's construction of a clinical-conceptual framework takes time, experience, and exposure to varied theoretical and research perspectives. One's clinical approach should be flexible, an amalgamation of knowledge and experience, consistent with one's values and beliefs. The previous seven chapters presented some of the ideas that an emerging clinician may consider in developing a leadership style, including:

- A sense of which **therapeutic factors** should be reinforced at any particular moment.
- An appreciation of those **regressive or restraining forces** that are likely to erupt.
- A sense of where the group is **developmentally** and what interventions are needed to help the group progress.
- A sensitivity to how group process is influenced by its **composition**, including kinds of psychopathology or stressors, demographics, cultural factors, ego strengths, and degree of homogeneity vs. heterogeneity.
- Ongoing awareness of **goals** and the processes of **therapeutic work**.
- A monitoring of the structural parameters and boundaries of the group, including its relationship to its immediate context (such as an agency or clinic).
- Access to the internal storehouse of our personal and clinical experiences, including the influences of our **training and supervision** and our observations as group members.

Given these variables, the leader should ideally create options of what to do at every moment to meet the needs of the members, options that range from:

- engaging a particular member,
- identifying and intervening to a particular dyad or subgroup,
- offering a group-as-a-whole interpretation or hypothesis,
- or even remaining silent.

For many, the prospect of becoming and being a *group* therapist is daunting, entailing a "radical transformation" of one's professional identity from the usual starting point of individual therapist to group therapist (Billow, 2012). The experiences of the group therapist are indeed vastly different from those of the individual therapist. Doing individual therapy, we can grow comfortable in the tempo and relative privacy of the dyadic dialogue, experiencing the luxury of time to consider what we would like to say. But as a group leader, we must consider:

- more than one client at every moment,
- the complex and shifting web of interpersonal relationships,
- and the overall functioning of the group.

Our group members have multiple and even conflicting wishes for how they would like us to be and behave. In individual therapy we can carefully explore the working relationship through teasing apart transference reactions and misunderstandings from accurate perceptions, but the group's multi-person field often encourages members to share their varied views of us in quick succession with little time for processing. No matter how neutral we might try to be in our leadership role, the many eyes focused on us can often see aspects of ourselves that may never have been highlighted in individual treatment. Sometimes group members clearly misperceive our intentions or interpersonal patterns, but at other times they can see us with uncanny accuracy. Groups often ask far more from their therapists in terms of disclosing details of our personal lives and the reasoning behind our actions, and are more likely to castigate us for our shortcomings much more than clients in individual therapy.

Group leadership is not for the faint of heart; it requires courage and an openness to vulnerability (Shapiro & Gans, 2008). And as Billow (2012) reminds us, while the neophyte group therapist may be particularly vulnerable to the powerful but invisible pushes and pulls of the group process, time and experience may lessen the emotional struggles of the group leader, "but they never disappear" (p. 385).

Recommended Resources

Billow, R. (Ed.) (2012). Special Issue: Essays on starting one's first therapy group. *International Journal of Group Psychotherapy, 62,* 341–390.

Shapiro, E. L., & Gans, J. S. (2008). The courage of the group therapist. *International Journal of Group Psychotherapy, 58(3),* 345–361.

Keeping the Group on Track and Task

Shaping Norms

While designing a meaningful and coherent group structure (Chapter 6) is part of the core preliminary work in establishing a viable therapy group, **attending to and reinforcing group boundaries, behavioral norms and the values inherent in the therapeutic work are part of the ongoing work of the group therapist.** The following material outlines some of the fundamental tasks required to have a successful group.

The group therapist is responsible for establishing and reinforcing **group norms**, those **behavioral expectations** that are in the service of therapeutic work, such as exploring here-and-now experiences in a relational or interpersonal group or complying with and reporting experiences with homework assignments in a cognitive behavioral group. These expectations are typically initially expressed in the review of group agreements, but the shaping and reinforcing of norms entails ongoing monitoring and managing. **Members may consciously or unconsciously want to enact their own agendas that collide, compete, or conflict with the leader's normative expectations.**

For example, in a group where the work is explicitly defined as learning and practicing skills, some members will want only to vent and complain about their current life events. Similarly, in a group where the work is explicitly defined as exploring here-and-now relationships, some group members will want to repeatedly focus on a specific childhood story, problem solve, or even engage in small talk.

Redirecting a group that is off track takes consistent, patient, and empathic effort. It is important for the therapist to appreciate that the process of therapy entails dealing with dialectics between:

- progressive and regressive forces,
- therapeutic and anti-therapeutic processes,
- driving and restraining forces,
- work and resistance.

Group psychotherapy is not a linear process. Groups will shift from work into a variety of non-work modes. As a leader it is important to note when the group is off task, attempting to understand why this is happening and inviting the group to be curious about what is happening in the moment. The leader and the group may come to understand that **being off track is an implicit communication and expression of needing a break from the hard work of therapy, an avoidance of certain content or processes, or an indirect message about an unresolved dynamic in the group. The leader's dual tasks are to empathically explore the meanings of the deviations and, at the same time, encourage a return to the group tasks.** After all, the primary task of the therapy group is therapy. The leader's steadfast reinforcing of therapeutic norms and values, that together constitute a therapeutic culture, is designed to help the group and all of its members psychologically grow and change.

Managing Time and Other Group Boundaries

As with all aspects of the therapeutic frame, the leader's management of time boundaries is ongoing and dynamic, not static. If the group comes to trust that it will begin and end on time, a greater sense of security and safety can ensue, which in turn can stir a greater freedom to take psychological risks in the protected time and space. If those boundaries are poorly regulated, all of the rules that constitute the therapeutic framework may feel undependable. The leader's competent management of the time boundaries leads to a sense that the group is well held and well contained. **Competency in management includes therapeutic handling of those inevitable instances and situations where members fail to comply with the time boundaries.** While wanting to restore and preserve the therapeutic frame, the leader's primary stance around such boundary issues is to be curious about what the behavior might signify and not to be either punitive or shaming. For example, if a member desires to leave early regularly, the leader might ask, "What would have to happen to avoid this conflict in the future?" If a member routinely arrives late, the leader might ask: "How are we to understand Dan's difficulty using his full time with us?" As a leader it is important to look for the meaning underlying such actions. Does the arriving late reflect, for example, a defensive maneuver of rejecting others before an anticipated rejection, an indirect and nonverbal communication about how out of control life feels, and how much containment is desired, or something else?

More generally, **all of the boundaries that define the therapy group** – both the external boundaries that define the time, space, and group task and the internal boundaries that define the work roles of members and leader – **need to be competently managed** in an ongoing manner. There are a vast array of boundary challenges, including failure to pay the fee, inappropriate touch or dress, efforts to assume the leadership role, or psychological withdrawal from the work of the group. The group leader must attempt to explore and understand the meanings of these violations and take steps to re-establish the formal boundaries that define the therapy group as social system. As suggested by Gutheil and Gabbard (1993, 1998), the study of these boundary challenges needs to incorporate considerations of:

1. whether harm to any patient or to the group-as-a-whole has occurred,
2. whether the infraction was motivated, consciously or unconsciously, as a message to the leader or another member,
3. whether it reflects the influence of cultural stylistic preferences (Chen, Kakkad, & Balzano, 2008).

It is important to underscore that while it is always preferable to work through and resolve boundary challenges with the group, it is ultimately the leader's responsibility and authority to preserve the framework of the group and set clear behavioral expectations. As a last resort, but in some instances, a member's boundary violation may be so severe that a leader might have to have the member leave the group.

Recommended Resources

Chen, E. C., Kakkad, D., & Balzano, J. (2008). Multicultural competence and evidence-based practice in group therapy. *Journal of Clinical Psychology*, 64(11), 1261–1278.

Gutheil, T. G., & Gabbard, G. O. (1993). The concept of boundaries in clinical practice: Theoretical and risk-management dimensions. *American Journal of Psychiatry*, 150, 188–196.

Gutheil, T. G. & Gabbard, G. O. (1998). Misuses and misunderstandings of boundary theory in clinical and regulatory settings. *American Journal of Psychiatry*, 155, 409–414.

Creating Safety

No matter the type or composition of the group, an **initial and fundamental task of the group therapist is to establish the group as a safe and dependable place**. This is primarily accomplished by paying careful attention to group norms and boundaries. It is also facilitated by the assumption that members are doing the best they can to be *in* relationship, no matter how awkward or maladaptive those attempts may be. Leading with empathy and curiosity and encouraging members to also be empathic and curious can foster a welcoming feeling. Threats to safety that stem from such hostile behaviors as:

- verbal attacks or bullying behavior,
- microaggressions,
- devaluing the work of the group

must be immediately addressed. Exploration of and empathic resonance with the many anxieties and fears associated with group membership can serve to enhance the sense of safety. The work of psychotherapy takes a degree of courage but also the assurance of sufficient security and safety in the group. Generally, as a leader we want to set and reinforce norms which promote a **sense of safety in the group** and thus facilitate **psychological risk-taking** – exploring new understandings of ourselves and others and trying different ways of relating.

Fostering Engagement and a Therapeutic Culture – the First Meeting and Beyond

Freud (1913/1958) compared psychotherapy to chess when he said, "Anyone who hopes to learn the noble game of chess from books will soon discover that only the opening and end games admit of an exhaustive systematic presentation." The first meeting of a group, though often filled with unique anxieties, is nonetheless one of the more straightforward meetings to lead because there is usually **only one core underlying theme – "Is this going to be a safe place?"**

Even prior to the arrival of members for this initial group meeting the therapist can take some steps to promote a sense of safety. As described in the pre-group preparation work (Chapter 7) the therapist should have fostered an initial sense of alliance and reviewed a set of agreements that serve to establish therapeutic norms and clarify expectations. And on the day of the initial group session, the therapist should prepare the group room as a quiet, comfortable space with the right number of chairs, a room with the potential to be transformed into **a reflective space** for the work of psychotherapy (Counselman, 2016).

Still, the members will anxiously be wondering what type of host the leader will be: warm and supportive, encouraging risk taking, modeling therapeutic behavior, probing and intrusive, remaining neutral, or potentially unpredictable. Do the members initiate introductions on their own, or do they wait for direction from the therapist? Does the leader leap to fill awkward and anxious silences, or is silence valued as part of the process? **All remains unknown; only the familiar interpersonal patterns that the members bring with them can be initially counted on.**

To bind some of the initial anxiety, the leader might begin this first meeting by restating the goals of the group and the group agreements. The leader could ask what it feels like to be in this group, what the hopes and worries are. In this first meeting it is almost always possible to observe that everyone is assessing how safe this group is going to be and **the leader can give voice to this universal anxiety.**

Remember, our patients tend not to come with *problems*, but rather with *solutions* (though perhaps solutions that have outlived their functionality). In this first meeting the therapist will begin to see how the members handle this unfamiliar and unknown situation: the new relationships, the emerging social dynamics, and the inevitable stress and defensive patterns of a first meeting and their idiosyncratic ways of coping with all of it.

The first group is usually what Bion (see Chapter 5) would call a Dependency Group, and the members are hypervigilant regarding all aspects of the leader's presence. The leader should remember that the leader role that is set in this first meeting is often hard to alter. Thus, if you are using a more psychodynamic model it is important in this first session to initiate a role that primarily expresses curiosity and reflection on the group process. If your role is more active, as in a psycho-educational group, you can begin providing more structure and guidance. **Consistency, reliability and dependability** are useful role traits in establishing a sense of security and safety.

One of the most important events in the first meeting (and all subsequent meetings) is the ending. Over the course of time, there will be many pressures to alter the ending, usually to extend it because something very important is occurring. Leaders, particularly those newer to group therapy, need remember that *we* do not end the group, the clock does. We simply note when the time has expired. The members know full well when the time is over, so it is often not random if important material flowers at the end of a session. It may appear then because the members expect to be protected by the boundary at the end of the time. Alternatively, this may be a test to see if the therapist "really cares" by extending the time. **It is vital to begin and end sessions on time and help the members understand the importance of this structure.**

Despite the high levels of anxiety and sometimes unrealistic catastrophic fantasies that members and leaders can bring into an initial group, first meetings often go far better than people expect. Usually, in the first meetings

- members begin to get to know one another,
- certain connections and similarities are discovered,
- some amount of acceptance or validation can occur,
- and nothing terrible happens.

It is always possible to summarize a first meeting by saying, "People have been saying hello in their own unique ways." If possible, a statement reinforcing hope about the process and acknowledging the members' courage to share and interact can help build momentum into the next week.

The importance of **engagement** as a core therapeutic factor is reflected in its prominence in multiple theories, research findings, and group process assessment instruments (Burlingame et al., 2006; Leszcz, 2017a; MacKenzie, 1983). Monitoring and facilitating engagement extends beyond the first session, and indeed throughout the life of the group. Those who are withdrawn or quiet may be at risk for early drop out, and efforts need to be made to bring them back into the group. In dynamically oriented groups, they might be asked directly for their reactions to what is being discussed, or connected to other members through linking (Bion, 1961) or bridging (Ormont, 1992), or encouraged to join like-minded others using functional subgrouping techniques (Agazarian, 2004), or asked empathic-oriented exploration questions ("What has stood out to you so far in the group today"). In CBT and psychoeducational groups they can be encouraged to share their experience of a group exercise or homework assignment (Bieling et al., 2013). To the extent such leader-initiated interventions succeed in fostering engagement in all of the members and the group as a whole, the leader may be able to gradually step more into the background and allow the group to function more independently.

Recommended Resources

Agazarian, Y. (2004). *System-centered therapy for groups* (2nd ed.). New York: Guilford.

Bieling, P. J., McCabe, R. E., & Antony, M. M. (2009). *Cognitive-behavioral therapy in groups*. New York: Guilford.

Burlingame, G. M., Strauss, B., Joyce, A., MacNair-Semands, R., MacKenzie, K. R., Ogrodniczuk, J., & Taylor, S. (2006). *Core Battery – revised: An assessment tool kit for promoting optimal group selection, process and outcome*. Available through the AGPA store.

Counselman, E. (2016). First you put the chairs in a circle: Becoming a group therapist. The Anne and Ramon Alonso Presidential Plenary Address presented at the 2016 Annual meeting of the American Group Psychotherapy Association, New York, NY.

Freud, S. (1958). On beginning the treatment. In J. Strachey (Ed. & Trans.), *The standard edition of the complete psychological works of Sigmund Freud* (Vol. 12, pp. 121–144). London: Hogarth Press. (Original work published 1913).

Leszcz, M. (2017). A relational approach to evidence-based group psychotherapy. The Louis R. Ormont Lecture presented at the annual meeting of the American Group Psychotherapy Association, New York, NY.

MacKenzie, K. R. (1983). The clinical application of a group climate measure. In R. R. Dies & K. R. MacKenzie (Eds.), *Advances in group psychotherapy: Integrating research and practice* (pp. 159–170). Madison, CT: International Universities Press.

Ormont, L.R. (1992). *The group therapy experience*. New York: St. Martin's Press.

Therapeutic Alliance or Collaboration

The therapeutic or working alliance has repeatedly been shown to be the most important dynamic to create positive change in all forms of psychotherapy (Arnow & Steidtmann, 2014; Leszcz, 2017a; Roth & Fonagy, 2013). Bordin's (1979) delineation of three components of the alliance in individual psychotherapy is still useful today:

- the **emotional bond** between patient and therapist,
- their **agreement on therapeutic tasks,**
- their **agreement on therapeutic goals**.

In group psychotherapy, the alliance extends to the **member's relationship not only to the group leader,** but also to **other members, and the group-as-a-whole** on these same three dimensions. (Rutan, Stone, & Shay, 2014).

Recommended Resources

Arnow, B. A., & Steidtmann, D. (2014). Harnessing the potential of the therapeutic alliance. *World Psychiatry, 13(3)*, 238–240.

Bordin E. S. (1979). The generalizability of the psychoanalytic concept of the working alliance. *Psychotherapy, 16*, 252–260.

Leszcz, M. (2017). A relational approach to evidence-based group psychotherapy. The Louis R. Ormont Lecture presented at the annual meeting of the American Group Psychotherapy Association, New York, NY.

Roth, A., & Fonagy, P. (2013). *What works for whom: A critical review of psychotherapy research, 2nd edition*. New York: Guilford.

Rutan, J., Stone, W., & Shay, J. (2014). *Psychodynamic group psychotherapy (5th ed.)*. New York: Guilford.

Alliance with the Leader

The alliance between individual members and the group leader is vital to positive group experiences. In the pre-screening interview, the leader has a chance to demonstrate empathy, insight, knowledge and skill through the processes of collecting history and collaboratively setting goals. The member gets an honest evaluation of what may be achieved and what type of participation is needed. The leader can demonstrate a therapeutic presence that helps build the alliance and has been shown to produce positive outcomes across theoretical models (Siegel, 2013; Wampold & Imel, 2015). Schneider (2015) suggests therapeutic presence includes appreciative openness, concerted engagement, support, and emotional expressiveness. For many members, **being seen, heard, engaged with emotionally, and reflected upon is tremendously helpful and can have positive impacts across group settings** (Leszcz, 2017a).

Several experiences **are seen as underlying the building of an alliance with the therapist** in group psychotherapy including:

- a developing trust, faith, and belief in the therapist's ability to help,
- experiencing the therapist as well attuned and empathic,
- feeling genuinely cared for and authentically related with,
- seeing the therapist as reliable, dependable, consistent,
- a growing conviction that the therapist is on the patient's side.

However, the growth of a therapeutic alliance is not a linear process, and often only through a series of **ruptures and repairs** does the alliance become stronger (Miller-Bottome, Safran, Talia, & Muran, 2018; Safran, Muran, & Eubanks-Carter, 2011). **Ruptures are inevitable;** despite our best efforts to attune to all our members at any given moment, some will at times feel misunderstood or malnourished. Within the same group, members will have different emotional needs vis-a-vis the leader: Some members might strongly prefer that the leader be active and directive, while other members might prefer to take more initiative themselves. Not everyone will feel gratified by or connected with the leader at any moment. But it is through such fissures in attunement and the leader's ability to understand and validate them that trust is strengthened. In **navigating a rupture,** it is useful for the therapist to:

- be curious about and validate the member's experience,
- not take the member's experience personally,
- acknowledge the rupture and be willing to work through the situation,
- ask the other members for help in understanding the rupture,
- understand that this may take time to work through.

A major piece of sustaining an alliance is connection and engagement, and as leaders, we may want to contact each group member at least once per group. This contact could range from:

- empathic response,
- expressing curiosity by asking questions,
- skillfully and preparedly teaching or presenting a helpful skill,
- offering an empathic interpretation and asking whether it fits with the patient's experience.

At other times the therapeutic alliance can be built and sustained through more subtle means such as:

- brief moments of eye contact with the member,
- a smile or head nod of acknowledgement when a member is working well,
- helping the group work on issues relevant to the member,
- even saying hello and goodbye.

Exercises

1) How do you try to establish a therapeutic alliance with your members?
2) How do you handle ruptures?

Recommended Resources

Miller-Bottome, M., Safran, J. D., Talia, A., & Muran, J. C. (2018). Therapeutic alliance, alliance ruptures, and the process of resolution. *Psychoanalytic Psychology, 35*(2), 175–183.

Safran, J. D., Muran, J. C., & Eubanks-Carter, C. (2011). Repairing alliance ruptures. In J. C. Norcross (Eds.). *Psychotherapy relationships that work: Evidence-based responsiveness* (2nd Ed) (pp. 224–238). New York: Oxford University Press.

Schneider, K. (2015). Presence: the core contextual factor of effective psychotherapy. *Existential Analysis, 26*(2), 304–313.

Siegel, D. J. (2013). *The mindful therapist: A clinician's guide to mindsight and neural integration.* New York: Norton.

Wampold, B. E., & Imel, Z. E. (2015). *The great psychotherapy debate: The evidence for what makes psychotherapy work.* New York: Routledge.

Alliance with Other Members

In group therapy, the notion of therapeutic alliance also extends to the individual member's relationship to other members. Other members can often provide support, insight, challenge, and relational opportunities for the individual participant beyond the limitations of our encumbered role. The **leader can reinforce these alliances between members through encouraging member to member engagement**. Alliances can be seen as akin to functional subgroups (from system centered groups) in terms of members sharing similarities of ideas, experiences, and challenges and building towards increased disclosure and depth. **Group member alliances can encompass many group therapeutic factors,** including

- universality,
- the experience of acceptance,
- instillation of hope,
- altruism,
- corrective recapitulation of family of origin challenges.

Similar to the alliance with the leader, the alliance between group members supports a sense of safety and promotes risk-taking, engagement, and commitment to the work of the group. In a mature working group, challenges and confrontation between members can be seen as evidence of an alliance as members have developed the ability to be more honest and authentic in their reactions with one another. Members challenging or having strong emotional reactions to one another can come from connection and care. However, it is best to check with each member about the interchange and use clinical judgment to interrupt any sadistic or destructive discharge. Over time, members can develop complex multifaceted relationships with one another that may include feelings of admiration, respect and deep intimacy, but also include moments of disagreement, and anger. Members can develop a full range of feelings towards one another within the overarching ground of relational commitment, care, and dedication to growth for all members

Alliance to the Group-As-A-Whole

Cohesion and alliance are closely related, and perhaps no other concepts are as empirically supported and central to productive group work. Cohesion may be seen as a general sense of belonging shared by all the members, while alliance is a more multidimensional concept entailing a sense of positive bonding and positive working relationships (Burlingame, McClendon, & Alonso, 2011). The leader works towards building cohesion and alliance through helping members talk with each other in ways that are both supportive and empathic and yet honest and authentic. The members may begin **to see the group as an entity onto itself, and feel as if they are a vital part of something important, that is acquiring both a positive sense of "we" and a conviction that the work and goals of the group are valuable.** This connection to the group entity provides the scaffolding for the group tasks, and serves to hold the challenging moments of misunderstanding, confusion, and the distress of group work.

Finally, as discussed in Chapter 3, recent research has suggested the importance of assessing the relationships among these three foci of alliance (i.e., towards the leader, the other members, and the group-as-a-whole). In general, positive alliances predict superior outcome, however mixed alliances as in **intrapersonal splitting** (e.g., when an individual member has positive feelings for the leader but not for the group) and **interpersonal splitting** (e.g., when the individual member holds feelings towards the leader that are very different from those held by other members), might negatively impact therapeutic progress (Kivlighan, Li, & Gillis, 2015; Kivlighan et al., 2017; Lo Coco, Gullo, & Kivlighan, 2012).

Recommended Resources

Burlingame G. M., McClendon D. T., Alonso J. (2011). Cohesion in group therapy. *Psychotherapy*, *48*, 34–42.

Kivlighan, D. M. Jr., Li, X., & Gillis, L. (2015). Do I fit with my group? Within-member and within-group fit with the group in engaged group climate and group members feeling involved and valued. *Group Dynamics*, *19*, 106–121.

Kivlighan, D. M. Jr., Lo Coco, G., Oieni, V., Gullo, S., Pazzagli, C., & Mazzeschi, C. (2017). All bonds are not the same: A response surface analysis of the perceptions of positive bonding relationships in therapy groups. *Group Dynamics*, *21*, 159–177.

Lo Coco, G., Gullo, S., & Kivlighan, D. M. Jr. (2012). Examining patients' and other group members' agreement about their alliance to the group as a whole and changes in patient symptoms using response surface analysis. *Journal of Counseling Psychology*, *59*, 197–207.

Concluding Thoughts

The overarching or unifying principle in leading effective therapy groups across approaches and populations is creating and managing a **therapeutic culture**. This ideally begins with the pre-screening interview (or first group session) through connecting with interest, curiosity, and emotional attunement, and supporting these types of interchanges in the group among members. While initially a leader may focus on boundary and task clarity, safety, and creating a sense of belonging in the group, over time the leader promotes a wider range of authentic engagements within the membership. The **therapeutic container** of the group can become a sacred space that allows our members to reveal more and more of themselves, their thoughts, histories, vulnerabilities, and explore a full range of behaviors and feelings. The leader task is to help members work along their growth edge without becoming chronically overwhelmed or commonly disengaged. Boundaries challenges, task drift, ruptures that go unaddressed can commandeer the productive power of group interactions. Lou Ormont (1992) used the metaphor of group leader as an orchestra conductor who balances different players, varied thoughts and feelings, and dynamics as they rise and fall throughout the symphony of the group. After all, group psychotherapy is a highly collaborative practice, and as leaders we simply model sincerity, effort, and trust in the process and allow the members to join in the music.

9 Advanced Skills

Les R. Greene, Francis J. Kaklauskas, and J. Scott Rutan

Introduction

Group psychotherapy introduces many variables and challenges that are different from those in individual therapy. However, group also potentially provides many unique rewards and therapeutic opportunities both for the members and for ourselves as group leaders. Motherwell and Shay (2014) highlight the intellectual and emotional trials of advancing group skills as well as the courage and openness to vulnerability needed to lead effectively:

> In this morass of complexity and high stress – not dissimilar from individual therapy but amplified by the number of people in the room – why then do we become and remain group therapists? For us, working with people who begin as strangers and who become intimate partners in learning about themselves and others is compelling, challenging, and often extremely moving. As leaders, we feel affectively engaged, and intellectually and emotionally stirred by our patients' courage, perseverance, and willingness to risk. This encourages *us* to risk the possibility of exposure *and* the possibility of self-knowledge and growth. To engage with others in such a difficult but rewarding process gives us hope and reinforces what we know about community and intimacy: that it is through respectful and positive attachments we become more resilient, empathic, and sympathetic to the pain and needs of the other.
>
> (p. 225)

Group leadership requires us to be **emotionally open**, and yet appropriately **contained and reflective**. We must be able to **think and feel**, and be ready **to respond at a moment's notice**. We wrestle **to make meaning** with the concrete and symbolic levels of language, subtle body movements, and our own internal dialogues (Billow, 2018). We need to listen with many ears (Horwitz, 2014), to accurately hear what is literally being said as well as to the masked affects, cognitive absurdities, disguised needs, hidden agendas and tests of the membership, and to tune into the larger undercurrents and stirrings of the group-as-a-whole. The movements of groups cycle through cacophony and harmony, crescendos and al niente, ballads, blues, passionate duets, and choral rounds. Part of the challenge is deepening our understanding of group processes (as covered in Chapters 4 and 5), including recognizing the lyricism below the singular notes.

If the newer leader focuses on the basics of **managing boundaries, feeling care and concern for the well-being of the members, facilitating here-and-now emotional experience as well as space for reflection and new understandings,** most group members will benefit and grow (cf. Bernard et al., 2008). The more advanced group leader will acquire and utilize additional skills to maximize the depth and breadth of the therapeutic change processes while at the same time preventing member and group-as-a-whole stagnation and deterioration (Leszcz, 2017a). Barlow (2013) has highlighted the unique multiple competencies needed for effective group leadership. Beyond the **foundational competencies** of mastery of knowledge of clinical theory, research, ethics, multiculturalism, and professionalism, we need to acquire **functional competencies** for deeply understanding the uniqueness of our members, groups and work roles. An advancing leader needs to develop the ability to:

- **Recognize and manage the multiple transferences** in the group, including individual and collective perceptions of the leader, of individual members, and of the group-as-a-whole,
- **Identify and work with subgroups and group-as-a-whole dynamics,**
- **Uncover and identify overarching themes** in what may seem like discordant or chaotic communications,
- **Balance the needs and goals of individual members with the group-as-a-whole,**
- **Assess clients' progress,**
- **Inquire into what may have been missed** in the previous group and what may be beneficial to the next group.

Recommended Resources

Barlow, S. H. (2013). *Specialty competencies in group psychology.* New York: Oxford University Press.

Bernard, H., Burlingame, G., Flores, P., Greene, L., Joyce, A., Kobos, J., Leszcz, M., MacNair-Semands, R.R., Piper, W. E., Slocum McEneaney, A. M.,& Feirman, D. (2008). Clinical practice guidelines for group psychotherapy. *International Journal of Group Psychotherapy, 58,* 455–542.

Billow, R. M. (2018). Doing our work: Words, deeds, and presence. *International Journal of Group Psychotherapy, 69*(1), 77–98.

Horwitz, L. (2014). *Listening with the fourth ear: Unconscious dynamics in analytic group psychotherapy.* London: Karnac.

Leszcz, M. (2017). A relational approach to evidence-based group psychotherapy. The Louis R. Ormont Lecture presented at the annual meeting of the American Group Psychotherapy Association, New York.

Motherwell, L., & Shay, J. J. (2014) *Complex dilemmas in group therapy: Pathways to resolution* [2nd Ed]. New York: Routledge.

Looking behind the Curtain

> Process is the here-and-now experience in the group that describes how the group is functioning, the quality of the relationships between members and with the leader, the emotional experiences and reactions of the group, and the group's strongest desires and fears.
>
> (Brown, 2003, p. 228)

Yalom and Leszcz (2005) stress the importance of **differentiating** *content* (what is actually and overtly said) from *process* (the underlying relationships and psychological themes arising in the here-and-now and associated thoughts, feelings, wishes, and needs) as well as **linking** content to process. Group members may be overtly discussing a certain topic, but underneath the surface more may be rousing. The unconscious or procedural processes occurring interpersonally and within the group-as-a-whole can have a private logic, and one of our tasks is to help them be **revealed, understood, and integrated** through our own intuitive, reflective, associative, and empathic processes. As leaders, we are looking to accurately identify our clients' **patterns and repetitions of thought, feeling and behavior** to help them **build more awareness and choice in their responses in interpersonal relations and to rely less upon automatic reactivity.**

To illustrate, if a patient relates a there-and-then story about feeling misunderstood, the leader needs to think about what might be stirring this story, whether the client is having a similar experience in the current group, what might have occurred in the group to unlock this memory, and what the member's current wish, fear, or need might be. Asking aloud or to oneself **"What is the telling of this story now serving for the member or the group?"** can offer clues about hidden motivations, affects, and needs. Similarly, if a member shares a long narrative about anger with, or love of, a teacher, the therapist might explore whether this is an indirect communication about the patient's feelings towards the therapist. A there-and-then story or memory reported in the present may offer insights into the person's experience currently in the group and the current group dynamics. **Helping members link the there-and-then past to the here-and-now present as well as content to process are important therapeutic tasks.**

It is important to note that even in structured nonprocess-oriented groups such as CBT or psychoeducation **internally considering and possibly intervening at the process level can help move the members and the group through potential blocks, heighten member engagement, and increase positive outcome** (Brown, 2011; Ettin, 1999; Sochting, 2014).

The in vivo aspects of group allow for our members' communication patterns, coping strategies, and relational styles to be revealed, and then allow for new opportunities to try new ways of thinking, feelings, acting, and being in the presence of others. New responses that may initially be practiced in the group circle will eventually extend out into our members' lives.

Recommended Resources

Brown, N. (2003). Conceptualizing process. *International Journal of Group Psychotherapy, 53(2)*, 225–244.

Brown, N. (2011). *Psychoeducational groups: Process and practice* [3rd Ed]. New York: Routledge.

Ettin, M. (1999). *Foundations and applications of group psychotherapy: A sphere of influence*. London: Jessica Kingsley.

Söchting, I. (2014). *Cognitive behavioral group therapy: Challenges and opportunities* [1st Ed.]. Wiley.

Yalom, I. D. & Leszcz, M. (2005). *The theory and practice of group psychotherapy* [5th Ed]. New York: Basic Books.

Working with Transference

Group psychotherapy has been empirically shown to highlight individuals' central relationship themes or transferences (Markin, 2009; Markin & Kivlighan, 2008), supporting the long held clinical theoretical notion that group psychotherapy is a microcosm that reflects individuals' characteristic relational approaches and social attribution processes (Yalom & Leszcz, 2005). Simply put, **transference is the process whereby members superimpose feelings and understandings from their past inaccurately into the current situation.** Transference as a clinical phenomenon was articulated by Freud more than a hundred years ago. Transference continues to be studied, clinically and empirically, as a ubiquitous social cognitive process by which people economically and expediently rely upon their early internalized self-other experiences as templates to make sense of new social experiences and thus create meaning (Andersen & Przybylinski, 2012). The identification and analysis of transferences provides opportunities to highlight and modify currently maladaptive patterns of cognition, affects, interpersonal relatedness, and resultant behaviors. As Janet Malcolm (1982) reminds us, however, the work is complex and arduous:

> The concept of transference at once destroys faith in personal relations and explains why they are tragic: we cannot know each other. We must grope around for each other through a dense thicket of absent others.

> (p. 6)

Analyzing transference, that is, exploring how we view others *as if* they were important historic figures rather than as they really are, is intricate enough when there is just a therapeutic dyad. In the group, the work becomes much more complicated, and much richer, because of the multiple transferences occurring simultaneously. Transference work is generally seen as best occurring during the middle or working phase of a group, rather than earlier phases of group life where building trust and safety are paramount.

Recommended Resources

Andersen, S. M., & Przybylinski, E. (2012). Experiments on transference in interpersonal relations: Implications for treatment. *Psychodynamic Psychotherapy*, 49 (3), 370–383

Markin, R. D. (2009). Exploring a method for transference assessment in group therapy using the social relations model: Suggestions for future research. *Journal for Specialists in Group Work, 34(4),* 307–325.

Markin, R. D., & Kivlighan, D. M. Jr. (2008). Central relationship themes in group psychotherapy: A social relations model analysis of transference. *Group Dynamics: Theory, Research, and Practice, 12*(4), 290–306.

Transferences Towards the Leader

Feelings and behaviors towards the group leader can take a variety of flavors from complete compliance and unrealistic adoration through thorough loathing, fear, and/or unyielding rebellion. In the interpersonal sphere of group, reality clashes with projections. **Sorting out transference distortions from realistic perceptions will always be partial, but a vital and beneficial exploration.** Sometimes a member, a subgroup, or the entire group will have projections or transference reactions towards the leader that can include feelings and ideas previously held towards a parent, sibling, partner, or another significant other from the past.

While transference-based experiences of the leader are wide ranging and idiosyncratic, typical perceptions range along such dimensions as seeing the group therapist as:

- Ideal or all knowing to incompetent and ineffective,
- Withholding and overly restrained to overly emotional and impulsive,
- Erotic and flirtatious to prudish and inhibited,
- Trustworthy and dependable to manipulative, unreliable and exploitative,
- Open and friendly to rejecting and dismissive.

As group leaders, **it is important not to get defensive in light of negative transferences and, just as importantly, not to get elevated or grandiose by idealizing projections.** While there may be a "kernel of reality" to them, **transference reactions toward us as leaders often say much more about the patients than about us as therapists.** And further, it is important to remember that transference distortions aimed at us as leaders in the group also likely are directed towards significant others in our patients' lives outside of group. A member who challenges everything the leader says may have wide ranging trust and relational issues with authority or intimate partnerships in many settings. Similarly, members who see the leader as omniscient may fail to rely upon their own intelligence and instincts, and be more dependent and naive than necessary in the various venues of their lives.

Transference reactions are usually resistant to quick change or correction as they have developed and been reinforced over many years, serving to provide an expedient means of interpreting, albeit inaccurately, any and every new social encounter, thus rendering the unknown familiar and comfortable. **Modifying transference reactions is a long process of working through** and rarely does cognitively explaining or confronting rapidly resolve the long standing interpersonal patterns. **The multi-person arena where members' views, beliefs and interpersonal stances can be validated or challenged is one of group therapy's most unique and powerful strengths.** Effective exploration of transference reactions toward leadership in the group depends upon the therapist's capacities to:

- Accept and experience all the varied and divergent feelings and reactions toward the leader,
- Avoid defensiveness (i.e., not taking the projections personally),
- Create and reinforce a culture of exploration and curiosity,
- Have and maintain accurate self-awareness to lead a discussion of contrasting perceptions of leadership.

Transferences can gradually be modified (through a process sometimes called the **corrective emotional experience**) as members experience the leader in ways that contradict previously held perceptions, anticipations and assumptions. Contrasting views of the leader, within a member over time and across the membership at any one time, can help to disconfirm deeply ingrained early perceptions and expectations. For example, clients who begin to recognize that the leader is neither sadistic nor attacking may come to the realization that others in their lives, from partners to bosses, may actually be caring for them and are trying to be supportive.

Many group leaders prefer to take on the work of analyzing transferences initially directed towards themselves before encouraging members to engage in this challenging work with each other. This leader-member dyadic work can provide modeling for the **containment, curiosity, reflection, and reality-testing** (i.e., assessing whether one's projections onto another person actually fit) that transference work entails.

Exercises

- Are you aware of your own predispositional tendencies, or transferences, towards authority figures? How successful are you usually in stepping back from automatic transference-driven reactions and in attempting to gain more accurate awareness and perceptions of specific authority figures? What helps in this process?
- What kind of transference reactions directed to you as group leader are particularly difficult for you to manage? How do you work with your reactions? Successfully or not?

Transferences Towards Other Group Members

While as leaders, we are trained to accept and manage transference reactions directed towards us; our members are often less comfortable with being projected upon inaccurately. However, learning how others view us, becoming **curious and not reactive**, being willing to see others' points of views, and considering changing aspects of our relational style while retaining our own integrity are powerful learning opportunities.

In working with transference reactions between members, the leader at times may need to step in to help maintain a sense of safety and facilitate emotional regulation. There are several common approaches for helping members work through transference reactions towards one another. For example, the leader could:

- Ask the member who is projecting whether similar feelings were experienced towards a historical person from the past or suggest this kind of connection by asking "Didn't you tell us your brother was also always putting you down?",

- Help to identify an underlying feeling such as fear, envy, or longing that may be fueling the transference,
- Wonder what needs the two members involved in the transference dynamic are serving for the group-as-a-whole,
- Provide psychoeducation about the ubiquitous social cognitive process of transference and provide a rationale for its study as part of psychotherapeutic work.

Often the member who is the target of transference reactions will need emotional support from the leader who can:

- Encourage the member to express the experience of being seen in this manner by another member (e.g. "How does it feel to be perceived in this way?"),
- Emphasize that just because someone experiences the member in a particular way, doesn't mean that the perception (projection) is accurate. Ask "Does this perception of you fit?",
- Point out how those who are projecting onto the member also likely project similar attributes onto others in their lives, thus encouraging the member not to take the perceptions personally,
- Join with the member by pointing out that you too have been perceived in a similar way, thus turning attention of the transference work towards yourself,
- Help to shift the focus away from content to process by focusing on the need for emotional regulation and effective and constructive interpersonal communication.

As the group engages in this type of work, members develop improved skills in presenting, hearing, and exploring their potential transferences. Of course, the leader must be aware of the potential for scapegoating and blaming dynamics. It is important to remember that being **the object of affectively charged negative transferences, particularly when presented without empathy or with limited reality testing, can be one of the most painful experiences for group members.** At times as leaders, we will need to step in strongly to protect the group as a place to work and explore our lives and interpersonal relationships and not to discharge destructively towards one another. Checking with those members who are the targets of transference is important, because at first they may report being fine, but may have deeper feelings of hurt, shame or confusion they are hesitant to disclose.

While clearly not every form of group therapy entails transference exploration and analysis, in those groups where it is part of the therapeutic work, the process is usually experienced as powerful, moving, and deeply authentic.

Group-as-a-Whole and Subgroup Transferences

All of us have had many meaningful and positive moments of connection with groups of all kinds – family, friends, clubs, teams, committees. However, likely, most of us have also had some painful and hurtful experiences in similar groups. Many of our group members have experienced being scapegoated, ostracized, ridiculed, and potentially abused by the groups in their lives. For many members, the courage to join a group is a leap of faith filled with suspiciousness and fear, but also with hope for new potential reparative experiences. It is not unusual to hear members say that they are feeling like they are back in their family of origin, and again playing the role of scapegoat, peacemaker, rescuer, truth teller, outcast, or forgotten child.

Members will project not only onto the leader or individual members but also onto subgroups and the group-as-a-whole affects, motives and attributes derived from their early life experience (Greene, 1999). When members experience that the group-as-a-whole is against them or hold some other destructive perception of the group, they are at risk for dropping out, withdrawing, and withholding a commitment to the group. In such situations the leader might ask if there is an unspoken desire or need that is not being met, ask others if they have similar experiences of the group, or shift the focus momentarily from the group transference by helping these members engage with either the leader or another member in the present. When members attack the entire group, they are often setting themselves up for a strong emotional response as others can feel personally misunderstood or put down. Trying to get the member and the entire group to become curious about what is occurring is vital. The leader can ask whether what is happening is a reflection of some unexamined need, vulnerability or anxiety.

Recommended Resource

Greene, L. R. (1999). Representations of the group-as-a-whole: Personality, situational and dynamic determinants. *Psychoanalytic Psychology, 16,* 403–425.

Group-as-a-Whole and Subgroup Interventions

The Tavistock Clinic in London is known for its adherence to group-as-a-whole theories and practice. In classic Tavistock and some group relational models, the group therapist (or "conductor") focuses primarily on subgroup and group-as-a-whole processes rather than on individual members. The theoretical rationale for this orientation was based in the Gestalt Psychology assumption that by changing the "ground" (the group), the "figures" (members) will change automatically.

Currently few group therapists practice pure group-as-a-whole group therapy nowadays, in part owing to a classic study (Malan, Balfour, Hood, & Shooter, 1976) that showed considerable dissatisfaction by patients undergoing this treatment; however, most group therapists acknowledge the presence of group-as-a-whole processes in all groups and the need to monitor them, regardless of the specific therapeutic approach. For example, **whenever there is a boundary breach (a new member, a termination, a leader's vacation or illness, etc.), one should be attentive to whole-group reactions.** In the initial session (See Chapter 6), group-as-a-whole interventions can help build cohesion and universality by the leader suggesting that likely everyone or at least most members of the group are feeling anxious. More generally, as Yalom and Leszcz (2005) suggest, **group-as-a-whole interpretations are particularly useful when group-wide forces are impeding the work of the group,** as when:

- The group or most of its members are using rigid defenses such as avoidance to cope with some underlying shared anxiety,
- When the group has adopted some rigid antitherapeutic norm such as "taking turns" in order to minimize the risks of spontaneity and free interactive exchange, or

- When the group is grappling with some common, but as yet unidentified, emotional issue, such as impending termination of the group or member.

A group-as-a-whole conception can help members begin to broaden their understanding of why they are acting like they are, as in understanding the impact of such group-induced processes as loss of individuality or obedience to authority. Even if the group dislikes these interventions, when used judiciously they help to refocus the group on what may actually be occurring in that moment, as in:

- Identifying underlying group-wide themes or dynamics,
- Exploring the symbolic meanings of the language or imagery being used in the group,
- Assessing the general emotional climate or "pulse" of the group,
- Commenting on how the embedding organizational context or socio-political environment may be impacting the group.

Group-as-a-whole interventions can help the group begin to see the forest from the trees. If the leader is able to pull together the more global themes that are occurring in the specific interchanges, it allows for the group to work more deeply with what are likely underlying tensions and issues affecting the whole group. Such interventions can promote cohesion and potentially help members combine cathartic discharge with cognitive understanding.

Recommended Resource

Malan, D. H., Balfour, F. H., Hood, V. G., & Shooter, A. M. (1976). Group psychotherapy: A long-term follow-up study. *Archives of General Psychiatry, 33,* 1303–1315.

Subgroups are collections of individuals who are connected to each other by virtue of their experiencing something in common with each other. These commonalities or "apparent similarities" may be demographic or sociocultural variables such as gender orientation, age, or race, or more psychological attributes such as shared feelings, beliefs, and needs. **Subgroups are an important way for members to begin to feel understood and not alone in the group.** For instance, in a group for individuals with anxiety disorders, subgroups may form on the basis of those having experienced panic symptoms and those who have not, or those who struggle with obsessive symptoms and those who do not.

Working with **functional subgroups** (i.e., those formed on the basis of here-and-now needs, beliefs, and affects) is a powerful tool that can help build both **cohesion** as members feel connected with others in their various subgroups, as well as **integration**, as members discover that they have commonalities with members of other subgroups who were initially seen as apparently very different (Gantt & Agazarian, 2010).

While leaders may wish to avoid conflict by emphasizing the overarching similarities of all group members, forming functional subgroups and promoting their engagement with each other are useful ways of uncovering cognitive distortions and transference reactions and deepening mutual understanding. Working in subgroups provides a vehicle for both gaining support from members within one's subgroups and coping with challenges and exploring differences from those in other subgroups.

Recommended Resource

Gantt, S. P., & Agazarian, Y. M. (2010). Developing the group mind through functional subgrouping: Linking systems-centered training (SCT) and interpersonal neurobiology. *International Journal of Group Psychotherapy*, 60(4), 515–544.

Utilizing Countertransference

Countertransference was identified by Freud in 1910 as the unconscious influence that the patient has on the analyst, and the therapist's reactions to the client's transference. Over time, and particularly due to the clinical contributions from object relations and relational theories, the ideas about and definitions of countertransference have evolved and broadened to include all conscious and unconscious reactions within the therapist. Currently countertransference is seen as not only inevitable but potentially helpful in the therapeutic relationship. Our feelings about our patients are not something to get rid of, but rather to be studied for everyone's benefit. As leaders, we need to work towards recognizing and becoming curious about the potential meanings of our feelings and attitudes towards our members and our groups.

Racker (1968) is frequently cited for his expanded notions of countertransference that distinguish:

- **Objective Countertransference** (feelings and reactions that many or most people have towards a member or member's behavior such as wanting to take care of the member or wanting to avoid conflict. The therapist's reactions are similar to most of the group members forming a kind of consensual validation),

  from

- **Subjective Countertransference** (a unique and idiosyncratic reaction based in the therapist personal history and personality),

  and

- **Concordant Identification** (having feelings similar to the client, for example, feelings of victimization, confusion or outrage),

  from

- **Complementary Identification** (identifying with some split off part of the patient's internal world and accepting the "invitation" to enact a unique role relationship with the patient, such as victim-tormentor).

Using Racker's taxonomy helps group leaders assess how best to utilize one's experience for the benefit of our members. A complementary countertransference may bring forth very strong impulses and inductions to react to members in ways that merely reinforce their existing scripts and attributions; more therapeutic is to understand our reaction as a potential reflection of an aspect of the patient's internal world. We want to find a way to work with objective countertransference reactions that members elicit and bring our subjective countertransference reactions to our own therapy and supervision.

It is important not to shy away from acknowledging our feelings towards our members. At times some will bring forth feelings of dislike, distrust, annoyance, eroticism, or friendship. These are not character critiques of the patients; but they may shed light on their histories and specific interpersonal needs and fears they are experiencing in the moment. Often if we feel ourselves being tempted to act in ways that seem foreign, it is helpful to ask **"what role in that member's history of interpersonal relationships am I being invited to perform?"**

To further complicate matters, we are not innocent blank screens. We bring our own interpersonal forces to the situation, and if we are to make maximum use of our affective responses in therapy it is imperative that we have sufficient self awareness so that we know when we are being impacted by "the other" versus when we are experiencing our own historic reactions. It is crucial, for the sake of understanding and therapeutic progress, that we do not accept the invitation by becoming the wished-for other and that we maintain the capacity to step back from the potential enactment in order to carefully explore and process it (Burke & Tansey, 1985).

What is of paramount importance is **countertransference management** (Hayes, Gelso, & Hummel, 2011), a process that refers to the **exploration of one's cognitive-affective reactions to our members or the group, without defensive avoidance, on one hand, or collusive enactments, on the other hand.** Successful countertransference management entails:

- **Self-insight**, referring to the therapists' awareness and understanding of their own feelings, attitudes, personalities, motives, and histories,
- **Self-integration**, reflecting the therapist's possession of an intact, basically healthy character structure,
- **Anxiety management**, referring to therapists' ability to control and understand their own anxiety so that it does not adversely affect their responses to patients,
- **Empathy**, or the ability to partially identify with a member, thus permitting the therapist to focus on the patient's needs despite difficulties one may be experiencing in the moment,
- Finally, **conceptualizing ability**, reflecting the therapist's ability to draw on theory and understand the patient's role in the therapeutic relationship.

There is some research evidence indicating that **competent countertransference management leads to better therapeutic outcomes** (Hayes, Nelson, & Fauth, 2015). The therapist **needs to routinely ask:**

- **What am I feeling** this moment?
- **Where are the feelings coming from?** Are these familiar feelings that are evoked in many situations and that derive from some early emotional issues within me or are they being induced in me by this particular patient, subgroup, or group as a whole?
- **Would other therapists feel similarly** (consensual validation) or are my reactions idiosyncratic?

- **What do I do with these feelings**? Can I use them to help me gain a better dynamic understanding of the patients and/or the group? Can they serve as the basis for a question or interpretation about what is happening in the group?

The vital message is that not only will we have strong thoughts and feelings towards our group members and our groups, but such experiences are welcome. **Counter-transference is another source of important information that can be used to understand your members and your groups, to more deeply attune to them, and to help us be responsive and not reactive.**

Exercises

Can you identify certain subjective countertransference potentials that can get in the way of the work? Are there particular patient behaviors that you tend to take personally?

How as a group therapist do you utilize your own feelings towards your members and the group for therapeutic work?

What do you see as the strengths and possible pitfalls of employing counter-transference material?

Recommended Resources

Burke, W. F., & Tansey, M. J. (1985). Projective identification and countertrans-ference turmoil: disruptions in the empathic process. *Contemporary Psycho-analysis, 21,* 372–402.

Hayes, J. A., Gelso, C. J., & Hummel, A. M. (2011). Managing countertransference. *Psychotherapy, 48,* 88–97.

Hayes, J. A., Nelson, D., & Fauth, J. (2015). Countertransference in successful and unsuccessful cases of psychotherapy. *Psychotherapy, 52,* 127–133.

Racker, H. (1968). *Transference and countertransference.* New York: International Universities Press.

Co-Leadership

Co-leadership or co-facilitation is having more than one leader conduct a group simultaneously (Freedman & Diederich, 2017), usually two, although in large groups settings there can be several. It is a structural arrangement that adds yet another layer of complexity to the already complicated situation of group therapy. It has long been recognized (Cooper, 1976; Gans, 1962; Luke & Hackney, 2007; Miles & Kivlighan, 2010) as offering a number of potential benefits but also poses several challenges to leadership. As there is relatively little empirical evidence to use as a guideline, choosing whether to lead solo or to co-lead is, in large measure, a personal preference: some group leaders will be drawn to co-leadership, while others prefer leading alone. While often used effectively in the training settings where a clear difference in role and authority exist between an experienced leader and newer group therapist (cf.

Goicoechea & Kessler, 2018), the practice is less utilized elsewhere, in part due to financial and resource constraints (Corey, Corey, & Corey, 2013).

Among the potential advantages of co-leadership are:

- Feelings of support, relational connectedness, and the rewards of positive collaboration,
- Decreased fatigue, effort, and anxiety by sharing the responsibilities,
- Another set of eyes to decrease a co-leader's subjectivity and bias, as well as capturing a fuller range of group dynamics,
- Ongoing learning from the close collaboration with another clinician,
- A wider range of transference and countertransference reactions available for exploration,
- Sharing the transferences, countertransference inductions, projective identifications, and other complexities and potential stressors of leadership,
- Increased variety of intervention styles to address the different ways members may progress,
- Ability in the co-leading relationship to positively model:
    - collegial support,
    - communication and conflict resolution skills,
    - acceptance and respect for differences,
    - a full variety of relational dynamics.

- Greater member satisfaction and less relational avoidance, as suggested by recent research (Kivlighan, London, & Miles, 2012).

The primary dynamic challenge has to do with both the **real differences** between the therapists in values, orientation and style and the **perceived differences,** based on projections onto them from the group. The group can construe the couple in a vast range of ways, from a fused, monolithic authority to a split dyad, polarized along such affective-cognitive dimensions as good-bad, powerful-weak, active-passive. The group can often projectively embellish real differences, for example in authority, by turning one into the omniscient therapist and the other into the ineffectual student. **How these differences are coped with** – in an open, nondefensive, exploratory mode versus a denied, countertransferentially enacted, or conflicted fashion – makes a crucial difference (Greene, Rosenkrantz, & Muth, 1986).

Co-leadership demands that individuals be committed to and valuing of the exploration of the co-therapy relationship as a vital source of information about group and individual dynamics. Further, the relationship, to be therapeutic for the group, requires:

- Respecting each other's views and ideas,
- Having an open communicative relationship in which ideas, feelings, and tensions can be discussed and examined,
- Not assuming your co-leader understands what you are thinking and actively communicating ideas and group plans prior to each group,
- Agreeing on how to share the leadership, work load, and talking time,
- Concurring on the type of culture to be created, change processes to be emphasized, and boundaries to be managed,

- Managing competitive feelings and not looking good at your co-leader's expense,
- Having good conflict resolution skills in the co-leadership team,
- Agreeing on an effective process for making clinically-relevant decisions,
- A willingness to seek outside supervision and consultation to help manage the dynamics when deemed necessary,
- Devoting time between groups to review the previous session and plan for the upcoming one.

Recommended Resources

Cooper, L. (1976). Co-therapy relationships in groups. *Small Group Behavior*, 7, 473–498.

Corey, M. S., Corey, G., & Corey, C. (2013). *Groups: Process and practice*. Independence, KY: Cengage Learning.

Freedman W., & Diederich, L. T. (2017). Group co-facilitation: Creating a collaborative partnership. In Ribeiro, M. D., Gross, J. M., & Turner, M. M. (Eds.), *The College Counselor's Guide to Group Psychotherapy* (pp. 159–172). New York: Routledge.

Gans, R. W. (1962). Group co-therapists and the therapeutic situation: A critical evaluation. *International Journal of Group Psychotherapy*, 12, 788–799.

Goicoechea, J., & Kessler, L. E. (2018). Competency-based training in interpersonal, process-oriented group therapy: An innovative university partnership. *Training and Education in Professional Psychology*, 12, 46–53.

Greene, L. R., Rosenkrantz, J., & Muth, D. (1986). Borderline defenses and countertransference: Research findings and implications. *Psychiatry*, 49, 253–264.

Kivlighan Jr, D. M., London, K., & Miles, J. R. (2012). Are two heads better than one? The relationship between number of group leaders and group members, and group climate and group member benefit from therapy. *Group Dynamics: Theory, Research, and Practice*, 16(1), 1–13.

Luke, M., & Hackney, H. (2007). Group coleadership: A critical review. *Counselor Education and Supervision*, 46(4), 280–293.

Miles, J. R., & Kivlighan Jr, D. M. (2010). Co-leader similarity and group climate in group interventions: Testing the co-leadership, team cognition-team diversity model. *Group Dynamics: Theory, Research, and Practice*, 14(2), 114–122.

Tracking Progress and Process

The goal of group psychotherapy, as with all therapeutic modalities, is to effect psychological change, that is, to produce positive outcomes and increasingly we as therapists are called upon to document therapeutic progress and be accountable for our therapeutic work (Leszcz, 2018) Therapeutic change can be viewed, and assessed, along such dimensions as:

- Attainment of the group member's **personally defined goals**, such as increased self esteem or better anger management skills,
- **Symptomatic change** (as in fewer panic attacks, decreased suicidal thoughts, or brighter mood),

- **Increased psychological vocabulary,** such as an understanding of triggers,
- **Shift in prominent cognitions** (from pathogenic beliefs to more realistic thoughts),
- **Increased insight, self awareness or psychological truths,** including clearer awareness of desires, values, anxieties, and defensive patterns (Billow, 2004),
- **Change in interpersonal behavior and dynamics** (from problematic relations such as conflicted, avoidant, overly domineering, hostile, anxious or enmeshed to more authentic, communicative and adaptive ones),
- **Enhanced emotional regulation, emotional intelligence, and impulse control,**
- **More adaptive and enhanced psychological resources** such as empathy, capacities for mindfulness and reflection, tolerance for ambiguity, sense of humor, regression in the service of the ego, self efficacy, self soothing, stress tolerance,
- **Client satisfaction with the therapeutic work.**

It is important for the group therapist to track therapeutic change for each group member, through clinical observation or formal assessment or both, to consider whether:

- Therapeutic progress is being achieved,
- No change is occurring, or
- Signs of deterioration are present.

What dimensions of change the therapist chooses to focus on depends on the task of the group, the theoretical orientation of the therapist, and the goals and needs of the client. In an open-ended psychodynamic group, the therapist might choose to primarily monitor increases in psychological mindedness and shifts from reliance on rigid or maladaptive defenses to more developmentally mature defenses, while in a time limited counseling group for substance abuse, the leader might focus on more overt behavioral dimensions, such as abstinence, and coping with "triggers." With respect to group psychotherapy, there is general agreement that it is **important to monitor not only each individual's progress** along the kinds of psychological dimensions of change or outcome listed above, but also **core group processes** that can facilitate or interfere with therapeutic progress. As suggested in AGPA's Core Battery-R (Burlingame et al., 2006), the therapist might usefully try to assess the individual member's experience of three core components of the group therapy experience:

- The **positive relational bonds** (How positively does this group member feel about my leadership, the other members and this group?),
- The **positive working relationships** (How much is this member committed to and valuing of the defined work of the group), and
- **Negative factors** (To what degree does this member experience negative reactions to me and the group?).

A recent trend in the practice of psychotherapy and group psychotherapy is **practice based evidence** that routinely administers psychological tests and inventories to assess the progress of each patient over the course of the group (Marmarosh, 2018; Tasca et al., 2016). It is important to note that the use of instruments to track therapeutic progress and group process is not a common practice and, in fact, is somewhat controversial. Some clinicians have expressed the view that it imposes an unnecessary interference into the group process and generates data that could be just as readily gathered by astute clinical observation. On the other hand, advocates argue that administering measures and receiving feedback routinely can:

- Increase the group therapist's awareness of where the group is emotionally and developmentally,
- Help the therapist proactively plan interventions,
- Allow the therapist to bring this information back to the group in varying degrees of explicitness,
- Track problematic cases and situations over time that might otherwise lead to treatment failures or drop outs and can thus provide opportunities to amend or alter treatment (Gleave, Beecher, Burlingame, Griner, & Hansen, 2016; Hansen, Beecher, Boardman, Burlingame, & Griner, 2017).

Advocates have further posited that **potential treatment failures** can be more readily identified by comparing the individual's performance trajectory with algorithms of those who have deteriorated or dropped out, arguing that research has demonstrated that the objective assessment of outcome (i.e., the use of instruments) has consistently outperformed clinicians' ability to predict which patients might become a treatment failure (Lambert, 2012). Further, there is even some intriguing evidence to suggest that routinely monitoring progress and giving feedback to clients in group therapy can lead to larger treatment gains, greater clinically significant change, and greater attendance rates than in groups without such monitoring (Slone, Reese, Mathews-Duval, & Kodet, 2015). Whether or not the therapist chooses to implement routine monitoring, an interesting recent thesis has been developed (Pascual-Leone & Andreescu, 2013) that learning about research outcome and process measures can help practitioners become more sensitive to and articulate about here-and-now dynamics of the therapy situation.

There is general agreement that **the use of instruments to "take the pulse of the group" should supplement, not supplant, clinical observation and judgment.** Further, there is no gold standard to guide how and when to collect inventory data and provide feedback to individual members or to the group as a whole (Jensen et al., 2012); the group therapist needs to use clinical judgment to determine in each specific situation how to best implement such monitoring and feedback procedures.

And as Strauss, Burlingame, and Bormann (2008) suggest, formal outcome and process measures may reveal some surprises for the practitioner. The general idea is **not to take the test responses as the absolute truth but rather to be curious and exploratory about what discrepancies between clinical observation and test data might mean.** For example, a patient who appears somewhat compliant, though reserved and deferential in the group may, on formal assessment, express considerable anger and disappointment at the group experience and towards the group therapist. How are these apparently inconsistent messages to be understood and reconciled? This of course is not easy to answer but does deserve some exploration and reflection by the therapist to develop some clinical hypotheses. Is the anger, expressed privately on a self-report measure but inhibited in real interpersonal interchanges, "real?" Is this an attempt to request or command the therapist's attention from an otherwise characterologically docile member? Is this an attempt to form a secret and private bond with the therapist or perhaps to engage in a clandestine sadistic attack? Again, the point is that one mode of communication and expression (in vivo versus self-report measure) is not more valid than the other; the **two modes differ in terms of how the message is communicated and may well reflect different but equally valid interpersonal needs and agendas.**

Exercises

1) Both as a member and therapist, how do you feel about implementing routine monitoring instruments to "take the pulse of the group?"
2) What are your reactions to the idea about the usefulness of learning about outcome research and process measures to enhance clinical sensitivity?

Recommended Resources

Billow, R. M. (2004). Truth and falsity in group. *International Journal of Group Psychotherapy, 54,* 321–345.

Burlingame, G. M., Strauss, B., Joyce, A., MacNair-Semands, R., MacKenzie, K. R., Ogrodniczuk, J., & Taylor, S. (2006). *Core Battery – Revised: An assessment tool kit for promoting optimal group selection, process and outcome.* Available through the AGPA store.

Gleave, R., Beecher, M., Burlingame, G., Griner, D. & Hansen, K. (2016). Practical and useful evidence-based practice: Using clinician-friendly process and outcome measures to enhance your groups. Open session presented at the 2016 AGPA annual meeting, New York City; audiotape available through AGPA store.

Hansen, K., Beecher, M., Boardman, R. D., Burlingame, G. M., & Griner, D. (2017). Practice-based evidence can help! Using clinician-friendly process and outcome measures to enhance your groups. Open session presented at the 2017 AGPA annual meeting, New York City; audiotape available through AGPA store.

Jensen, D. R., Abbott, M. K., Beecher, M. E., Griner, D., Golightly, T. R., & Cannon, J. A. N. (2012). Taking the pulse of the group: The utilization of practice-based evidence in group psychotherapy. *Professional Psychology: Research and Practice, 43,* 388–394.

Lambert, M. (2012). Helping clinicians to use and learn from research-based systems: The OQ-analyst. *Psychotherapy, 49,* 109–114.

Leszcz, M. (2018). The evidence-based group psychotherapist. *Psychoanalytic Inquiry, 38*(4), 285–298.

Marmarosh, C. L. (2018). Introduction to special issue: Feedback in group psychotherapy. *Psychotherapy, 55,* 101–104.

Pascual-Leone, A., & Andreescu, C. (2013). Repurposing process measures to train psychotherapists: Training outcomes using a new approach. *Counseling and Psychotherapy Research, 13,* 210–219.

Slone, N., Reese, R., Mathews-Duval, S., & Kodet, J. (2015). Evaluating the efficacy of client feedback in group psychotherapy. *Group Dynamics, 19,* 122–136.

Strauss, B., Burlingame, G. M., & Bormann, B. (2008). Using the CORE-R battery in group psychotherapy. *Journal of Clinical Psychology, 64,* 1225–1237.

Tasca, G. A., Cabrera, C., Kristjansson, E., MacNair-Semands, R., Joyce, A. S., & Ogrodniczuk, J. S. (2016). The Therapeutic Factors Inventory-8: Using item response theory to create a brief scale for continuous process monitoring for group psychotherapy. *Psychotherapy Research*, 26, 131–145.

Concluding Thoughts

The advancing path of group leaders has a paradox. While one improves and gains a level mastery of working in many situations, the challenge is that one never finishes building one's skills to a finite place of completion. Continual opportunities arise for expansion into new areas that can make the career journey enlivening, exciting, and endlessly interesting, but also challenging, imprecise, and unpredictable. Areas of life long development for group leaders can include refining many of the interpersonal skills covered in this chapter. Others may take time to focus on areas such as deepening one's ability at case conceptualization, building realistic collaborative goals and timelines with members, honing our presentation of didactic material to match a variety of learning styles and cultural locations, increasing our cultural proficiency, mentoring younger leaders, and onward.

Advanced skills and mastery take time. Since the journey is never ending, one task that becomes paramount is the pacing and enjoyment of the journey. Remember we are models for our members; they pick up on our tenets and lifestyle. For us, it should include continued professional development, but in our modeling we can also continue to grow in our private lives through sustaining mutual caring relationships, work-life balance, social advocacy, enjoyments, and other enriching experiences that provide us with meaning and purpose. To be our best healthy selves, and to foster that in our members, is also an advanced skill.

Module 5

Group Psychotherapy in Action

Ethics, Neuroscience and Personal Style

10 The Ethical Group Psychotherapist

Francis J. Kaklauskas and Elizabeth A. Olson

Introduction

At every moment, group psychotherapists have multiple matters that require their attention, but none is more important than sustaining an ethical practice. As Bricklin (2001) emphasized, ethics are central to all psychological processes and procedures, and should not be seen as an "add on." Traditionally, in the training of the group therapists, matters of theory and technique dominate, while the study of ethical and legal considerations garners less focus. However, state and federal governing bodies have increased their focus on ethical practice in recent years and have **stiffened the penalties and sanctions for unethical behavior** (MacNair-Semands, 2005).

Group therapists are frequently confronted with disturbing stories about criminal behaviors, child and elder abuse, substance misuse, secret affairs, bigotry, and abuses of power and privilege. Having the ability to **ethically, legally, clinically, and personally** navigate these situations can be challenging. In many ways, the group therapist is **uniquely prepared to address ethical dilemmas** given the need to understand situations from **multiple perspectives**.

Today, virtually all professional mental health organizations have **guidelines for ethical practice, the following specifically geared for the group therapist:**

- AGPA and IBCGP Guidelines for Ethics (2002). Available at www.agpa.org/home/practice-resources/ethics-in-group-therapy
- Brabender, V. (2007). The ethical group psychotherapist: A coda. *International Journal of Group Psychotherapy, 57*(1), 41–48.
- MacNair-Semands, R. (2005). *Ethics in group psychotherapy.* New York: American Group Psychotherapy Association.
- Thomas, R. V., & Pender, D. A. (2008). Association for Specialists in Group Work: Best Practice Guidelines 2007 Revisions. *Journal for Specialists in Group Work, 33,* 111–117.
- International Association for Group Psychotherapy and Group Process (2009). Ethical Guidelines and Professional standards for Group Psychotherapists. Available at: www.iagp.com/about/ethicalguidelines.htm

---

Recommended Resources

Bricklin, P. (2001). Being ethical: More than obeying the law and avoiding harm. *Journal of Personality Assessment, 77*(2), 195–202.

MacNair-Semands, R. (2005). *Ethics in group psychotherapy*. New York: American Group Psychotherapy Association.

Principle-Based and Virtue Ethics

Psychotherapy ethics are based in **religious and philosophical traditions** that attempt to outline **proper, just, and beneficial behaviors** (MacNair- Semands, 2005). **The primary purpose of ethical standards is to protect clients** and an ethical approach to the practice of psychotherapy entails adherence to an underlying philosophical system such as **principle-based ethics** or **virtue ethics**.

One well-respected **principle-based approach to ethical conduct** identifies five core principles (Kitchener, 1984; Kitchener & Anderson, 2011):

- **Autonomy** addresses clients' independence and freedom to choose their own course of action. Clients are not only allowed, but encouraged to follow the direction they feel is best. As group therapists, we can help clients understand how their decisions and their values impact their lives and the lives of others. Yet, clinicians need to refrain from demanding that clients proceed in the manner we determine is best for them. For the group therapist this can be important as the power of group can dramatically impact members' choices through peer pressure or groupthink dynamics. **The leader must work diligently to help members retain their own power of choice and autonomy.**

- **Nonmaleficence** harkens back to the often quoted maxim, *"primum non nocere" (do no harm)*. This goes beyond the prohibition of inflicting intentional harm, but also brings forth the idea of increasing one's awareness to foresee and prevent situations that could inadvertently harm. In the group psychotherapy situation, members experience various levels of discomfort as they receive feedback from other members. Leaders must stay sensitive to how much each group member can tolerate and interrupt the process if someone is being scapegoated or "invited" to play some other emotionally difficult role for the group, receiving unhelpful guidance, or becoming emotionally overwhelmed.

- **Beneficence** is in many ways the opposite of nonmaleficence, and speaks to working for the benefit of our clients. As group leaders, this principle entails such activities as helping someone find the best group fit regardless of its impact upon our agency or our own practice, as well as continuing our education and training to provide the best services we can. It also involves our capacity to appropriately manage our countertransference feelings (Chapter 9). Whether we are activated by certain issues in the group that resonate with similar issues in our personal histories or are induced into difficult emotional roles by various projections onto us, we need to work diligently at not losing our capacities for empathy, curiosity, non-defensiveness, and beneficence. Finding the balance of nonmaleficence and beneficence can be challenging and group therapists should explore whether they tend to lean towards one at the expense of the other.

- **Justice** guides clinicians towards finding ways for all individuals to receive equal opportunities to engage in optimal treatment without being subjected to bias and discrimination (MacNair-Semands, 2007). Given that individuals have different strengths and challenges a one-size-fits-all approach may not be fair or just (Chen, 2012). Therapists are increasingly encouraged to engage more fully in social justice perspectives and advocacy (Ratts, Singh, Nassar-McMillian, Butler, & McCullough, 2016). Such paradigms are also increasingly understood as enhancing clinical outcomes and broadening psychological perspectives and values to social issues (Nadal, 2017), as well as potentially enriching the therapist's personal communal life (Kozan & Blustein, 2018; Pease, Vreugdenhil, & Stanford 2017).
- **Fidelity** refers to faithfulness and loyalty. Group therapists must honor their commitments and follow through with mutually agreed upon obligations with their clients. A core aspect of this principle is to prepare contingencies in case of illness or disability, as well as having a professional will (Steiner, 2011), so that treatment is not unduly disrupted. The group therapist must respect and care for their clients' long term well being and actively advocate for their care.

Exercise

What are the ethical principles that come from your family or culture that may impact your ethical values and beliefs?

In contrast to a principles-based code of ethical behavior that emphasizes rules and duties, virtue ethics focuses on the moral character of the person carrying out an action. The following **virtue-based guidelines** identify core character traits **for the moral practitioner** (Beauchamp & Childress, 2001):

- **Compassion** is a prerequisite for effective group leadership and, unfortunately, somewhat neglected in therapist training. The ability to empathize and connect with our group members facilitates the development of the therapeutic alliance and helps them endure the often challenging work of the group by knowing that the leader is working towards a better life for them.
- **Discernment** requires the ability to think critically and rationally and to be able to carefully weigh the best interests of the varied stakeholders and legal requirements of any specific clinical situation. In addition, the ability to examine factors that may be influencing our moral perspective, such as our feelings and biases towards specific clients, helps guide one's best decisions (Betan & Stanton, 1999).
- **Trustworthiness** is the ability to weigh complex factors for the best possible outcome of all involved. Members who view a leader as trustworthy are more likely to be committed to the work in the group.
- **Integrity** is the ability to avoid duplicitous or reactive destructive behaviors. The therapist will act in ways that serve everyone's best interest, and not take action based on the therapist's personal or defensive needs.
- **Conscientiousness reflects a keen** awareness and anticipation of how actual or potential group processes could impact group members. A conscientious leader is

often able to avoid ethical and legal dilemmas by maintaining a **predictive, thoughtful, and reflective attitude** even in the emotional storms of group life.

Exercise

In reviewing these ethical principles and virtues, which ones come easiest to you? Which are more challenging for you?

Recommended Resources

Beauchamp, T. L., & Childress, J. F. (2001). *Principles of biomedical ethics*. Cary, NC: Oxford University Press.

Betan, E. J., & Stanton, A. L. (1999). Fostering ethical willingness: Integrating emotional and contextual awareness with rational analysis. *Professional Psychology: Research and Practice*, 30(3), 295–301.

Brabender, V. (2007). The ethical group psychotherapist: A coda. *International Journal of Group Psychotherapy*, 57(1), 41–48.

Chen, E. C. (2012). Multicultural competence and social justice advocacy in group psychology and group psychotherapy. *The Group Psychologist*, 22(2), 10.

Kitchener, K. S. (1984). Intuition, critical evaluation and ethical principles: The foundation for ethical decisions in counseling psychology. *The Counseling Psychologist*, 12(3), 43–55.

Kitchener, K. S., & Anderson, S. K. (2011). *Foundations of ethical practice, research, and teaching in psychology and counseling*. New York: Routledge.

Kozan, S., & Blustein, D. L. (2018). Implementing social change: A qualitative analysis of counseling psychologists' engagement in advocacy. *The Counseling Psychologist*, 46(2), 154–189.

MacNair-Semands, R. R. (2007). Attending to the spirit of social justice as an ethical approach in group therapy. *International Journal of Group Psychotherapy*, 57(1), 61–66.

Nadal, K. L. (2017). "Let's get in formation": On becoming a psychologist–activist in the 21st century. *American Psychologist*, 72(9), 935.

Pease, B., Vreugdenhil, A., & Stanford, S. (Eds.). (2017). *Critical ethics of care in social work: Transforming the politics and practices of caring*. London: Routledge.

Ratts, M. J., Singh, A. A., Nassar-McMillian, S., Butler, S. K., & McCullough, J. R. (2016). Multicultural and social justice counseling competencies: Guidelines for the counseling profession. *Journal of Multicultural Counseling and Development*, 44, 28–48.

Steiner, A. (2011). The therapist's professional will: A backup plan every clinician needs. *Group*, 35(1), 33–40.

Ethical Decision Making Models

Clinical situations that demand ethical and legal considerations can be **emotionally charged** for both group members and leaders. Bricklin (2001) suggests that as a therapist gains experience, a feeling of unease can serve as a signal of a brewing ethical dilemma. Having a **structured procedure** for addressing such situations assists in creating **the best course of action**. The literature offers a number of paths towards ethical decision making (Bush, Connell, & Denney, 2006; Forester-Miller & Davis, 1996; Koocher & Keith-Spiegel, 2008; Sileo & Kopala, 1993; Stadler, 1986; Van Hoose & Paradise, 1979), including some that take into account **feminist, social justice and multicultural perspectives** (Anderson, 1997; Brown, 2010; Knapp & VandeCreek, 2007).

Knapp, VandeCreek, and Fingerhut (2017) identify **five general steps useful in ethical decision making:**

- **Identification of the problem.** This step is designed to simplify the situation and maintain rationality in potentially emotionally charged situations. The first goal is to gather as much information as possible, detailing the problematic situation as rationally as possible and distinguishing between **facts,** innuendoes or subjective impressions. **What is the problem and who does it involve** – a member, the whole group, the group therapist, and/or the agency in which the treatment is conducted?
- **Development of alternatives.** Next, the group therapist needs to develop **potential courses of actions entailing all relevant ethical principles, virtues and legal considerations.** This can be a brain storming process that is often useful to do in consort with others as long as proper confidentiality of the members and other shareholders is intact.
- **Evaluation of alternatives.** Once possible actions have been identified, the therapist tries to think through the likely impact and consequences of each plan for all stakeholders involved. Sometimes from one course of action, **multiple new scenarios** emerge that also need to be considered over the long term. Removing plans that are unlikely to yield positive results or that may cause harm is a good place to start. As the list of plans gets shorter, you may need to get creative and combine aspects of several plans.
- **Implementation of the best option.** After settling on a course of action, it is best to assess it once more to see if it would benefit from any adjustments by asking (Stadler, 1986):

  - Would you recommend a similar course of action to another therapist?
  - Would you treat other clients in this same situation similarly?
  - If this became public are you satisfied with your course of action?

Taking this step of implementing your plan can be challenging, as often with complex ethical dilemmas **no choice seems ideal or perfect.** Knowing you have diligently and strategically evaluated the situation along with support from colleagues makes it easier to put the plan into action.

- **Evaluating the results.** Once a plan begins to move into action the therapist should follow its impact to see if any unforeseen adverse events have occurred that require revisions or extensions of the plan.

Recommended Resources

Anderson, G. (1997). Children, adolescents and their powerholders in therapy settings. *Women and Therapy*, 20, 1–6.

Brown, L. S. (2010). *Feminist therapy*. Washington, DC: American Psychological Association.

Bush, S. S., Connell, M. A., & Denney, R. L. (2006). *Ethical practice in forensic psychology: A systematic model for decision making*. Washington, DC: American Psychological Association.

Forester-Miller, H., & Davis, T. E. (1996). A Practitioner's Guide to Ethical Decision Making. Retrieved from www.counseling.org/docs/ethics/practitioners_guide.pdf?sfvrsn=2

Knapp, S., & VandeCreek, L. (2007). When values of different cultures conflict: Ethical decision making in a multicultural context. *Professional Psychology: Research and Practice*, 38(6), 660–666.

Knapp, S. J., VandeCreek, L. D., & Fingerhut, R. (2017). *Practical ethics for psychologists: A positive approach* (3rd Ed). Washington, DC: American Psychological Association.

Koocher, G. P., & Keith-Spiegel, P. (2008). *Ethics in psychology and the mental health professions: Standards and cases*. Oxford: Oxford University Press.

Sileo, F. J., & Kopala, M. (1993). An A-B-C-D-E worksheet for promoting beneficence when considering ethical issues. *Counseling and Values*, 37(2), 89–95.

Stadler, H. A. (1986). Making hard choices: Clarifying controversial ethical issues. *Counseling and Human Development*, 19, 1–10.

Van Hoose, W. H., & Paradise, L. V. (1979). *Ethics in counseling and psychotherapy: Perspectives in issues and decision making*. Cranston, RI: The Carroll Press.

General Practice Principles

Disclosure Forms and Confidentiality

It is surprising how many therapists do not provide disclosure forms to their clients, or provide disclosures that do not have up to date information required by law. Taking time to review your disclosure form annually is a helpful practice, as this is a commonly sanctioned misstep when a therapist faces a grievance. Disclosure forms usually include:

- Name, degrees and institutions, licenses.
- Fees, billing, and scheduling practices.
- Brief description of practice and specialty areas.
- Confidentiality and its limits.
- Names and contact information of relevant regulatory agencies.
- Information about the nature of group psychotherapy and of the risks, benefits, rights and obligations as a member of a therapy group.
- Dated signatures of client and therapist.

Confidentiality is vitally important to most clients. Psychotherapy communication is privileged and confidential as outlined in federal law:

> Effective psychotherapy . . . depends upon an atmosphere of confidence and trust in which the patient is willing to make a frank and complete disclosure of facts, emotions, memories, and fears. Because of the sensitive nature of the problems for which individuals consult psychotherapists, disclosure of confidential communications made during counseling sessions may cause embarrassment or disgrace. For this reason, the mere possibility of disclosure may impede development of the confidential relationship necessary for successful treatment.
>
> (Jaffe v Redmond, 2017)

Limits to confidentiality should be explicitly listed in your disclosure form and discussed with your client at the beginning of treatment and in best practice brought up as treatment continues. Conditions that limit confidentiality include:

* The presence of suicidal or homicidal ideation,
* Child or elder abuse,
* Grave disability,
* Terrorist threats against the United States.

Recommended Resource

Jaffee v. Redmond (2017). Available at https://en.wikipedia.org/wiki/Jaffee_v._ Redmond

---

Confidentiality and Group Psychotherapy

Maintaining confidentiality in group therapy is complicated because while as leaders we are required to respect confidentiality, our clients are not legally bound. When there are two or more clients involved in the same treatment (group, couple, and family therapies) courts have upheld decisions that other clients are not bound by confidentiality (MacNair- Semands, 2005; Woods & Ruzek, 2017).

While we can strongly encourage our clients to uphold confidentiality and provide a compelling rationale for doing so, we **cannot secure confidentiality from group members.** It is important to stress this point to your clients so they can reveal at a level and rate that feel best for them. Members may decline to participate in certain activities, exercises or discussions, and should be supported in their choices around their own feelings of safety. In rare cases, group members could be called into court by a judge's order to testify about disclosures made by other members. All of this information should be included on a disclosure form for members joining a group. **Best practice is to have this discussion at the beginning of group and intermittently throughout the group to help the members understand and build a collaborative and realistic agreement among all involved** (McClanahan, 2014).

Recommended Resources:

MacNair-Semands, R. (2005). *Ethics in group psychotherapy*. New York: American Group Psychotherapy Association.

McClanahan, K. (2014). Can Confidentiality be Maintained in Group Therapy? Retrieved from http://nationalpsychologist.com/2014/07/can-confidentiality-be-maintained-in-group-therapy/102566.html

Woods, J., & Ruzek, N. (2017). Ethics in group psychotherapy. In M. D. Ribeiro, J. Gross, & M. M. Turner (Eds.). *The college counselor's guide to group psychotherapy* (pp. 83–100). New York: Routledge.

Release of Information

Therapists are not to release any information about a client without a signed release of information form except under a judge's order. Release of information forms should be as detailed as possible including:

- Purpose of release,
- Identification of the specific persons to receive the information,
- Specific information that can or cannot be released,
- Expiration dates,
- Signature of a witness.

Documentation

The documentation of clients' progress is an important aspect of ethical professional practice, serving to explicate treatment needs, goals, plans and progress (Knauss, 2006). To insure confidentiality in group progress notes, the names of the other group members are never disclosed. Clinicians often choose to use pseudonyms, one or two initials, or another coding system to capture the significant clinical events. Typically, the note includes both group level themes, issues, and processes, which may be the same for each member in the session, and salient aspects of the member's participation, both qualitative and quantitative, such as:

- **Adherence to the therapeutic framework or group agreements,**
- **Commitment to the work and agreement on the tasks,**
- **Therapeutic alliance,** with the leader, other members and the group-as-a-whole.

Where risk is an issue, a **risk assessment** for suicide, homicide, or grave disability is needed along with the current plans for safety.

Increasingly, awareness and impact of **cultural and sociopolitical factors** are expected to be documented including:

- Extent of family support (or disintegration of family),
- Access to and availability of community resources,
- Change in social status as a result of immigration to this country,
- Level of stress related to acculturation, identity, cultural position and social status.

In addition, in response to the need for increasing accountability when providing mental health services, the implementation and documentation of **routine monitoring measures** are becoming more frequent in clinical practice (see Chapter 9).

Recommend Resource

Knauss, L. K. (2006). Ethical issues in recordkeeping in group psychotherapy. *International Journal of Group Psychotherapy*, 56(4), 415–430.

Impaired Professionals

The work of psychotherapy, and perhaps group psychotherapy in particular, is intense, emotional, and complex. We hear endless painful stories of trauma, grief, and despair. Often times in agency work, the focus is on productivity without the sufficient emphasis placed upon therapist self care. Empathic burnout and secondary trauma impact our ability to work constructively and compassionately. Some therapists turn to **substance abuse**, others fall into **clinical depression**, and others participate in a variety of non-healthy coping strategies. **Continual self care is part of our vocation** (cf. Chapter 12).

If you witness a colleague who is struggling, it is important to remember our ethical duty to protect all psychotherapy clients and the integrity of the profession. While not always met with openness, expressing concern is advised. In certain situations after you have spoken with your colleague and no changes are made, one may be forced to express concern to a state regulatory agency or national organization.

Boundaries

Some therapists can lose their boundaries with clients and enact inappropriate and unethical relationships. These enactments can range from small infractions such as laxness in starting or ending the group on time to beginning to socialize with clients. In some cases, therapists will develop **intimate and sexual relationships** with their clients to everyone's tremendous detriment. Even well trained and well meaning therapists can trick themselves into thinking that their situation is unique. The **intimacy** of group psychotherapy can sometimes bring forth sexual and/or romantic feelings. Clients may also develop erotic transferences towards us and we may lose site of the extreme power differential between our roles. Such enactments are extremely destructive; research has shown that clients who have had sex with their therapist are much more vulnerable to attempt suicide (Pope & Vasquez, 2016a). Continuous supervision and consultation in a forum where a therapist can be completely honest is essential to avoid boundary violations.

Recommended Resource

Pope, K. S. & Vasquez, M. J. (2016). Sexual attraction to patients, therapist. In Pope, K. S., & Vasquez, M. J. *Ethics in psychotherapy and counseling: A practical guide*. Hoboken, NJ: John Wiley & Sons.

Concurrent Therapies

Concurrent therapies refer to clinical situations where a patient is simultaneously treated in two modalities, either with the same (combined) or different (conjoint) therapists.

- While combining group therapy with another therapeutic modality, typically individual psychotherapy, can offer a deeper and broader understanding of the client that can help develop case formulations and guide interventions, it also poses a number of ethical challenges that the therapist needs to attend to, such as the handling of complex transferences (such as a when a group member boasts about having a "special relationship" with the leader because of their also engaging in individual therapy), intensified dependence dynamics, and issues of confidentiality (Brabender & Fallon, 2009a; Roth, 2009; Taylor & Gazda, 1991). Generally speaking, combined therapy is not encouraged without many years of experience, close supervision, and a specific rationale that spells out why this arrangement is in the best interest of the client.
- In **Conjoint** therapy, it is important that all treaters involved have releases of information to enable them to share and integrate relevant clinical information and concerns, including the monitoring of potential splitting dynamics across the modalities.

Many group clients may also be participating in a variety of support groups such as Alcoholics Anonymous and ideally the group leader facilitates an exploration of the impact and interactions of these ancillary treatments on the group members.

Recommended Resources

Brabender, V. M., & Fallon, A (2009). Ethical hot spots of combined individual and group therapy: Applying four ethical systems. *International Journal of Group Psychotherapy*, 59(1), 127–147.

Roth, B. E. (2009). Some problems with treatment: Destructive enactments in combined therapy. *International Journal of Group Psychotherapy*, 59(1), 47–66.

Taylor, R. & Gazda, G. M. (1991). Concurrent individual and group therapy: The ethical issues. *Journal of Group Psychotherapy, Psychodrama & Sociometry*, 44 (2), 51–59.

Internet Groups

Internet support and therapy groups for a variety of mental health and personal growth topics emerged in the early eighties and the clinical-theoretical literature shows an increasing interest and exploration of their use (Hsiung, 2002; Weinberg, 2001, 2014). Developing research into their effectiveness and comparability to in-person groups has been promising (cf. Morland et al., 2010) and studies of therapeutic processes such as the therapeutic alliance and patient satisfaction suggest considerable, although not complete, overlap in change mechanisms between in-person and online groups (Greene et al.,

2010). Clearly more conceptual and empirical study of the ways in which therapeutic change is effected in online groups is needed (Berger, 2016; Goodwin et al., 2018).

Legal statutes and ethical practice considerations for Internet group therapy vary across states and countries and in many ways have not kept up with the rate of technology advancement and utilization (Haberstroh, Barney, Foster, & Duffey, 2014). Generally speaking, the online clinician needs to follow procedures as similar as possible to in-person therapy practices including proper documentation, treatment goals and plans, as well as adherence to all other legal constraints and ethical principles. The clinician should utilize online resources supplied by state licensing boards and professional organizations to keep abreast of ethical and legal considerations in this emerging field, although they may not answer every specific question that arises. **Supervision with an experienced clinician with expertise in this area is strongly recommended.** One may also want to consult with a knowledgeable telecommunication attorney in setting up and running such a practice.

Salient among the clinical challenges for leadership is how to develop and maintain a therapeutic presence and how to reinforce therapeutic values and norms via the Internet, given that the leader has less control over the immediate environment than in in-person groups. In this regard, clinicians need to take steps to make the online environment as secure as possible and make explicit the details and limitations of confidentiality. As in all forms of group therapy, communication and collaboration remain essential and the clinician needs to be assured clients realistically understand the opportunities, limitations, and risks of online group psychotherapy.

Recommended Resources

Berger, T. (2016). The therapeutic alliance in internet interventions: A narrative review and suggestions for future research, *Psychotherapy Research*, 27(5), 511–524.

Goodwin, B. C., Ford, D. E., Hsiung, R. C., Houston, T. K., Fogel, J., & Van Voorhees, B. W. (2018). First, do no harm: Referring primary care patients with depression to an internet support group. *Telemedicine and e-Health*, 24, 37–44.

Greene, C. J., Morland, L. A., Macdonald, A., Frueh, B. C., Grubbs, K. M., & Rosen, C. S. (2010). How does tele-mental health affect group therapy process? Secondary analysis of a noninferiority trial. *Journal of Consulting and Clinical Psychology*, 78, 746–750.

Haberstroh, S., Barney, L., Foster, N., & Duffey, T. (2014). The ethical and legal practice of online counseling and psychotherapy: A review of mental health professions. *Journal of Technology in Human Services*, 32(3), 149–157.

Hsiung, R. C. (2002). *E-therapy: Case studies, guiding principles, and the clinical potential of the Internet*. New York: Norton.

Morland, L. A., Greene, C. J., Rosen, C. S., Foy, D., Reilly, P., Shore, J., He, Q., & Frueh, B. C. (2010). Telemedicine for anger management therapy in a rural population of combat veterans with posttraumatic stress disorder: A randomized noninferiority trial. *Journal of Clinical Psychiatry*, 71, 850–863.

Weinberg, H. (2001). Group process and group phenomena on the Internet. *International Journal of Group Psychotherapy*, 51(3), 361–378.

Weinberg, H. (2014). *The paradox of internet groups: Alone in the presence of others*. London: Karnac.

Standards of Care

Group psychotherapists are expected to use best practice standards of care guidelines that include:

- Gaining a full history, including previous mental health treatment, to provide a detailed case conceptualization and psychodiagnostic formulation.
- Documenting of treatment plan and its rationale, therapeutic goals and progress.
- Incorporating evidence supported approaches to meet client needs, including culturally informed approaches.
- Keeping well-informed of the recent theoretical, practical and empirical advances in the field.

Concluding Thoughts

Brabender (2007) highlighted five domains to ensure ethical and legal practice for the group therapist.

- **Acquiring solid understanding** of ethical principles and virtues, as well as knowing pertinent laws and best practice guidelines. This knowledge base will allow us to foresee ethical situations and intervene quickly and effectively when they arise.
- **The Person of the Group Therapist** refers to the virtues and qualities that facilitate ethical decision making, including:
- Courage (Mangione, Forti, & Iacuzzi, 2007).
- Humility (Exline & Hill, 2007).
- Multicultural curiosity and knowledge (Debiak, 2007; Knapp & VandeCreek, 2007).
- **Self Awareness** of our characteristic response tendencies, especially in the context of others' anxieties, disappointments and criticisms as we take an ethical stand. Examining our underlying motivations, emotions and worries allows us to steer clear of our own biases and defensive needs in ethical decision making.
- **Examining Information Within a Larger Context** allows us to not erroneously over- or under-emphasize any one aspect of a dilemma and to consider any situation from multiple perspectives.
- **A Continuous Rather than Episodic Focus** encourages us to engage in ongoing explorations of ethical and legal perspectives with peers and supervisors and in formal trainings.

As group therapists we are lucky to do work we enjoy and that benefits others, but with this comes ethical responsibilities. Despite the complexities, sustaining an ethical group practice is within everyone's reach.

Exercise

Think of previous situations you were involved in that presented ethical choices and challenges.

How did you decide what to do in those situations? Would your decisions be any different currently?

Recommended Resources

Brabender, V. (2007). The ethical group psychotherapist: A coda. *International Journal of Group Psychotherapy, 57*(1), 41–48.

Debiak, D. (2007). Attending to diversity in group psychotherapy: An ethical imperative. *International Journal of Group Psychotherapy, 57*(1), 1–12.

Exline, J. J., & Hill, P. C. (2012). Humility: A consistent and robust predictor of generosity. *The Journal of Positive Psychology, 7*(3), 208–218.

Knapp, S., & VandeCreek, L. (2007). When values of different cultures conflict: Ethical decision making in a multicultural context. *Professional Psychology: Research and Practice, 38*(6), 660–666.

Mangione, L., Forti, R., & Iacuzzi, C. M. (2007). Ethics and endings in group psychotherapy: Saying good-bye and saying it well. *International Journal of Group Psychotherapy, 57*(1), 25–40.

11 Implications of Neuroscience for Group Psychotherapy

Susan Gantt

Introduction

Up until recently tracking the connections between psychotherapy and physiological changes in the brain were very limited. However, the advent of advanced brain imaging in the 1990s heralded a new wave of neurobiological research. This spawned novel integrations of neurobiology and psychotherapy, pioneered by Dan Siegel (2000, 2012) and Allan Schore (2003, 2012), leading to an innovative focus on "interpersonal neurobiology (IPNB)" or relational neuroscience (Badenoch, 2016). This focus has exploded in the last decade, resulting in more than 45 texts in the Norton series on interpersonal neurobiology alone and many articles, including a special issue of *International Journal of Group Psychotherapy* published in 2010 devoted to the **integration of neurobiology and group and couples psychotherapy** (Gantt & Cox, 2010), and the book, *The Interpersonal Neurobiology of Group Psychotherapy and Group Process* (Gantt & Badenoch, 2013).

With respect to group psychotherapy, the primary thesis based on these works is that this modality, with its emphasis on here-and-now interpersonal experience that can activate new neural firing patterns, provides a uniquely rich environment for neuropsychological healing. For many patients, group psychotherapy may be the most powerful setting in which to alter brain circuitry.

As Denninger (2010) asserts:

> just as we are hard-wired for attachment, we are hard-wired for groups; these two forces together ultimately form one of the most potent sources of change in the central nervous system", (p. 597) ... Not only is group psychotherapy a brain treatment and, more specifically, a social brain treatment, it is also, arguably, the most targeted type of treatment available for social brain dysfunction.
>
> (p. 599)

Recommended Resources

Badenoch, B. (2016, May). A symphony of gifts from relational neuroscience. How understanding our embodied brains can support lives of hope & resilience. The Neuroscience Training Summit. Retrieved from www.soundstrue.com/store/neu roscience-summit

Denninger, J.W. (2010). Commentary on the neurobiology of group psychotherapy: Group and the social brain: Speeding toward a neurobiological understanding of group psychotherapy. *International Journal of Group Psychotherapy, 60(4)*, 595–604. doi: 10.1521/ijgp.2010.60.4.595

Gantt, S.P., & Badenoch, B. (Eds.) (2013). *The interpersonal neurobiology of group psychotherapy and group process*. London, UK: Karnac Books.

Gantt, S.P., & Cox, P. (Eds.) (2010). Neurobiology and building interpersonal systems: Groups, couples, and beyond [Special issue]. *International Journal of Group Psychotherapy, (60)4*.

Norton Series on Interpersonal Neurobiology: http://books.wwnorton.com/books/book-template.aspx?ser=Norton+Series+on+Interpersonal+Neurobiology

Schore, A. N. (2003). *Affect regulation and repair of the self*. New York: Norton.

Schore, A. N. (2012). *The science or the art of psychotherapy*. New York, NY: Norton.

Siegel, D. J. (2000). *The developing mind*. New York: Guilford.

Siegel, D.J. (2012). *The developing mind [2nd ed.]: How relationships and the brain interact to shape who we are*. New York, NY: Guilford Press.

Neuroscientific advances have led us to more fully consider the ongoing plasticity of our brains and the ways that interpersonal experiences may impact and change our brains, in developing, strengthening or weakening neural pathways and networks and increasing neural integration, particularly under certain social conditions. Drawing from the work of Siegel (2000, 2012), Schore (2003, 2012), and Cozolino (2010, 2014), **specific psychotherapeutic conditions have been identified that appear to promote neural development and integration, namely:**

- The establishment of safe, trusting and attuned interpersonal relationships,
- In a climate of moderate emotional arousal,
- With the provision of emotional support for experiential awareness of significant early personal memories,
- And with the acquisition of new experiences that disconfirm earlier implicit memories, beliefs and assumptions.

With regard to the group psychotherapy context, Badenoch and Cox (2010) conclude:

> One of the strengths of group therapy is the high likelihood that the neural networks holding early implicit experience will be triggered as other members bring their struggles into the group. At the same time, group can become an empathy-rich environment for holding the pain and fear that emerges. In our clinical experience, as both therapist and group members understand more about brain development, they become more capable of seeing other members (and themselves) with understanding and compassion. Such attunement helps to repair the circuits of regulation not only for the receiver of care but for the giver of care as well.
>
> (p. 468)

Flores (2010) draws a similar conclusion:

> ... the field of "interpersonal neurobiology" helps validate the venerable notion that talking with someone will alter neural pathways and synaptic strength – especially if the encounter is meaningful and occurs within the context of emotional arousal, attunement, and a strong emotional bond. All forms of group psychotherapy, from psychodynamic, interpersonal, and systems-centered theory (SCT) to cognitive behavioral therapy (CBT), are successful to the degree to which they accomplish this task and enhance growth in relevant neuron-circuitry.
>
> (Flores, 2010, p. 565)

Exercise:

Think of groups you have led or been part of, in what way did the group provide the conditions for neural development as listed above? Did some groups provide more of this than others?

Recommended Resources

Badenoch, B., & Cox, P. (2010). Integrating interpersonal neurobiology with group psychotherapy. *International Journal of Group Psychotherapy*, 60(4), 462–481. doi: 10.1521/ijgp.2010.60.4.462

Cozolino, L. (2010). *The neuroscience of psychotherapy: Healing the social brain* (2nd ed.). New York, NY: Norton.

Cozolino, L. (2014). *The neuroscience of human relationships: Attachment and the developing social brain.* [Kindle version]. New York, NY: Norton.

Denninger, J.W. (2010). Commentary on the neurobiology of group psychotherapy: Group and the social brain: Speeding toward a neurobiological understanding of group psychotherapy. *International Journal of Group Psychotherapy*, 60(4), 595–604. doi: 10.1521/ijgp.2010.60.4.595

Flores, P.J. (2010). Group psychotherapy and neuro-plasticity: An attachment theory perspective. *International Journal of Group Psychotherapy*, 60(4), 546–570. doi: 10.1521/ijgp.2010.60.4.546

Gantt, S.P., & Badenoch, B. (Eds.) (2013). *The interpersonal neurobiology of group psychotherapy and group process.* London, UK: Karnac Books.

Gantt, S.P., & Cox, P. (Eds.) (2010). Introduction to the special issue: Neurobiology and building interpersonal systems: Groups, couples, and beyond. *International Journal of Group Psychotherapy*, (60)4, 455–461. doi: 10.1521/ijgp.2010.60.4.455

Siegel, D.J. (2010). Commentary on "Integrating interpersonal neurobiology with group psychotherapy": Reflections on mind, brain, and relationships in group psychotherapy. *International Journal of Group Psychotherapy*, 60(4), 483–485. doi: 10.1521/ijgp.2010.60.4.483

Brain Models

There are many conceptual models for understanding brain functioning. Three models are highlighted here that are useful in conceptualizing the relationship between brain functioning and the group psychotherapy context:

- Triune brain (MacLean, 1990),
- Social brain (Cozolino, 2010; Siegel, 2012),
- Right and left brains (McGilchrist, 2009; Siegel, 2012).

The Triune Brain

The long-standing model of the triune brain provides a simple framework for understanding some of the complex functioning of our brains (Bentzen, 2015; MacLean, 1990; Neuropsychotherapy, 2016). In this model, there are three components:

- The brain stem processes and regulates the basic physiological state of the body, such as breathing, heart rate, blood pressure and is involved in quick responses about safety or danger.
- Immediately adjacent is the limbic brain, often called the emotional brain, where significant emotional processing happens in the hippocampus (compiles explicit memories starting around the age of 18–24 months), thalamus, hypothalamus, amygdala (implicit memory and quick judgment of safety or danger), and other structures.
- The cerebral cortex is the site of what is called executive action and is especially important in emotional regulation of limbic activation, attachment, integrating memories and modulating fear as well as in attuned communication and empathy (Siegel, 2012).

Recommended Resources

Bentzen, M. (2015). *The neuroaffective picture book*. Rothersthorpe, UK: Paragon Publishing.

MacLean, P.D. (1990). *The triune brain in evolution: Role in paleocerebral functions*. New York, NT: Springer Science & Business Media.

Neuropsychotherapy. (2016, August 22). The triune brain in 60 seconds [Video file]. Retrieved from www.youtube.com/watch?v=7uVSGbnEHOg

---

The Social Brain

Anthropologist Robin Dunbar (1998) proposed the **social brain hypothesis**, namely that the size of the human brain evolved to manage the complexities of interacting with larger social groups. Increasingly, relational neuroscience and interpersonal neurobiology have emphasized the human brain as a social brain.

This focus on the social brain stresses that our interactions with others are continually shaping our brains and that our brains are always adapting to our social groups and in interactions with others. Siegel (2012) emphasizes that interpersonal integration facilitates greater integration of neural patterns in the brain. While it is well known from developmental theory that the containing function of the mother-infant relationship helps brain development, an appreciation of the neuroplasticity of the brain leads us to theorize that **throughout our lifespan secure and attuned interpersonal experiences can modify and develop brain circuitry in our social brains**, most especially in our limbic region, middle prefrontal cortex and anterior cingulate.

As Cozolino (2010) posits:

> Affect regulation, especially the modulation and inhibition of anxiety and fear, allows for continued cortical processing in the face of strong emotions, allowing for ongoing cognitive flexibility, learning, and neural integration. In this process the therapist plays essentially the same role as a parent, providing and modeling the regulatory functions of the social brain. **As affect is repeatedly brought into the therapeutic relationship and successfully managed, the client gradually internalizes these skills by sculpting the neural structures necessary for autoregulation.**
>
> (p. 21)

Importantly, as group therapists we know that most of the major theories of group psychotherapy emphasize the development of precisely the empathic and authentic connections that directly affect both brain functioning and psychological well being. Group therapy can help both the brain and mind of the dysregulated individual through processes of containment and attunement, and the under-activated and disengaged individual through such means as linking and encouragement (Coan, 2014; Cozolino, 2014).

Recommended Resources

Coan, J. (2014, January 25). Why we hold hands [Video file]. Retrieved from www. youtube.com/watch?v=1UMHUPPQ96c

Cozolino, L. (2010). *The neuroscience of psychotherapy: Healing the social brain* (2nd ed.). New York, NY: Norton.

Dunbar, R.I. (1998). The social brain hypothesis. *Evolutionary Anthropology: Issues, News, and Reviews*, 6(5), 178–190.

Siegel, D.J. (2012). *The developing mind, second edition: How relationships and the brain interact to shape who we are*. New York, NY: Guilford Press.

Right and Left Brain Function

Considerable neuroscience research demonstrates that the two brain hemispheres function differently, both perceiving and creating different worlds (McGilchrist, 2009). While the complexity of the differences is beyond the scope of this manual, Siegel (2009, 2012) describes some of the distinct differences that are relevant for our work as group therapists.

The right hemisphere focuses on sensory, emotional, and contextual processing, in assessing the emotions of others and attending to what is emerging in the present moment, including the sense of being in connection with each other. In contrast the left hemisphere attends more to what has already been experienced, to specific details and to problem solving by logically putting pieces together.

The right hemisphere more fully "sees the world for what it is", whereas the left hemisphere must reduce the world much more into mentally defined, often socially constructed chunks of information.

(Siegel, 2012, p. 237)

Neither way of attending is sufficient unto itself. When left hemisphere attending is disconnected from the right, we lose our sense of the context and our resonance and connectedness with others. We are less able to use the resources of our right-centric social brain. Instead, we begin to focus on the task of controlling and mastering a situation. When right hemisphere attending is not integrated with left brain function, we lose our ability to observe and reality-test our right brain sense. We need our left brain function to master problems in reality, put language to what we sense in our right brain, to communicate in words to others, and to generalize from our experience.

(Gantt & Badenoch, 2017)

Different kinds of groups may differentially influence the two hemispheres. While all groups in some ways will impact both right and left-centric brain function, below are some examples of group models and their potential hemispheric focus.

- Attachment-focused groups orient to greater right-centric social brain development.
- Psychodynamic groups aim to influence greater integration between the two hemispheres.
- Systems-centered therapy orients first to modifying left-centric restraining forces to reality-testing (explaining) to enable more right-centric apprehensive exploration (exploring), and ultimately to better integration between right- and left-centric functioning.
- Cognitive behavioral therapy groups generally focus more on improving left-centric functioning.
- Interpersonal groups focus on developing the social brain, more right-centric function.
- Mindfulness and compassion-based group therapy orient more to left-centric function in strengthening observational capacity.

Recommended Resources

Gantt, S.P., & Badenoch, B. (2017). Systems-centered group psychotherapy: Developing a group mind that supports right brain function and right-left-right hemispheric integration. In R. Tweedy (Ed.), *The divided therapist: Hemispheric difference and contemporary psychotherapy*. London, UK: Karnac Books.

McGilchrist, I. (2009). *The master and his emissary: The divided brain and the making of the western world*. New Haven, CT & London, UK: Yale University Press.

Siegel, D.J. (2009). On Integrating the Two Hemispheres of Our Brains. Retrieved from www.youtube.com/watch?v=xPjhfUVgvOQ

Siegel, D.J. (2012). *The developing mind (2nd ed.): How relationships and the brain interact to shape who we are*. New York, NY: Guilford Press.

Polyvagal Theory

While not without some critics who believe the research remains inconclusive, polyvagal theory greatly enriches our understanding of how group therapy influences autonomic nervous system regulation. Porges' (2011, 2014) research on the evolution of our autonomic nervous system has enabled us to move beyond our long held understanding that the autonomic nervous system contains only two branches, the sympathetic and parasympathetic nervous systems, the former system serving as the accelerator and the parasympathetic as the brake to conserve resources when in defense. Importantly Porges adds a third branch to create a model where the three branches of our autonomic nervous system are constantly adjusting to protect us if needed or enable us to open if the context is right. Porges refers to the process of this third branch as **social engagement** where we first look to others to see if they are present to us or absent, friend or foe so to speak. Porges calls this process of assessing "**neuroception**," in that it is largely not in our consciousness but, as we look and listen, we pick up cues in others' faces and tone about whether we are safe or not, whether to protect or open. When our neuroception registers safety, we relax, our heart rate slows, our voices become more melodic, the striated muscles of our face become more mobile, the muscles in our ears relax, and others whom we are relating to respond in turn. This process of neuroception is largely right-centric as our ventral vagal nerve lateralizes right. In this state of social engagement, we make resonant connections to others and others to us, in effect, co-regulation.

If instead, our neuroception registers danger, (e.g., if we say something in a group and everyone looks away and no one responds) our sympathetic system mobilizes for flight or fight, our face tightens, our voice changes, and we become less able to hear others as we are listening only for sounds of danger. And our communications, verbal and nonverbal, will induce others into sympathetic activation. If the threat escalates further, our dorsal vagal parasympathetic system activates and we collapse or dissociate, both forms of resource conservation (Badenoch, 2016).

These newer perspectives provide important guidance for group leaders in recognizing the autonomic nervous system conditions in groups that promote open exploration versus those that activate the physiology of old survivor roles. It also raises an important issue for group leaders of how to influence the group communication patterns in the direction of social engagement. For example, Ormont's bridging technique around similarities is likely to increase social engagement and lower flight/fight responses. Similarly, systems-centered's functional subgrouping starts by requiring that the first person to talk is reflected by the next person speaking before adding new information resulting in social engagement and developing the capacity for greater resonance and attunement. Also important are the implications for training group leaders, as when a leader works from greater social engagement (ventral vagal activation), the leader will have a very different impact on the group's social engagement than when distracted, preoccupied, or withdrawn.

Recommended Resources

Badenoch, B. (2016, May). A symphony of gifts from relational neuroscience. How understanding our embodied brains can support lives of hope & resilience. The Neuroscience Training Summit. Retrieved from www.soundstrue.com/store/neu roscience-summit

Flores, P. J., & Porges, S. W. (2017). Group psychotherapy as a neural exercise: Bridging polyvagal theory and attachment theory. *International Journal of Group Psychotherapy, 67*(2), 202–222.

Porges, S.W. (2011). *The polyvagal theory: Neurophysiological foundations of emotions, attachment, communication, and self-regulation.* New York, NY: Norton.

Porges, S. (2014). Human nature and early experience. Retrieved from www.youtube.com/watch?v=SRTkkYjQ_HU&t=639s

Resonance Circuitry, Mirror Neurons and Brain Coupling

Mirror neurons were identified in the 1990's when researchers discovered that when a monkey saw a researcher eating a peanut a part of its brain fired as if the monkey was also eating a peanut. Importantly, animal research with mirror neurons demonstrates that activation of mirror neurons is in response to observing a goal-oriented act (Di Pellegrino, Fadiga, Fogassi, Gallese, & Rizzolatti, 1992). In 2010, mirror neurons were also observed in human brains. Mirror neuron research has led to greater understanding and interest in resonance circuitry.

Iacoboni (2008) proposes that mirror neurons enable us to create a map of another person's state of mind. Mirror neurons also influence activation of our own internal subcortical arousal and emotional states when we see goal directed actions in another person. This is likely part of what enables us to have resonance with others. Many observations link the notions of imitation, the development of mirror neurons, and the capacity for empathy and emotional resonance.

- Imitation in early life appears essential to the development of mirror neurons (Iacoboni, 2008).
- Mirror neurons code facial movements (Ferrari, Gallese, Rizzolatti, & Fogassi, 2003) suggesting that mirror neurons facilitate emotional understandings between people.
- Imitating begins in infants and leads to increased liking and empathy for others. (Chartrand & Bargh, 1999).
- Group psychotherapy is a rich environment for being able to learn by imitating in the context of support (Gantt & Agazarian, 2013).

Resonance circuitry refers to not only the mirror neurons in our brains that fire similarly to the other's brain when we observe other's goal-directed actions, but to the larger circuitry in our brains involved with resonance with others including the insula, limbic, brainstem, and prefrontal cortex. Mirror neuron firing patterns stimulate and shape our subcortical feeling so that we feel similarly to the other person. These feelings then enable us to map in our middle prefrontal cortex the other's experiences and thus feel compassion, resonance, and empathy.

Brain coupling (Hasson, 2016; Hasson, Ghazanfar, Galantucci, Garrod, & Keysers, 2012) refers to the phenomenon in interpersonal communication when the brain of a listener begins to fire in synchrony with the brain of a speaker. Importantly, this happens when the listener is understanding the speaker. When there is little understanding, the brains do not fire in alignment. This is especially useful in thinking through the challenges in all psychotherapy groups of managing differences in interpersonal relations since reactions to differences can readily activate our sympathetic nervous system and lead to fight-flight behavior with little opportunity to explore the differences and understand each other.

Recommended Resources

Chartrand, T.L., & Bargh, J. A. (1999). The chameleon effect: The perception-behavior link and social interaction. *Journal of Personality and Social Psychology, 76*, 893–910.

di Pellegrino, G., Fadiga, L., Fogassi, L., Gallese, V., & Rizzolatti, G. (1992). Understanding motor events: A neurophysiological study. *Experimental Brain Research, 91*, 176–180.

Ferrari, P.F., Gallese, V., Rizzolatti, G., & Fogassi, L. (2003). Mirror neurons responding to the observation of ingestive and communicative mouth actions in the monkey ventral premotor cortex. *European Journal of Neuroscience, 17*, 1703–1714.

Gantt, S.P., & Agazarian, Y.M. (2013). Developing the group mind through functional subgrouping: Linking systems-centered training (SCT) and interpersonal neurobiology. In S.P. Gantt, & B. Badenoch (Eds.), *The interpersonal neurobiology of group psychotherapy and group process* (pp. 73–102). London, UK: Karnac Books.

Hasson, U. (2016, June 3). This is your brain on communication: Uri Hasson [Video file]. Retrieved from www.youtube.com/watch?v=FDhlOovaGrI

Hasson, U., Ghazanfar, A. A., Galantucci, B., Garrod, S., Keysers, C. (2012). Brain-to-Brain coupling: A mechanism for creating and sharing a social world. *Trends in Cognitive Sciences, 16(2)*: 114–121.

Iacoboni, M. (2008). *Mirroring people: The new science of how we connect with others.* New York, NY: Farrar, Straus & Giroux.

Iacoboni, M. (2013, August 1). "Are we wired for empathy?" [Video file]. Retrieved from www.youtube.com/watch?v=pXTZLTJbU8g

---

Instinctive Emotional Patterns

In his research with animals, Panksepp (Panksepp & Biven, 2012) has identified seven primary emotional systems inherent in all mammals identifiable with specific subcortical regions:

- SEEKING/desire system. Activates searching for resources and sense of purpose.
- CARE/maternal nurturance system. Related to protection and care of offspring.
- GRIEF/separation distress. Activated by loss of nurturance; often functions to restore social-attachment bonding.
- FEAR/anxiety. System goal is protection from pain and destruction.
- RAGE/anger system. Activates aggressive energy and is aroused when freedom of action, often related to seeking, is thwarted. Intense psychological energy from this system. Situated close to and interacts with FEAR system.

- PLAY/social engagement system. Enables learning social rules of interaction. Assertive energy to go back and forth with others, usually with positive feelings, sometimes joy.
- LUST/sexual system. Activates search for sexual rewards.

It is the interaction of these systems within the individual group member, between group members, and between members and the group leader that may help regulate our emotional functioning and well-being. For example, when a group member experiences grief over separation, others' responses of care or even joining with curiosity lower the pain of grief and offer experiencing of grief linked with support. In effect, the CARE system activation in response to the GRIEF system provides needed relief. In contrast, disruptive encounters in the group can activate the FEAR and RAGE systems, manifested in a group's flight-fight pattern. Such emotional action patterns are present as regulating and dysregulating patterns in the group and its members. In a well-functioning group, the group itself may function to provide CARE, sometimes called the maternal function in the group. **Importantly, in all groups, as soon as SEEKING is evidenced, manifested by curiosity and exploration, the activation of FEAR and RAGE systems may typically be lowered.**

Recommended Resources

Panksepp, J., & Biven, L. (2012). *The archaeology of mind: Neuroevolutionary origins of human emotions*. New York, NY: Norton.
Panksepp, J. (2014, January 13). The science of emotions. [Video file]. Retrieved from www.youtube.com/watch?v=65e2qScV_K8

Implicit Memory and Implicit and Top-Down Emotional Regulation

There are two different kinds of memory: implicit and explicit. **Explicit memory**, which first begins around 12–18 months, refers to specific conscious experiences that we can recall that link to a time frame. Earlier than this, we have only **implicit memories**, which are coded as unverbalized impulses, emotions, sensations, perceptions, and images (Badenoch, 2008). Implicit memories are the neural substrate through which we experience and relate to the world and are indirectly manifested through

- our assumptions about, attitudes towards and perceptions of the world,
- our beliefs about ourselves and our relationships,
- and our sense of our trust in the world.

In group therapy, implicit memories and experiences are apparent in our group members' behavior, thus **rendering the therapy group as a unique context for identifying implicit memories**. For example, a group member who describes the leader as being cold and unavailable while other group members experience the group leader as very present may be enacting a deep basic mistrust derived from implicit experience (Gantt & Agazarian, 2013).

Schore's (2010) work further extends our understanding of implicit memory in its impact on our emotional or arousal regulation processes which originate in right brain to right brain communication patterns, initially between mothering figure and infant. The co-regulatory nonverbal interactions first between infant and mother and later between self and others are implicitly encoded in our right brains and form the basis of our internal regulation within ourselves and with others; that is, **the implicit memories of our early co-regulating processes are reflected in the nature of our self-regulating and co-regulating processes in later life.**

As Schore (2010) describes it, in psychotherapy there is a kind of implicit right-brain experiential learning where

> a dysregulating affective experience ... is communicated to an empathic other [the caregiver originally] ... with an opportunity for interactive affect regulation, a process which is the core of [secure] attachment.

(p. 194)

Importantly, we now increasingly believe that **co-regulation of affect occurs throughout lifetime, including in the therapeutic interaction between patient and therapist in their right brain to right brain communications, enhancing emotional regulatory capacities that are further stored in implicit memory.** Schore stresses that the heart of change in psychotherapy is in the interpersonal regulation of "affective-autonomic arousal that allows for repair and re-organization" (Schore, 2010, p. 194) of right brain implicit functioning. Badenoch (2011) builds on this in her work on training therapists in emotional presence and the importance of interpersonal emotional regulation so that the therapist learns to open to the range of implicit emotional experience that patients communicate in their session.

A second kind of emotional regulation repair focuses on improving executive function by means of the greater activation of the middle prefrontal cortex regulating our limbic activation. Siegel's (2013) "hand" model of the brain is useful in understanding this type of emotional regulation. Siegel uses our hand as a brain model where when we fold our fingers over our thumb, the fingers (representing our prefrontal cortex) calm our limbic system (represented by our thumb). So when we are angry and have the impulse to hit someone, the prefrontal cortex enables us to consciously pause and settle the activation in our limbic system. When our prefrontal cortex is not active, we act out more easily. Mindfulness training strengthens this function of our middle prefrontal cortex to enable us to better control strong emotion.

This kind of top-down regulation is commonly taught in cognitive behavioral groups where members are taught to modify maladaptive thought patterns that create fear and anxiety and to learn soothing thoughts to calm themselves when anxious, using the middle prefrontal cortex to settle the activation in the limbic system. In a similar yet different fashion, mindfulness group therapy trains the middle prefrontal cortex to observe the subcortical activations, again providing vertical regulation where the cortex is regulating downward in influencing the limbic system.

Recommended Resources

Badenoch, B. (2008). *Being a brain-wise therapist: A practical guide to interpersonal neurobiology.* New York, NY: Norton.

Badenoch, B. (2011). The Integrated and Mindful Therapist. Retrieved from: www.youtube.com/watch?v=eOPr8MPzdvA&index=1&list=PLdVCA4bAqgHsggm7zn3nSSRzw7B39-q_G

Leszcz, M. (2017). How understanding attachment enhances group therapist effectiveness. *International Journal of Group Psychotherapy*, 67(2), 280–287.

Schore, A.N. (2010). The right brain implicit self: A central mechanism of the psychotherapy change process. In J. Petrucelli (Ed.), *Knowing, not-knowing and sort-of-knowing: Psychoanalysis and the experience of uncertainty* (pp. 177–202). London, UK: Karnac Books.

Siegel, D. (2013, April 16). Mindfulness. Brain hand model. [Video file]. Retrieved from www.youtube.com/watch?v=vESKrzvgA40

Group therapy offers potential for both kinds (i.e., right brain to right brain co-regulation and top down prefrontal cortex containment of the limbic system) of repair to our emotional processing systems. For example, often a group member who is dysregulated will become more regulated as they hear others talk about how they regulate themselves, potentially understood as one part of the group providing middle prefrontal cortex regulation of the limbic system arousal in the group, or what many group leaders have conceptualized psychologically as containment. The other form of regulation – group co-regulation – occurs as group members join each other in emotional resonance and attunement providing the emotional responsiveness to each other that is settling (in Panksepp's model, CARE system responding to FEAR system) and over time providing new implicit emotional patterning, closer to more secure attachments, and similar to Schore's (2010) conceptualization of right brain to right brain regulation. Many group approaches can be viewed in terms of the interactions of these right brain systems. For example, systems-centered training teaches functional subgrouping where members learn to reflect the heart of each other's communication in attunement and resonance, thus providing strong right-centric regulation. In interpersonal and psychodynamic groups, members' responses to each other often function as co-regulation.

Memory Reconsolidation

Ecker (Ecker, Ticic, & Hulley, 2012) has integrated the research on memory reconsolidation and, importantly, identified how implicit memories can be modified. He utilized this work to develop the psychotherapy process he calls "Coherence Psychotherapy" which focuses on memory reconsolidation. The thesis of this work is that symptoms represent an adaptation related to our implicit memories. Change or memory reconsolidation occurs when we identify an implicit memory entailing some implicit interpersonal schema and beliefs about self and the world, and re-experience the implicit memory within the context of a secure relationship and emotional connection that simultaneously provide what Ecker calls a "disconfirming reparative experience." Having a disconfirming experience within a few hours of re-experience of an early implicit memory enables "erasure" of the original memory and re-stabilization with new learning. It is this combination that "unlocks" the brain irrespective of therapeutic orientations and enables what Ecker calls "transformation learning" in which symptoms abate. In summary, early emotional learnings are implicit and they drive symptoms. The process of transformative change is the unlearning of old implicit memories and integrating new memories. This is highly relevant in understanding what group psychotherapy can offer, which can provide a secure emotional context and here-and-now experiences that disconfirm long held implicit emotional assumptions.

Recommended Resources

Ecker, B. (2014, April 10). Memory reconsolidation: Key to transformational change in psychotherapy [Video file]. Retrieved from www.youtube.com/watch?v=_V_rI2N6Fco

Ecker, B., Ticic, R., & Hulley, L. (2012). *Unlocking the emotional brain: Eliminating symptoms at their roots using memory consolidation.* New York, NY: Routledge.

Developing Mindfulness and the Group Mind

> Mindfulness … is about waking up from life on automatic, and being sensitive to novelty in our everyday experiences. Mindfulness awareness … involves more than just simply being aware: It involves being aware of aspects of the mind itself. Instead of being on automatic and mindless, mindfulness helps us awaken, and by reflecting on the mind, we are enabled to make choices and thus change becomes possible. How we focus attention helps directly shape the mind. When we develop a certain form of attention to our here-and-now experiences and to the nature of our mind itself, we create the special form of awareness, mindfulness.
>
> (Siegel, 2007, p. 6)

In many ways, mindfulness captures the work of all therapy (Campbell, 2008; Siegel, 2007, 2012), learning to focus our attention on ways that help shape our mind. This expands exponentially in group as our focus on here-and-now experience relates not only to ourselves but also to other group members and to the group itself. **Neuroscience enables us as group therapists to think through how to heighten the mindful function of our groups and strengthen the capacity of our groups to shape the minds of their members.** It is likely that all group therapies can be strengthened by an increased focus on mindful attention and function.

Siegel (2007) defines "mind" as a relational process that regulates the flow of energy and information "at the interface of neurophysiological processes and interpersonal relationships". Gantt and Agazarian (2010) expanded this view of mind to group therapy and proposed the idea of a "group mind" that regulates the flow of energy and information in the group system.

All groups develop norms which influence group patterns of emotional regulation that either enhance development or stabilize the group but at the expense of development. For example, a scapegoating pattern regulates emotion yet does so at the expense of both group development and emotional exploration within and between group members, instead leading to fixation as well as pain and frustration for members. A group's patterns of co-regulation function as an implicit group mind. **Recognizing the group processes that emotionally regulate the group and its flow of energy and information enables group leaders to influence group norms that promote neural regulation and integration in the service of development.**

Applying principles of neuroscience in working with groups enables group leaders to more deliberately enhance both the group mind and its interpersonal regulation patterns and neuroplasticity and neural integration in group members in the direction of development rather that reinforcing survival roles and group patterns. The group mind then provides the context for regulating the brains and minds of group members, parallel to how the primary caregiver-infant system regulates the infant. Conceptualizing the group mind enables a mindful understanding of explicit and implicit regulation patterns in the group system. Group leaders can then monitor these emotional relational patterns as information about the neurobiological arousal in the group and support the group developing explicit and implicit regulating patterns that function in the service of greater neural integration and increased plasticity. The developments in neuroscience reviewed here can enable group therapists to more explicitly develop a group mind that potentiates problem-solving, as well as experiences that regulate and develop the minds and brains of the group members.

Specific mindfulness techniques have been incorporated into many group therapies (see Chapter 1). Zindel Segal's work has been very influential starting in the 1980s with mindfulness-based cognitive therapy for depression to prevent relapse. Since that time, mindfulness and variants of it have been incorporated in many group therapies and used with a variety of populations, such as cancer patients, for stress reduction, PTSD, depression, and social anxiety.

Recommended Resources

Gantt, S.P., & Agazarian, Y.M. (2010). Developing the group mind through functional subgrouping: Linking systems-centered training (SCT) and interpersonal neurobiology. *International Journal of Group Psychotherapy, 60(4)*, 515–544. doi: 10.1521/ijgp.2010.60.4.515

Campbell, V. (2008). Brain science podcast: Meditation and the brain with Dan Siegel, MD [Transcript]. Retrieved from docartemis.com/brain%20science/44-brainscience-Siegel.pdf

Segal, Z.V., Williams, J.M.G., & Teasdale, J.D. (2001). Mindfulness-based cognitive therapy for depression: A new approach to preventing relapse. New York, NY: Guilford Press.

Siegel, D.J. (2007). *The mindful brain*. New York, NY: Norton.

Siegel, D. (2012, May 2). Mindfulness and neural integration [Video file]. Retrieved from www.youtube.com/watch?v=LiyaSr5aeho

---

Concluding Thoughts

Group psychotherapy with its breadth and depth of interpersonal processes may provide a rich resource for changing the function and structure of our brains toward greater neural integration, and specifically greater:

- right and left hemispheric integration,
- vertical integration from the body up, from the vagal nerve to the brain stem to the limbic and into the cortex,

- interpersonal integration making greater use of our social brain function and building the sense of "we",
- memory integration of implicit and explicit memories,
- secure attachment patterns reflective of emotional integration,
- capacity for emotional co-regulation with an increasingly wider range of emotional experiences and greater development and use of our social brains.

Understanding of contemporary neuroscience perspectives enables group leaders to deliberately enhance the impact of psychotherapeutic processes on neuroplasticity, neural integration, and emotional co-regulation and our attachment patterns.

> Maximizing neuroplasticity requires that we create an experiential group environment that provides a secure relational context, with neural and emotional regulation within and between brains, where moderate levels of emotion can be experienced with the right-brain resonance and responsiveness that enables modulation, development, and greater implicit integration. This facilitates the integration and reintegration of cognitive and implicit emotional elements of human experience that, in turn, increase access to the range of human experience and capacity for implicit and explicit regulation of one's experience with one's self and with others.
>
> (Gantt & Agazarian, 2013, pp. 81–82)

12 Finding the Leader in You

Francis J. Kaklauskas and Les R. Greene

Developing proficiency as a group leader requires desire, effort, practice, and patience. One must stay open to new ideas, have a willingness to make mistakes, to prognosticate realistic plans that may or may not come to fruition, be ready to respond to unanticipated events, to trust oneself, and also to seek guidance. Many feel that being a group leader is much more than a profession, but rather one's life work or an occupational calling. It is a lifelong journey of learning about oneself, learning about others, contributing to the creation of meaningful constructive relationships, and a way of contributing to the world one group at a time.

Training Recommendations

The path towards proficiency is likely unique for each person, but these journeys may share some common elements. **Anxiety** is typically a common experience for the neophyte group leader, but this and other unsettling emotional reactions can be worked with constructively through organizational support, training, additional experience, and importantly a positive supervisory relationship (Murphy, Leszcz, Collings, & Salvendy, 1996).

Barlow (2012) and Goicoechea and Kessler (2018) detail the two unique knowledge domains that need to be acquired to achieve group leadership competency.

- **Foundational knowledge** that includes a mastery of sociopsychological theory such as recognizing the complex relationships among personality, role, and group dynamics for each group member.
- **Functional competencies** that include capacities to formulate sophisticated hypothesis to guide meaningful and effective clinical interventions, ranging from efforts at establishing a positive therapeutic culture as a group forms to commenting about subtle and unspoken group processes as the group progresses.

In a unique series of studies that underscores the fundamental importance and impact of training, Kivlighan and colleagues (Kivlighan, Markin, Stahl, & Salahuddin, 2007; Kivlighan & Tibbits, 2012; Li, Kivlighan, & Gold, 2015) identify important differences between newer and seasoned group leaders both with respect to conceptualization of the group and in choices regarding intervention strategies. In general, the **findings suggest that trainees lack depth and complexity in their thinking about groups and have narrower ranges of interventions that are deemed therapeutic.** For example, novice therapists tend to view leader silence as hostile and, unlike experienced group leaders, not consider that silence can provide an opportunity to convey empathy and create space for reflection. Over time with clinical experience and training the conscious options of intervention strategies in any situation become broader (Zukor, 2017).

Over the years, several models for the development of group leadership skills have been proposed. In an early model, Zaslav (1988) describes a journey from

- **Group Shock** as the novice clinician experiences a buzzing array of stimulation and utilizes familiar but not so useful techniques (such as doing individual therapy in the group or focusing exclusively on content) through
- prolonged processes of reappraisal and then
- a gradual internalizing of group skills and knowledge (such as increased appreciation of here-and-now activation) and eventually reaching a point of
- integrating multiple templates and recognizing process phenomena in the **Polishing Skills** stage.

More recently, Brabender (2010) describes a prototypical developmental pathway where the group therapist trainee progresses over 5 stages.

1) Decisional-anticipatory stage where the idea of pursuing work in group psychotherapy is initially formed
2) Basic training stage where foundational knowledge and basic functional skills are acquired
3) Nice stage where the individual identifies self as a group psychotherapist and forges ties to other group therapists and group therapy organizations to develop further knowledge and skills
4) Proficiency stage where the individual has internalized a substantial body of knowledge and valid set of practices based on accumulated training, supervision, and clinical experience
5) Stage of achieving, and maintaining expertise reflecting very high levels of group experience and the acquisition of very sophisticated conceptual and technical skills.

With regard to **methods of training**, Yalom and Leszcz (2005), while hesitating to endorse a universal blueprint for training group leaders, do endorse several time-honored practices:

- **observations** of experienced group leaders at work
- close clinical **supervision** at the beginning of one's experience leading groups
- **personal experience** as a group member
- **personal psychotherapeutic work**.

Similarly, Stockton, Morran, and Chang (2013) summarize the best practice approach for group leadership training as emphasizing:

- **Didactic learning** of theoretical and practical material
- **Observing** groups and **practicing** skills before leading groups
- **Personal development** including experience as a group member
- Practice leading or co-leading under close **supervision**.

Through observing an experienced group leader, theory and research come alive in actual practice. The opportunity to discuss the observed group with the leader provides many learning experiences including:

- Understanding **choice points and clinical decision making processes**
- Learning to see both **content and process** and to develop an understanding of their interrelationship
- Understanding the application of didactic or theoretical material to actual group experiences.

In the past, many training facilities used two-way mirrors for group observation for trainees. In contemporary settings the opportunity for observation is provided more often through co-leading a group with a more experienced clinician as part of an internship, training program, or other professional development opportunity (cf. Goicoechea & Kessler, 2018). This experience provides the direct opportunity for newer leaders to observe and participate without having to hold all of the clinical responsibility. After the group, the co-leaders discuss the group and this form of impromptu supervision is a great chance for the newer leader to ask questions, discuss interventions and to get support around such typical reactions as anxiety, confusion, and countertransference experiences. In addition to this post-group review and analysis, regular supervision on groups provides opportunities for increased depth into case conceptualization, treatment planning, and potential interventions.

Joining a group as a member provides a wonderful opportunity to observe another clinician navigate the various aspects of group life, including keeping the group on task, managing group boundaries and reinforcing a therapeutic culture and norms, and handling disruptions to the therapeutic frame and ruptures in here-and-now relationships. Additionally, membership in a group, whether this be a formal psychotherapy group or a process group, provides unique insight and experientially-based learning about the challenges, dilemmas, and anxieties of group life, on one hand, and hopes, gratifications and opportunities for growth and change, on the other.

There are a number of models available that utilize the unique experiences of small process group membership to enhance deep learning about self-in-relationship, learning that is directly applicable not only in developing group leadership skills, but more generally in developing skills as a therapist and clinician (Menter, 2018; Stone, 2010). For example, Scharff and Scharff (2017) offer an innovative model on the use of the small process group to enhance learning and understanding about such complex clinical concepts as countertransference and projective identification. In their view, the process group

> becomes an expanded setting in which concepts can be taken in, reacted to, rejected, accepted, mulled over, modified and become part of the student's therapeutic instrument….a potential space for intense experience, exploration of symbolic meaning, creative thinking and reflection.
>
> (p. 1621)

In the same vein, the more familiar Balint group model (McKensey & Sullivan, 2016) provides opportunities for deeper learning about self in relation to difficult or disturbing clinical situations.

Finally there are a variety of process groups all designed to enhance a deeper understanding of self-in-relation-to-others. Popularized in the 1960's under a variety of names such as Tavistock group relations training, encounter groups, t-groups, growth groups, and sensitivity training groups (cf. Lieberman, Miles & Yalom, 1973), this invaluable learning afforded by these kinds of groups is championed currently by the process groups run by the American Group Psychotherapy Association.

Recommended Resources

Barlow, S. H. (2012). An application of the competency model to group-specialty practice. *Professional Psychology: Research and Practice, 43,* 442–451.

Brabender, V. (2010). The developmental path to expertise in group psychotherapy. *Journal of Contemporary Psychotherapy, 40,* 163–173.

Goicoechea, J. & Kessler, L. E. (2018). Competency-based training in interpersonal, process-oriented group therapy: An innovative university partnership. *Training and Education in Professional Psychology, 12,* 46–53.

Kivlighan, Jr., D. M., & Tibbits, B. M. (2012). Silence is mean and other misconceptions of group counseling trainees: Identifying errors of commission and omission in trainees' knowledge structures. *Group Dynamics: Theory, Research, and Practice, 16*(1), 14–34.

Kivlighan, D. M. Jr., Markin, R. D., Stahl, J. V., & Salahuddin, N. M. (2007). Changes in the ways that group trainees structure their knowledge of group members with training. *Group Dynamics: Theory, Research, and Practice, 11,* 176–186.

Li, X.; Kivlighan, D. M. Jr. & Gold, P.B. (2015). Errors of commission and omission in novice group counseling trainees' knowledge structures of group counseling situations. *Journal of Counseling Psychology, 62,* 159–172.

Lieberman, M.A., Yalom, I.D. & Miles, M.B. (1973). *Encounter groups: First facts.* New York: Basic Books

McKensey, A. & Sullivan, L. (2016). Balint groups – Helping trainee psychiatrists make even better use of themselves. *Australasian Psychiatry, 24,* 84–87.

Menter, P. (2018). Training residents in empathic attunement and emotional process: Four group models. Presented at AGPAConnect 2018. Available at http://member.agpa.org/imis/agpa/store

Murphy, L., Leszcz, M., Collings, A. K., & Salvendy, J. (1996). Some observations on the subjective experience of neophyte group therapy trainees. *International Journal of Group Psychotherapy, 46*(4), 543–552.

Stockton, R., Morran, D. K., Chang, S. H. (2013). An overview of current research and best practices for training beginning group leaders. In J. L. DeLucia-Waack, D. A. Gerrity, C. R. Kalodner, M. T. Riva (Eds.), *Handbook of group counseling and psychotherapy* (2nd ed., pp. 133–145).Thousand Oaks, CA: Sage.

Scharff, J. S., & Scharff, D. E. (2017). Group affective learning in training for psychotherapy and psychoanalysis. *The International Journal of Psychoanalysis, 98*(6), 1619–1639.

Stone, W. (Ed.) (2010). Training in group psychotherapy (Special Issue). *Group, 34(4).*

Yalom, I.D. & Leszcz, M. (2005). *The theory and practice of group psychotherapy.* New York: Basic Books.

Zaslav, M. R. (1988). A model of group therapist development. *International Journal of Group Psychotherapy, 38,* 511–519

Zukor T. (2017). Trainee development in group psychotherapy. In M. D. Ribeiro, J. Gross, & M. M. Turner (Eds.). *The college counselor's guide to group psychotherapy* (pp. 101–113). New York City: Routledge.

Self-Care

Group therapy is a very powerful medium, and those who lead groups volunteer to board a rollercoaster of emotions week after week, that can include often painful affects such as shame (Weber & Gans, 2003) and anxiety (Billow, 2001). As leaders, we will be exposed to stories of tragedy and trauma, while attempting to maintain empathic attunement and managing the diverse needs of all the members. **Therapists owe it to themselves and their patients to make self-care part of the profession** (Pope & Vasquez, 2016b) Despite the often endless pull for more client contact, training, and study in this profession, it is easier to try to prevent burnout than recover once you are depleted. Your career can be envisioned more as a marathon then a sprint and proper pacing is essential.

Many clinicians will experience the symptoms of **burnout, secondary trauma reactions, and compassion fatigue** throughout their careers. Common indicators include (Barnett, 2014; Harrison & Westwood, 2009; Killian, 2008, Smith, 2007):

- Loss of pleasure and enjoyment in work and life
- Decreased self-care
- Intrusive thoughts about your work or clients (not the same as deliberate and focused reflection)
- Affective symptoms including increased reactivity or persistent negative emotional states
- Somatic symptoms of agitation, sleep difficulties, and compromised health and recovery functions.

The classic Benjmin Franklin adage that an ounce of prevention is worth a pound of cure may be true in this situation. Underestimating the impact of this work on oneself will lead to poor work performance and compromises in other areas of one's life. Beck (2012) suggests group leaders engage in such good-for-you practices as:

- Balancing work and play
- Connecting with others (friends, family, and peers)
- Caring for our bodies and our physical health
- And taking personal time to rejuvenate, reflect, and refill our tanks.

Norcross and Guy (2007) provide an even more comprehensive checklist of items that assess the degree to which we routinely take care of our selves, our bodies and our therapeutic roles. Examples of their checklist items are shown below in the following headings:

- **valuing the person of the psychotherapist** (e.g., Assess your deep motives for becoming a psychotherapist beyond the altruism of "to help people." How are these motives facilitating or hindering your effective self-care?)

- **refocusing on the rewards** (e.g., Variety and intellectual stimulation are indispensable. What can you do to increase their impact on your schedule and professional duties?)
- **recognizing the hazards** (e.g., Reflect on the number of clients that you've said good-bye to over the years. What has been the cumulative impact of these terminations?)
- **minding the body** (e.g., Stretch your muscles and reconnect to your body as antidotes to the sedentary nature of psychotherapy.)
- **nurturing relationships** (e.g., Identify the three most nurturing people in your life. What can you do to increase the amount of support you receive from them?)
- **setting boundaries** (e.g., Begin by understanding concretely your roles, responsibilities, and limitations as a psychotherapist; only then can you communicate and establish these boundaries with patients.)
- **restructuring cognitions** (e.g., Think through the transferential feelings directed to you; to whom are they aimed and to whom do they belong?)
- **sustaining healthy escapes** (e.g., Follow Freud's example: every year take several weeks away from the office, and stay largely out of contact.)
- **creating a flourishing environment** (e.g., Increase sensory awareness: using vision, hearing, touch, and olfaction counterbalances the cognitive and affective work of psychotherapy.)
- **undergoing personal therapy** (e.g., Heed the evidence: personal therapy is an emotionally vital and professionally nourishing experience central to self-care. And pursue other personal development activities that interest you, such as the creative arts, mindfulness seminars, dream work, or self-help groups.
- **cultivating spirituality and mission** (e.g., Create a hope-protecting philosophy of life that will help inoculate you from the despair that can come with the work at times.)
- **fostering creativity and growth** (e.g., Imagine periodically your future possible selves as a psychotherapist and then set sail in that direction.)

Exercise:

What are your self-care practices? How effective are they for you?

Recommended Resources

Barnett, J. (2014, December). Distress, burnout, self-care, and the promotion of wellness for psychotherapists and trainees: Issues, implications, and recommendations. [Web article]. Retrieved from: http://www.societyforpsychotherapy.org/distress-therapist-burnout-self-care-promotion-wellness-psychotherapists-trainees-issues-implications-recommendations

Beck, R. (2012). Care for the caregivers, In J. L. Kleinberg (Ed.), *The Wiley-Blackwell Handbook of Group Psychotherapy* [pp. 571–585]. West Sussex, UK: John Wiley.

Billow, R.M. (2001). The therapist's anxiety and resistance to group therapy. *International Journal of Group Psychotherapy, 51*, 225–242.

Harrison, R. L. & Westwood, M.J. (2009). Preventing vicarious traumatization of mental health therapists: Identifying protective practices. *Psychotherapy Theory, Research, Practice, Training* 46(2), 203–213.

Killian, K. D. (2008). Helping till it hurts? A multimethod study of compassion fatigue, burnout, and self-care in clinicians working with trauma survivors. *Traumatology*, 14(2), 32–44.

Norcross, J. C., & Guy, J. D. (2007). Psychotherapist Self-Care Checklist. In J. C. Norcross & J.D. Guy, *Leaving it at the office: A guide to psychotherapist self-care*. New York: Guilford. Retrieved from: https://www.researchgate.net/publication/300580928_Psychotherapist_Self-Care_Checklist

Pope, K.S. & Vasquez, M.J. (2016). Creating and using strategies for self care. In Pope, K. S., & Vasquez, M. J. (2016), *Ethics in psychotherapy and counseling: A practical guide*. Hoboken, NJ: John Wiley & Sons.

Smith, P. (2017). How to Manage Compassion Fatigue in Caregiving | TEDxSanJuanIsland Talk. [video] Retrieved from https://www.youtube.com/watch?v=7keppA8XRas

Weber, R. L. & Gans, J. S. (2003). The group therapist's shame: A much undiscussed topic. *International Journal of Group Psychotherapy*, 53, 395–416.

Boundaries

As shown above, an important means of self care is diligently protecting one's own boundaries and personal space, that is, giving ourselves permission to say "no." By virtue of becoming a group therapist, one automatically increases one's caseload substantially. With this increase in patients comes an expansion of administrative duties and documentation, as well as likely more phone calls, emails, texts, or requests for your time, energy and expertise. There are times when each of those requests is warranted and of critical importance, but there are many times when the therapist (and the therapy) are best served by protecting a boundary between the group and out-of-group contact. Discernment takes time, practice, knowledge of the client, and ethical considerations. Answering a client's request initially with the old adage, "Let me think about it" may allow time to consider what is best for the client, yourself, and the work over the long term.

> **Exercise:**
>
> How comfortable are you in saying "no," that is in setting limits and maintaining the boundaries of the therapeutic contract? Can you think of an example when you said "yes," but may have been better off saying "no?"

Supervision

While it is true that our groups are ultimately our best supervisors and we should always solicit our members' ideas, opinions and views, it is equally true that at times it is helpful to have an outside set of eyes and ears evaluate what is going on not only in our groups, but also what is going on for us personally. Personal therapy or a supervisory relationship that includes personal elements is strongly recommended as part of ongoing self-care. For neophyte group therapists, close supervision is imperative; but continual supervision is recommended for all. **Supervision, after all, is simply a loaning out of experience, a process that can help moderate our emotional reactions so we can return to our own thoughts and feelings, to ourselves, and to our own lives.**

Most of what happens for a new group therapist has occurred in other groups and a senior supervisor can guide a therapist through the sometimes troubled waters of a therapy group, provide needed support, ideas, and practical interventions, and emotional connection. Most group therapists seek clinical supervision throughout their careers as group psychotherapy presents complex dynamics that can bring forth strong feelings and require strong containment.

Also over the course of one's career, additional supervision or training can be beneficial if you are leading groups with new populations, incorporating new theories and techniques, and working with a patient who is complex or outside of one's previous expertise. Group supervision of groups is a popular method of both gaining continual insight into oneself, group leadership, and group membership; as well as providing peer connection and emotional support.

Recommended Resources

Riva, M. T. (2014). Supervision of group leaders. In J. L. DeLucia-Waack, D. A. Gerrity, C. R. Kalodner, M. T. Riva (Eds.), *Handbook of group counseling and psychotherapy* (2nd ed., pp. 146–158). Thousand Oaks, CA: Sage.

Shay, J. & Motherwell, L. (2014). Why do we continue to do this work? The power of the group. In. L. Motherwell & J. Shay (Eds.) *Complex dilemmas in group therapy: pathways to resolution* [2nd ed.]. New York, NY: Routledge.

Your Journey

What Drew You to the Group Leadership?

Self-understanding informs our work and helps us work constructively with our countertransference experiences. Self-exploration also helps us live better lives, and be more effectively connected with those around us. There are many possible professions and many modalities even within this field. An interesting question to consider is **why did you want to become a group leader?** Your answers could be numerous, ranging from conscious and simple to more distal and complex. What are all of your motivations?

- To help others?
- To quench your thirst for mastery of complex ideas?
- To be in a position of power, influence, or attention?
- To heal some old wounds in yourself or in others?
- Other reasons?

First Models

Just as children learn from and imitate adults, as beginning group leaders we often try to identify with a mentor or someone more experienced than ourselves. Over time, we may rely less on the external role model and begin to experiment towards developing more of our distinctive personal style. Similar to the uniqueness of our group members, leaders bring their own histories, psychological resources, and vulnerabilities into the group room. As developing leaders, some individuals will be very skilled at and comfortable with employing more structured psychoeducational formats, while others will be more naturally adept at feeling and exploring the tenor of group-as-a-whole dynamics. Even among those individuals adopting similar theoretical approaches and specific treatment modalities, leadership styles vary. Our preferences about what to do and how to be in the group, influenced by comfort level, past experiences in groups and our internal worlds, range widely across individuals. Of vital importance, however, is to **deeply understand that we are different from our members and our members are different from each other** – even if they share similar symptoms, histories, or challenges. Over time, as we increasingly appreciate the uniqueness of the individual, we will want to develop and integrate a variety of approaches that can be maximally effective. **With experience, the integration of nomothetic and ideographic approaches can become more natural, authentic, and nurturing to you and the members in your groups.**

For the novice leader, focusing on one style or theory may be a pragmatic and productive manner to initially work with our members and ourselves. Over time, some leaders will continue on one theoretical path with increasing **depth and nuance**, while others will travel through many approaches towards a more **integrative** style. Changes in settings, populations, clinical focus, and the larger culture will demand that we continue to grow and adjust.

Expecting to become a flawless leader is an aspirational, albeit unrealistic, ambition. It is possible, however, to lead groups that benefit the majority of our members, especially with ongoing practice, learning, and experience. Mistakes – in technique, timing, and understanding – are inevitable, but with supervision, temperance, and patience, they can provide opportunities for growth and thus add to the further development of our skills, competence and effectiveness. Remember that despite the inevitable shock of relational ruptures, it is often the willingness and vulnerability expressed in the efforts at repair that can benefit our members. The leader and the members are growing together collaboratively.

Exercise

- Who were your first models of group leadership? Parents? Teachers? Coaches? Community leaders? Clergy? Someone in the popular culture or media?
- What did you like about this observed leadership style? What was disappointing?
- How specifically have you been influenced by these role models, either through a positive identification or by negative reaction to?

Choices

The landscape of contemporary group approaches continues to broaden. Many leaders' approaches are influenced by their initial and subsequent trainings, the needs of the individuals they serve, the treatment models endorsed by the agencies or organizations in which they work, and their own personal interests. As reflected in chapter 4 on therapeutic factors, group leaders typically develop their own beliefs and hypotheses about what the "active ingredients" of effective psychotherapy are – both technical and common factors – and notions about what dimensions of change (chapter 9) are particularly important to monitor.

Ideally one's group leadership methods bring together sound clinical theory and applicable research with the presenting needs of the clients. For instance, the group therapist wishing to treat those suffering from chronic pain might well utilize mindfulness skills training as a theory- and research-based approach for enhancing patients' self-compassion, acceptance, hope and the ability to selectively choose areas of mental focus. Similarly, a group therapist wanting to help new parents enhance their skills and wellbeing might use psychoeducational formats to teach relevant child development concepts, skills to enhance emotional regulation particularly in conditions of sleep deprivation, and ways to increase the acceptance of a wide range of feelings, including frustration, anxiety, and stress.

Personal Style

Carl Jung brought the idea of personality typology into the forefront of psychology. The Myers Briggs type inventories are assessments most of us have taken. Many therapists joke that they identify as introverts who work hard to develop constructive social skills.

Rutan, Stone, and Shay (2010) describe how leadership styles can vary along several dimensions, reflecting personal preferences, from:

- Transparency versus opaqueness
- Activity versus nonactivity
- Gratification versus Frustration (of clients' request and desires).

Still other stylistic dimensions of leadership include:

- Promoting safety to promoting spontaneous risk taking
- Maintaining flexible boundaries to reinforcing stricter boundaries
- Adhering to one treatment model to integrating multiple models
- Being supportive to being challenging
- Practicing time limited to open ended groups.
- Interpretive and exploratory to teaching of skills and concepts.

This list could go on as group leaders have many choices to make about their style. Moreover, styles are not static; most leaders try to adapt their leadership style to meet the needs of a particular group, its stage of group development and the current dynamic issues and tensions.

Exercises:

What stylistic attributes apply in general to your group leadership? Which do you think are particularly helpful? Which have caused problems in the work?
How has your style evolved or changed?

Bringing Out the Best in Yourself

An unfortunate tendency of many therapists is to be very self-critical. **Undoubtedly fearless self-inquiry is a part of personal and professional development but a part that should be balanced with honest and accurate self-appreciation.** Not attending to either part will be limiting.

Exercises:

1. What thoughts or feelings get in the way of your best work? (anxiety, desire for success, fear of failure or criticism, or others?) How can you address these with yourself?

2. What are your unique gifts, talents, and experiences that you could embrace more? (Examples may include unique life experiences, emotional openness, rigorous study, an empathic heart, sense of humor or others?) Is there a way to allow these positive attributes more into your own identity and into your life and work?

Concluding Thoughts

While group psychotherapy can be complex, interpersonally intense, and demanding of our focus, it is also a wonderfully unique experience. For many group therapists, leading group is a wonderful addition to a rewarding professional career and an interesting, meaningful life. As leaders, we are privileged to experience great moments of intimacy, witness positive changes and growth, and embrace a full range of human feelings in our members and inside ourselves. Groups are not static, but alive with life, spontaneity, and movement. By leading groups we embrace this vitality of connectedness in all its varied forms.

References

Abernethy, A.D. (2012). A spiritually informed approach to group psychotherapy. In J.L. Kleinberg (Ed.), *The Wiley-Blackwell handbook of group psychotherapy* (pp. 681–705). West Sussex: John Wiley & Sons.

Agazarian, Y.M. (1982). Role as a bridge construct in understanding the relationship between the individual and the group. In *The Individual and the Group* (pp. 181–192). Boston, MA: Springer.

Agazarian, Y. M. (1983). Theory of the invisible group applied to individual and group-as-a-whole interpretations. *Group*, 7(2), 27–37.

Agazarian, Y.M. (2004). *System-centered therapy for groups* (2nd ed.). New York: Guilford.

Agazarian, Y.M. & Gantt, S. (2003). Phases of group development: Systems-centered hypotheses and their implications for research and practice. *Group Dynamics: Theory, Research, and Practice*, 7(3), 238–252.

Agazarian, Y., & Gantt, S. (2012). "The interpersonal neurobiology of building mindful systems through functional subgrouping" Retrieved from: www.youtube.com/watch?v=p3UE3c_ndxw

Agazarian, Y.M., & Peters, R. (1981). *The visible and invisible group*. London: Routledge & Kegan Paul.

American Psychological Association. (2003). Guidelines on multicultural education, training, research, practice and organizational change for psychologists. *American Psychologist*, 58, 377–402.

American Psychological Association. (2015). Guidelines for psychological practice with transgender and gender nonconforming people. Retrieved from www.apa.org/practice/guidelines/transgender.pdf

American Psychological Association. (2017). Multicultural guidelines: An ecological approach to context, identity, and intersectionality, 2017 Retrieved from www.apa.org/about/policy/multicultural-guidelines.pdf

American Psychological Association Presidential Task on Evidence Based-Practice in Psychology. (2006). Evidence-based practice in psychology. *American Psychologist*, 61, 271–285.

Andersen, S.M., & Przybylinski, E. (2012). Experiments on transference in interpersonal relations: Implications for treatment. *Psychodynamic Psychotherapy*, 49(3), 370–383.

Anderson, G. (1997). Children, adolescents and their powerholders in therapy settings. *Women and Therapy*, 20, 1–6.

Anthony, E.J. (1971). The history of group psychotherapy. In H. Kaplan, & B. Sadock (Eds.), *Comprehensive group psychotherapy* (pp. 4–31). Baltimore, MD: Williams and Wilkens.

Arnow, B.A., & Steidtmann, D. (2014). Harnessing the potential of the therapeutic alliance. *World Psychiatry*, 13(3), 238–240.

Arredondo, P., & Tovar-Blank, Z.G. (2014). Multicultural competencies: A dynamic paradigm for the 21st century. In F.T.L. Leong (Ed.), *APA handbook of multicultural psychology vol. 2: Applications and training* (pp. 19–34). Washington, DC: American Psychological Association.

Asch Conformity Experiment. (2007). Retrieved from www.youtube.com/watch?v=TYIh4MkcfJA

Badenoch, B. (2008). *Being a brain-wise therapist: A practical guide to interpersonal neurobiology.* New York, NY: Norton.

Badenoch, B. (2011). The integrated and mindful therapist. Retrieved from www.youtube.com/watch?v=eOPr8MPzdvA&index=1&list=PLdVCA4bAqgHsggm7zn3nSSRzw7B39-q_G

Badenoch, B. (2016, May). A symphony of gifts from relational neuroscience. How understanding our embodied brains can support lives of hope & resilience. The neuroscience training summit. Retrieved from www.soundstrue.com/store/neuroscience-summit

Badenoch, B., & Cox, P. (2010). Integrating interpersonal neurobiology with group psychotherapy. *International Journal of Group Psychotherapy*, 60(4), 462–481.

Baer, R.A. (Ed.) (2015). *Mindfulness-based treatment approaches: Clinician's guide to evidence base and applications.* New York: Academic Press.

Barlow, S., Burlingame, G.M., Greene, L.R., Joyce, A., Kaklauskas, F., Kinley, J., Klein, R.H., Kobos, J.C., Leszcz, M., MacNair-Semands, R., Paquin, J.D., Tasca, G.A., Whittingham, M., & Feirman, D. (2015). Evidence-based practice in group psychotherapy [American Group Psychotherapy Association Science to Service Task Force web document]. Retrieved from www.agpa.org/home/practice-resources/evidence-based-practice-in-group-psychotherapy

Barlow, S.H. (2012). An application of the competency model to group-specialty practice. *Professional Psychology: Research and Practice*, 43, 442–451.

Barlow, S.H. (2013). *Specialty competencies in group psychology.* Oxford: Oxford University Press.

Barlow, S.H., & Burlingame, G.M. (2006). Essential theory, processes, and procedures for successful group psychotherapy: Group cohesion as exemplar. *Journal of Contemporary Psychotherapy*, 36, 107–112.

Barlow, S.H., Fuhriman, A.J., & Burlingame, G. (2004). The history of group counseling and psychotherapy. In J.L. Delucia-Waack, D.A. Gerrity, C.R. Kalodner, & M.T. Riva (Eds.), *Handbook of group counseling and psychotherapy* (pp. 3–22). Thousand Oaks, CA: Sage.

Barnett, J. (2014, December). Distress, burnout, self-care, and the promotion of wellness for psychotherapists and trainees: Issues, implications, and recommendations. [Web article]. Retrieved from www.societyforpsychotherapy.org/distress-therapist-burnout-self-care-promotion-wellness-psychotherapists-trainees-issues-implications-recommendations

Beauchamp, T.L., & Childress, J.F. (2001). *Principles of biomedical ethics.* Cary, NC: Oxford University Press.

Beck, R. (2012). Care for the caregivers. In J.L. Kleinberg (Ed.), *The Wiley-Blackwell handbook of group psychotherapy* (pp. 571–585). Chichester: John Wiley.

Bemak, F., & Chung, R.C.Y. (2004). Teaching multicultural group counseling: Perspectives for a new era. *Journal for Specialists in Group Work*, 29, 31–41.

Benish, S.G., Quintana, S., & Wampold, B.E. (2011). Culturally adapted psychotherapy and the legitimacy of myth: A direct-comparison meta-analysis. *Journal of Counseling Psychology*, 58(3), 279–289.

Bennett, M.J. (1986). A developmental approach to training for intercultural sensitivity. *International Journal of Intercultural Relations*, 10(2), 179–196.

Bennis, W.G., & Shepard, H.A. (1956). A theory of group development. *Human Relations*, 9, 415–457.

Ben-Noam, S. (2010). The fee: A clinical tool in group therapy. In S.S. Fehr (Ed.), *101 interventions in group therapy* (Rev. ed.) (pp. 539–542). New York: Routledge: Routledge/Taylor & Francis Group.

Bentzen, M. (2015). *The neuroaffective picture book.* Rothersthorpe: Paragon Publishing.

Berg-Cross, L., & So, D. (2011). The start of a new era: Evidence-based multicultural therapies. *The Register Report*, 37, 8–15. [Web page]. Retrieved from www.nationalregister.org/pub/the-national-register-report-pub/the-register-report-fall-2011/evidence-based-multicultural-therapies-the-start-of-a-new-era/

Berger, T. (2016). The therapeutic alliance in internet interventions: A narrative review and suggestions for future research. *Psychotherapy Research*, 27(5), 511–524.

Berman, M.I., Chapman, N., Nash, B., Kivlighan, D.M., & Paquin, J.D. (2017). Sharing wisdom: Challenges, benefits, and developmental path to becoming a successful therapist-researcher. *Counselling Psychology Quarterly*, 1–21.

Bernal, G., & Domenech Rodríguez, M.M. (2013). Tailoring treatment to the patient's race and ethnicity. In G. Koocher, J. Norcross, & B. Greene (Eds.), *Psychologists' desk reference* (3rd ed.) (pp. 310–313). Oxford University Press.

Bernard, H., Burlingame, G., Flores, P., Greene, L., Joyce, A., Kobos, J.C., Leszcz, M., MacNair-Semands, R.R., Piper, W., Slocum McEneaney, A.M., & Feirman, D. (2008). Clinical practice guidelines for group psychotherapy. *International Journal of Group Psychotherapy*, 58, 455–542.

Bernard, H.S., & MacKenzie, K.R. (1994). *Basics of group psychotherapy*. New York: Guilford.

Berne, E. (1966). *Principles of group treatment*. New York: Grove Press.

Betan, E.J., & Stanton, A.L. (1999). Fostering ethical willingness: Integrating emotional and contextual awareness with rational analysis. *Professional Psychology: Research and Practice*, 30(3), 295–301.

Bieling, P.J., McCabe, R.E., & Antony, M.M. (2013). *Cognitive-behavioral therapy in groups*. New York: Guilford.

Bieling, P.J., Milosevic, I., & McCabe, R.E. (2014). Groups for depression. In J.L. DeLucia-Waack, C.R. Kalodner, & M.T. Riva (Eds.), *Handbook of group counseling and psychotherapy* (2nd ed.) (pp. 367–380). Sage Publications.

Billow, R. (Ed.) (2012). Special issue: Essays on starting one's first therapy group. *International Journal of Group Psychotherapy*, 62, 341–390.

Billow, R.M. (2001). The therapist's anxiety and resistance to group therapy. *International Journal of Group Psychotherapy*, 51, 225–242.

Billow, R.M. (2004). Truth and falsity in group. *International Journal of Group Psychotherapy*, 54, 321–345.

Billow, R.M. (2006). The three R's of group: Resistance, rebellion, and refusal. *International Journal of Group Psychotherapy*, 56, 259–284.

Billow, R. M., 2012. Transforming the professional self. *International Journal of Group Psychotherapy*, 62(3), 381–386.

Billow, R.M. (2015). *Developing nuclear ideas: Relational group psychotherapy*. London: Karnac.

Billow, R.M. (2018). Doing our work: Words, deeds, and presence. *International Journal of Group Psychotherapy*, doi: 10.1080/00207284.2018.1483197

Bion, W. (1961). *Experiences in groups and other papers*. London: Tavistock.

Bordin, E.S. (1979). The generalizability of the psychoanalytic concept of the working alliance. *Psychotherapy*, 16, 252–260.

Borgogno, F., & Merciai, S. A. (2000). Searching for Bion: Cogitations, a new 'clinical diary'? In W. R Bion, F. Talamo, F. Borgogno and S. Merciai (Eds.), *W.R. Bion: Between past and future*. London: Karnac.

Bowen, S., Vieten, C., Witkiewitz, K., & Carroll, H. (2015). A mindfulness-based approach to addiction. In K.W. Brown, J.D. Creswell, & R.M. Ryan (Eds.), *Handbook of mindfulness: Theory, research, and practice* (pp. 387–404). New York: Guilford.

Brabender, V. (2007). The ethical group psychotherapist: A coda. *International Journal of Group Psychotherapy*, 57(1), 41–48.

Brabender, V. (2010). The developmental path to expertise in group psychotherapy. *Journal of Contemporary Psychotherapy*, 40, 163–173.

Brabender, V. (2016). Chaos theory and group psychotherapy 15 years later. *Group*, 40(1), 9–15.

Brabender, V., & Fallon, A. (2009a). *Group development in practice: Guidance for clinicians and researchers on stages and dynamics of change*. Washington, D.C.: American Psychological Association.

Brabender, V.M., & Fallon, A. (2009b). Ethical hot spots of combined individual and group therapy: Applying four ethical systems. *International Journal of Group Psychotherapy*, 59(1), 127–147.

Brabender, V.M., & Fallon, A. (2019). *Group psychotherapy in context. Inpatient, partial hospital and residential care*. Washington, D.C: American Psychological Association.

Bricklin, P. (2001). Being ethical: More than obeying the law and avoiding harm. *Journal of Personality Assessment*, 77(2), 195–202.

Brown, L.S. (2010). *Feminist therapy*. Washington, DC: American Psychological Association.

Brown, N.W. (2003). Conceptualizing process. *International Journal of Group Psychotherapy*, 53 (2), 225–244.

Brown, N.W. (2011). *Psychoeducational groups: Process and practice*. London: Routledge/Taylor & Francis Group.

Brown, N. W. (2018). *Psychoeducational groups: Process and practice*. New York: Routledge.

Bullock, M. (2012). International psychology. In D.K. Freedheim, & B. Weiner (Eds.), *Handbook of psychology: History of psychology* (2nd ed.) (pp. 562–596). Hoboken, NJ: Wiley.

Burke, W.F., & Tansey, M.J. (1985). Projective identification and countertransference turmoil: Disruptions in the empathic process. *Contemporary Psychoanalysis*, 21, 372–402.

Burlingame, G., Fuhriman, A., & Johnson, J. (2002). Cohesion in group psychotherapy. In J. Norcross (Ed.), *Psychotherapy relationships that work: Therapist contributions and responsiveness to patients* (pp. 71–87). New York: Oxford University Press.

Burlingame, G., Strauss, B., & Joyce, A. (2013). Change mechanisms and effectiveness of small group treatments. In M.J. Lambert (Ed.), *Bergin & Garfield's handbook of psychotherapy and behavior change* (6th ed.) (pp. 640–689). New York: Wiley & Sons.

Burlingame, G.M., Cox, J.C., Davies, D.R., Layne, C.M., & Gleave, R. (2011). The group selection questionnaire: Further refinements in group member selection. *Group Dynamics: Theory, Research, and Practice*, 15(1), 60–74.

Burlingame, G.M., McClendon, D.T., & Alonso, J. (2011). Cohesion in group therapy. *Psychotherapy*, 48, 34–42.

Burlingame, G.M., McClendon, T., & Yang, C. (2018). Cohesion in group therapy: A meta-analysis. *Psychotherapy*, 55, 384–398.

Burlingame, G.M., Strauss, B., Joyce, A., MacNair-Semands, R., MacKenzie, K.R., Ogrodniczuk, J., & Taylor, S. (2006). *Core battery – revised: An assessment tool kit for promoting optimal group selection, process and outcome*. Available through the AGPA store.

Bush, S.S., Connell, M.A., & Denney, R.L. (2006). *Ethical practice in forensic psychology: A systematic model for decision making*. Washington, DC: American Psychological Association.

Campbell, V. (2008). Brain science podcast: Meditation and the brain with Dan Siegel, MD [Transcript]. Retrieved from http://docartemis.com/brain%20science/44-brainscience-Siegel.pdf

Chang, C., Ciliberti, A., & Kaklauskas, F.J. (2017). Mindfulness approaches for groups in college counseling centers. In M.D. Ribeiro, J. Gross, & M.M. Turner (Eds.), *The college counselor's guide to group psychotherapy* (pp. 218–238). New York: Routledge/Taylor & Francis Group.

Chang-Caffaro, S., & Caffaro, J. (2018). Differences that make a difference: Diversity and the process group leader. *International Journal of Group Psychotherapy*, 68, 483–497.

Chartrand, T.L., & Bargh, J.A. (1999). The chameleon effect: The perception-behavior link and social interaction. *Journal of Personality and Social Psychology*, 76, 893–910.

Chávez, V. (2012) *Cultural humility: People, principles, and practices*. [Video file]. Retrieved from: www.youtube.com/watch?v=SaSHLbS1V4w

Chen, E.C. (2012). Multicultural competence and social justice advocacy in group psychology and group psychotherapy. *The Group Psychologist*, 22(2), 10.

Chen, E.C., Budianto, L., & Wong, K. (2010). Professional school counselors as social justice advocates for undocumented immigrant students in group work. *The Journal for Specialists in Group Work*, 35(3), 255–261.

Chen, E.C., Kakkad, D., & Balzano, J. (2008). Multicultural competence and evidence-based practice in group therapy. *Journal of Clinical Psychology, 64*(11), 1261–1278.

Chu, J., & Leino, A. (2017). Advancement in the maturing science of cultural adaptations of evidence-based interventions. *Journal of Consulting and Clinical Psychology, 85*(1), 45–57.

Chu, J., Leino, A., Pflum, S., & Sue, S. (2016). A model for the theoretical basis of cultural competency to guide psychotherapy. *Professional Psychology: Research and Practice, 47*(1), 18–29.

Cloitre, M., & Koenen, K.C. (2001). The impact of borderline personality disorder on process group outcome among women with posttraumatic stress disorder related to childhood abuse. *International Journal of Group Psychotherapy, 51*, 379–398.

Coan, J. (2014, January 25). Why we hold hands [Video file]. Retrieved from www.youtube.com /watch?v=1UMHUPPQ96c

Cohn, B. (2014). Creating the group envelope. In L. Motherwell, & J. Shay (Eds.), *Complex dilemmas in group therapy: Pathways to resolution* (2nd ed.), (pp. 27–35). New York: Routledge/Taylor & Francis Group.

Cone-Uemura, K., & Bentley, E.S. (2017). Multicultural/Diversity issues in groups. In M. D. Ribeiro, J. Gross, & M.M. Turner (Eds.), *The college counselor's guide to group psychotherapy* (pp. 21–35). New York City: Routledge.

Constantine, M.G. (2002). Predictors of satisfaction with counseling: Racial and ethnic minority clients' attitudes toward counseling and ratings of their counselors' general and multicultural counseling competence. *Journal of Counseling Psychology, 49*(2), 255–263.

Cooper, L. (1976). Co-therapy relationships in groups. *Small Group Behavior, 7*, 473–498.

Corey, M.S., Corey, G., & Corey, C. (2013). *Groups: Process and practice.* Independence, KY: Cengage Learning.

Corsini, R.J., & Rosenberg, B. (1955). Mechanisms of group psychotherapy: Processes and dynamics. *Journal of Abnormal and Social Psychology, 51*, 406–411.

Counselman, E. (2016) First you put the chairs in a circle: Becoming a group therapist. The Anne and Ramon Alonso Presidential Plenary Address presented at the 2016 Annual meeting of the American Group Psychotherapy Association, New York.

Cozolino, L. (2010). *The neuroscience of psychotherapy: Healing the social brain* (2nd ed.). New York: Norton.

Cozolino, L. (2014). *The neuroscience of human relationships: Attachment and the developing social brain.* [Kindle version]. New York: Norton.

D'Andrea, M. (2014). Understanding racial/cultural identity development theories to promote effective multicultural group counseling. In J.L. DeLucia-Waack, C.R. Kalodner, & M.T. Riva (Eds.), *Handbook of group counseling and psychotherapy* (2nd ed.) (pp. 196–208). Thousand Oaks, CA: Sage.

Davis, D.M., & Hayes, J.A. (2011). What are the benefits of mindfulness? A practice review of psychotherapy-related research. *Psychotherapy, 48*(2), 198–208.

Debiak, D. (2007). Attending to diversity in group psychotherapy: An ethical imperative. *International Journal of Group Psychotherapy, 57*(1), 1–12.

Deiner, E. (1979). Deindividuation: The absence of self-awareness and self-regulation in group members. In P. Paulus (Ed.), *The psychology of group influence* (pp. 209–242). Hillsdale, NJ: Lawrence Erlbaum Associates.

Denninger, J.W. (2010). Commentary on the neurobiology of group psychotherapy: Group and the social brain: Speeding toward a neurobiological understanding of group psychotherapy. *International Journal of Group Psychotherapy, 60*(4), 595–604.

Di Pellegrino, G., Fadiga, L., Fogassi, L., Gallese, V., & Rizzolatti, G. (1992). Understanding motor events: A neurophysiological study. *Experimental Brain Research, 91*, 176–180.

Domenech Rodríguez, M.M., & Bernal, G. (2012). Bridging the gap between research and practice in a multicultural world. In G. Bernal, & M. Domenech Rodríguez (Eds.), *Cultural adaptations:*

Tools for evidence-based practice with diverse populations (pp. 265–287). Washington, DC: American Psychological Association.

Dunbar, R.I. (1998). The social brain hypothesis. *Evolutionary Anthropology: Issues, News, and Reviews*, 6(5), 178–190.

Ecker, B. (2014, April 10). Memory reconsolidation: Key to transformational change in psychotherapy. [Video file] Retrieved from www.youtube.com/watch?v=_V_rI2N6Fco

Ecker, B., Ticic, R., & Hulley, L. (2012). *Unlocking the emotional brain: Eliminating symptoms at their roots using memory consolidation.* New York: Routledge/Taylor & Francis Group.

Ettin, M. (1992). Managing group process in non process group: Working with structured theme-centered tasks. In M. Ettin (Ed.), *Foundations and applications of group psychotherapy* (pp. 233–259). Boston, MA: Allyn & Bacon.

Ettin, M. (1999). *Foundations and applications of group psychotherapy: A sphere of influence.* London: Jessica Kingsley.

Exline, J.J., & Hill, P.C. (2012). Humility: A consistent and robust predictor of generosity. *The Journal of Positive Psychology*, 7(3), 208–218.

Experimental Studies in the Social Climate of Groups. (1953 (2013)). Retrieved from www.youtube.com/watch?v=J7FYGn2NS8M

Ferrari, P.F., Gallese, V., Rizzolatti, G., & Fogassi, L. (2003). Mirror neurons responding to the observation of ingestive and communicative mouth actions in the monkey ventral premotor cortex. *European Journal of Neuroscience*, 17, 1703–1714.

Flores, P.J. (2010). Group psychotherapy and neuro-plasticity: An attachment theory perspective. *International Journal of Group Psychotherapy*, 60(4), 546–570.

Flores, P.J., & Porges, S.W. (2017). Group psychotherapy as a neural exercise: Bridging polyvagal theory and attachment theory. *International Journal of Group Psychotherapy*, 67(2), 202–222.

Fonagy, P., Campbell, C., & Bateman, A. (2017). Mentalizing, attachment, and epistemic trust in group therapy. *International Journal of Group Psychotherapy*, 67(2), 176–201.

Forester-Miller, H., & Davis, T.E. (1996). A practitioner's guide to ethical decision making. Retrieved from www.counseling.org/docs/ethics/practitioners_guide.pdf?sfvrsn=2

Forsyth, D.R. (2000). The social psychology of groups and group psychotherapy: One view of the next century. *Group*, 24(2–3), 147–155.

Forsyth, D.R. (2010). The nature and significance of groups. In R.K. Conyne (Ed.), *The Oxford handbook of group counseling* (pp. 19–35). New York: Oxford University Press.

Forsyth, D.R. (2018). *Group dynamics.* Boston, MA: Cengage Learning.

Foulkes, S.H. (1990). *Selected papers of S.H. Foulkes: Psychoanalysis and group analysis.* London: Karnac.

Foulkes, S.H., & Anthony, E.J. (1965). *Group psychotherapy: The psycho-analytic approach.* London: Karnac.

Free, M. (2007). *Cognitive therapy in groups: Guidelines and resources for practice* (2nd ed.). Chichester: Wiley.

Freedman, W., & Diederich, L.T. (2017). Group co-facilitation: Creating a collaborative partnership. In M.D. Ribeiro, J.M. Gross, & M.M. Turner (Eds.), *The college counselor's guide to group psychotherapy* (pp. 159–172). New York: Routledge/Taylor & Francis Group.

Freud, S. (1921). Group psychology and the analysis of the ego. *Standard Edition, 18*. London: Hogarth.

Freud, S. (1958). On beginning the treatment. In J. Strachey (Ed. & Trans.), *The standard edition of the complete psychological works of Sigmund Freud* (Vol. 12, pp. 121–144). London: Hogarth Press. (Original work published 1913).

Gallagher, M.E., Tasca, G.A., Ritchie, K., Balfour, L., & Bissada, H. (2014). Attachment anxiety moderates the relationship between growth in group cohesion and treatment outcomes in group psychodynamic interpersonal psychotherapy for women with binge eating disorder. *Group Dynamics*, 18, 38–52.

Gans, J.S. (1992). Money and psychodynamic group psychotherapy. *International Journal of Group Psychotherapy, 42*(1), 133–152.

Gans, J.S., & Counselman, E.F. (2000). Silence in group psychotherapy: A powerful communication. *International Journal of Group Psychotherapy, 50*(1), 71–86.

Gans, J.S., & Counselman, E.F. (2010). Patient selection for psychodynamic group psychotherapy: Practical and dynamic considerations. *International Journal of Group Psychotherapy, 60*(2), 197–220.

Gans, R.W. (1962). Group co-therapists and the therapeutic situation: A critical evaluation. *International Journal of Group Psychotherapy, 12,* 788–799.

Gantt, S.P., & Agazarian, Y.M. (2010). Developing the group mind through functional subgrouping: Linking Systems-Centered Training (SCT) and interpersonal neurobiology. *International Journal of Group Psychotherapy, 60*(4), 515–544.

Gantt, S.P., & Agazarian, Y.M. (2013). Developing the group mind through functional subgrouping: Linking Systems-Centered Training (SCT) and interpersonal neurobiology. In S.P. Gantt, & B. Badenoch (Eds.), *The interpersonal neurobiology of group psychotherapy and group process* (pp. 73–102). London: Karnac.

Gantt, S.P., & Badenoch, B. (Eds.) (2013). *The interpersonal neurobiology of group psychotherapy and group process.* London: Karnac.

Gantt, S.P., & Badenoch, B. (2017). Systems-centered group psychotherapy: Developing a group mind that supports right brain function and right-left-right hemispheric integration. In R. Tweedy (Ed.), *The divided therapist: Hemispheric difference and contemporary psychotherapy.* London, UK: Karnac.

Gantt, S.P., & Cox, P. (Eds.) (2010a). Neurobiology and building interpersonal systems: Groups, couples, and beyond [Special issue]. *International Journal of Group Psychotherapy, 60*(4).

Ganzarain, R. (1989). *Object relations group psychotherapy.* Madison, CT: International Universities Press.

Gemmill, G. (1989). The dynamics of scapegoating in small groups. *Small Group Behavior, 20,* 406–418.

Gibbard, G.S. (1974). Individuation, fusion and role specialization. In G.S. Gibbard, J.J. Hartman, & R.D. Mann (Eds.), *Analysis of groups* (pp. 247–265). San Francisco, CA: Jossey-Bass.

Gibbard, G.S., & Hartman, J.J. (1973). The significance of utopian fantasies in small groups. *International Journal of Group Psychotherapy, 23,* 125–147.

Gibbard, G.S., Hartman, J.J., & Mann, R.D. (1974). Group process and development. In G. S. Gibbard, J.J. Hartman, & R.D. Mann (Eds.), *Analysis of groups* (pp. 83–93). San Francisco, Jossey-Bass.

Gilligan, C. (1977). In a different voice: Women's conceptions of self and of morality. *Harvard Educational Review, 47*(4), 481–517.

Gleave, R., Beecher, M., Burlingame, G., Griner, D., & Hansen, K., (2016). Practical and useful evidence-based practice: Using clinician-friendly process and outcome measures to enhance your groups. Open session presented at the 2016 AGPA annual meeting, New York City. Audiotape available through AGPA store.

Goicoechea, J., & Kessler, L.E. (2018). Competency-based training in interpersonal, process-oriented group therapy: An innovative university partnership. *Training and Education in Professional Psychology, 12,* 46–53.

Goodwin, B.C., Ford, D.E., Hsiung, R.C., Houston, T.K., Fogel, J., & Van Voorhees, B.W. (2018). First, do no harm: Referring primary care patients with depression to an internet support group. *Telemedicine and e-Health, 24,* 37–44.

Gorski, P.C., & Goodman, R.D. (2015). Introduction: Toward a decolonized multicultural counseling and psychology. In R. Goodman, & P.C. Gorski (Eds.), *Decolonizing "multicultural" counseling through social justice* (pp. 1–10). New York: Springer.

Gough, B., & Madill, A. (2012). Subjectivity in psychological science: From problem to prospect. *Psychological Methods*, 17(3), 374–384.

Greene, C.J., Morland, L.A., Macdonald, A., Frueh, B.C., Grubbs, K.M., & Rosen, C.S. (2010). How does tele-mental health affect group therapy process? Secondary analysis of a noninferiority trial. *Journal of Consulting and Clinical Psychology*, 78, 746–750.

Greene, L.R. (1999). Representations of the group-as-a-whole: Personality, situational and dynamic determinants. *Psychoanalytic Psychology*, 16, 403–425.

Greene, L.R. (2012). Group therapist as social scientist, with special reference to the psychodynamically oriented psychotherapist. *American Psychologist*, 67(6), 477.

Greene, L.R. (2016). Group psychotherapy research studies that therapists might actually read: My top 10 list. *International Journal of Group Psychotherapy*, 67, 1–26.

Greene, L.R., Rosenkrantz, J., & Muth, D. (1986). Borderline defenses and countertransference: Research findings and implications. *Psychiatry*, 49, 253–264.

Gross, J.M. (2017). The group coordinator: Promoting group culture by managing stages of program development. In M.D. Ribeiro, J. Gross, & M.M. Turner (Eds.), *The college counselor's guide to group psychotherapy* (pp. 131–144). New York City: Routledge.

Grossmark, R. (2015). The edge of chaos: Enactment, disruption, and emergence in group psychotherapy. In R. Grossmark, & F. Wright (Eds.), *The one and the many: Relational approaches to group psychotherapy* (pp. 57–74). Routledge/Taylor & Francis Group.

Gutheil, T.G., & Gabbard, G.O. (1993). The concept of boundaries in clinical practice: Theoretical and risk-management dimensions. *American Journal of Psychiatry*, 150, 188–196.

Gutheil, T.G., & Gabbard, G.O. (1998). Misuses and misunderstandings of boundary theory in clinical and regulatory settings. *American Journal of Psychiatry*, 155, 409–414.

Haberstroh, S., Barney, L., Foster, N., & Duffey, T. (2014). The ethical and legal practice of online counseling and psychotherapy: A review of mental health professions. *Journal of Technology in Human Services*, 32(3), 149–157.

Haen, C., & Aronson, S. (Eds.) (2017). *Handbook of child and adolescent group therapy: A practitioner's reference*. New York: Routledge/Taylor & Francis Group.

Haen, C., & Thomas, N.K. (2018). Holding history: Undoing racial unconsciousness in groups. *International Journal of Group Psychotherapy*, 68, 498–520.

Haldeman, D. (2011). Diversity training: Multiple minority awareness. In R. Nettles, & R. Balter (Eds.), *Multiple minority identities: Applications for research, practice and training* (pp. 231–247). New York: Springer.

Haldeman, D. (2012). Guidelines for psychological practice with lesbian, gay, and bisexual clients. *American Psychologist*, 67(1), 10–42.

Hansen, K., Beecher, M., Boardman, R.D., Burlingame, G.M., & Griner, D. (2017). Practice-based evidence can help! Using clinician-friendly process and outcome measures to enhance your groups. Open session presented at the 2017 AGPA annual meeting, New York City. Audiotape available through AGPA store.

Harrison, R.L., & Westwood, M.J. (2009). Preventing vicarious traumatization of mental health therapists: Identifying protective practices. *Psychotherapy: Theory, Research, Practice, Training*, 46(2), 203–213.

Hartman, J.J., & Gibbard, G.S. (1974). Anxiety, boundary evolution and social change. In G. S. Gibbard, J.J. Hartmna, & R.D. Mann (Eds.), *Analysis of groups*, (pp. 154–176). San Francisco, CA: Jossey-Bass.

Hasson, U. (2016, June 3). This is your brain on communication: Uri Hasson [Video file]. Retrieved from www.youtube.com/watch?v=FDhlOovaGrI

Hasson, U., Ghazanfar, A.A., Galantucci, B., Garrod, S., & Keysers, C. (2012). Brain-to-Brain coupling: A mechanism for creating and sharing a social world. *Trends in Cognitive Sciences*, 16(2), 114–121.

Hayes, J.A., Gelso, C.J., & Hummel, A.M. (2011). Managing countertransference. *Psychotherapy, 48*, 88–97.

Hayes, J.A., Nelson, D., & Fauth, J. (2015). Countertransference in successful and unsuccessful cases of psychotherapy. *Psychotherapy, 52*, 127–134.

Hays, D.G., Arredondo, P., Gladding, S.T., & Toporek, R.L. (2010). Integrating social justice in group work: The new decade. *The Journal for Specialists in Group Work, 35*(2), 177–206.

Hays, P.A. (2016). *Addressing cultural complexities in practice: Assessment, diagnosis, and therapy* (3rd ed.). Washington, D.C: American Psychological Association.

Helms, J.E., Malone, L.S., Henze, K., Satiani, K., Perry, J., & Warren, A. (2003). First annual diversity challenge: How to survive teaching courses on race and culture. *Journal of Multicultural Counseling and Development, 31*, 3–11.

Hewitt, P.L., Mikail, S.F., Flett, G.L., & Dang, S.S. (2018). Specific formulation feedback in dynamic-relational group psychotherapy of perfectionism. *Psychotherapy, 55*, 179–185.

Holmes, D.E. (2012). Multicultural competence: A practitioner-scholar's reflections on its reality and its stubborn and longstanding elusiveness. *Register Report*, 1–18. Retrieved from www.national register.org/pub/the-national-register-report-pub/spring-2012-issue/multicultural-competence-a-practitioner-scholars-reflections-on-its-reality-and-its-stubborn-and-longstanding-elusiveness/

Hook, J.N., Davis, D.E., Owen, J., Worthington, Jr, E.L., & Utsey, S.O. (2013). Cultural humility: Measuring openness to culturally diverse clients. *Journal of Counseling Psychology, 60*(3), 353.

Hopper, E. (2003). *Traumatic experience in the unconscious life of groups: The fourth basic assumption: Incohesion: Aggregation/massification or (ba)I:A/M.* London: Jessica Kinglsey.

Hopper, E. (2007) Moral corruption and ethical dilemmas in professional life. Paper presented at the 64th Annual Meeting of the American Group Psychotherapy Association, Austin, TX.

Hornsey, M., Olsen, S., Barlow, F.K., & Oei, T.P.S. (2012). Testing a single-item visual analogue scale as a proxy for cohesiveness in group psychotherapy. *Group Dynamics, 16*, 80–90.

Horwitz, L. (1983). Projective identification in dyads and groups. *International Journal of Group Psychotherapy, 33*, 259–279.

Horwitz, L. (2014). *Listening with the fourth ear: Unconscious dynamics in analytic group psychotherapy.* London: Karnac.

Hsiung, R.C. (2002). *E-therapy: Case studies, guiding principles, and the clinical potential of the Internet.* New York: Norton.

Iacoboni, M. (2008). *Mirroring people: The new science of how we connect with others.* New York: Farrar, Straus & Giroux.

Iacoboni, M. (2013, August 1). 'Are we wired for empathy?' [Video file]. Retrieved from www.youtube.com/watch?v=pXTZLTJbU8g

Imel, Z., Baldwin, S., Bonus, K., & MacCoon, D. (2008). Beyond the individual: Group effects in mindfulness-based stress reduction. *Psychotherapy Research, 18*(6), 735–742.

Jaffee v. Redmond. (2017). Retrieved from https://en.wikipedia.org/wiki/Jaffee_v._Redmond

Janis, I.L. (1972). *Victims of groupthink.* Boston, MA: Houghton Mifflin.

Jensen, D.R., Abbott, M.K., Beecher, M.E., Griner, D., Golightly, T.R., & Cannon, J.A.N. (2012). Taking the pulse of the group: The utilization of practice-based evidence in group psychotherapy. *Professional Psychology: Research and Practice, 43*, 388–394.

Jensen, H.H., Mortensen, E.L., & Lotz, M. (2014). Drop-out from a psychodynamic group psychotherapy outpatient unit. *Nordic Journal of Psychiatry, 68*(8), 594–604.

Johnson, J., Burlingame, G.M., Olsen, D., Davies, R., & Gleave, R.L. (2005). Group climate, cohesion, alliance, and empathy in group psychotherapy: Multilevel structural equation models. *Journal of Counseling Psychology, 52*, 310–321.

Joyce, A.S., MacNair-Semands, R., Tasca, G.A., & Ogrodniczuk, J.S. (2011). Factor structure and validity of the therapeutic factors inventory – Short form. *Group Dynamics: Theory, Research, and Practice, 15*, 201–219.

Jun, H. (2018). *Social justice, multicultural counseling, and practice: Beyond a conventional approach*. New York: Springer.

Kabat-Zinn, J. (1994). *Wherever you go, there you are: Mindfulness meditation in everyday life*. New York: Hyperion.

Kabat-Zinn, J. (2011). Some reflections on the origins of MBSR, skillful means, and the trouble with maps. *Contemporary Buddhism, 12*(01), 281–306.

Kaklauskas, F.J., & Olson, E.A. (2008). Large group process: Grounding Buddhist and psychological theory in experience. In F.J. Kaklauskas, S. Nimanheminda, L. Hoffman, & M.S. Jack (Eds.), *Brilliant sanity: Buddhist approaches to psychotherapy* (pp. 133–160). Colorado Springs, CO: University of the Rockies Press.

Kaplan, S.A. (2017). The art of the sell: Marketing groups. In M.D. Ribeiro, J. Gross, & M.M. Turner (Eds.), *The college counselor's guide to group psychotherapy* (pp. 117–130). New York City: Routledge/Taylor & Francis Group.

Kealy, D., Ogrodniczuk, J.S., Piper, W.E., & Sierra-Hernandez, C.A. (2016). When it is not a good fit: Clinical errors in patient selection and group composition in group psychotherapy. *Psychotherapy, 53*(3), 308–313.

Kegel, A.F., & Flückiger, C. (2015). Predicting psychotherapy dropouts: A multilevel approach. *Clinical Psychology & Psychotherapy, 22*(5), 377–386.

Kernberg, O. (1975). Systems approach to priority setting of interventions in groups. *International Journal of Group Psychotherapy, 25*, 251–275.

Kernberg, O. (1980). Regression in groups. In O. Kernberg (Eds.), *Internal world and external reality: Object relations theory applied*. New York: Jason Aronson.

Killian, K.D. (2008). Helping till it hurts? A multimethod study of compassion fatigue, burnout, and self-care in clinicians working with trauma survivors. *Traumatology, 14*(2), 32–44.

Kitchener, K.S. (1984). Intuition, critical evaluation and ethical principles: The foundation for ethical decisions in counseling psychology. *The Counseling Psychologist, 12*(3), 43–55.

Kitchener, K.S., & Anderson, S.K. (2011). *Foundations of ethical practice, research, and teaching in psychology and counseling*. New York: Routledge/Taylor & Francis Group.

Kivlighan, Jr., D.M., (2014). Three important clinical processes in individual and group interpersonal psychotherapy sessions. *Psychotherapy, 51*, 20–24.

Kivlighan, Jr., D.M., & Holmes, S.E. (2004). The importance of therapeutic factors: A typology of therapeutic factors studies. In J.L. DeLucia-Waack, D.A. Gerrity, C.R. Kalodner, & M.T. Riva (Eds.), *Handbook of group counseling and psychotherapy* (pp. 23–36). Thousand Oaks, CA: Sage.

Kivlighan, Jr., D.M., & Kivlighan, D.M.III (2014). Therapeutic factors. In J.L. DeLucia-Waack, D.A. Kalodner, & M.T. Riva (Eds.), *Handbook of group counseling and psychotherapy* (2nd ed., p. 46). Thousand Oaks, CA: Sage.

Kivlighan, Jr., D.M., Li, X., & Gillis, L. (2015). Do I fit with my group? Within-member and within-group fit with the group in engaged group climate and group members feeling involved and valued. *Group Dynamics, 19*, 106–121.

Kivlighan, Jr., D.M., Lo Coco, G., Gullo, S., Pazzagli, C., & Mazzeschi, C. (2017). Attachment anxiety and attachment avoidance: Members' attachment fit with their group and group relationships. *International Journal of Group Psychotherapy, 67*(2), 223–239.

Kivlighan, Jr., D.M., Lo Coco, G., Oieni, V., Gullo, S., Pazzagli, C., & Mazzeschi, C. (2017). All bonds are not the same: A response surface analysis of the perceptions of positive bonding relationships in therapy groups. *Group Dynamics, 21*, 159–177.

Kivlighan, Jr, D.M., London, K., & Miles, J.R. (2012). Are two heads better than one? The relationship between number of group leaders and group members, and group climate and group member benefit from therapy. *Group Dynamics: Theory, Research, and Practice, 16*(1), 1–13.

Kivlighan, Jr., D.M., Markin, R.D., Stahl, J.V., & Salahuddin, N.M. (2007). Changes in the ways that group trainees structure their knowledge of group members with training. *Group Dynamics: Theory, Research, and Practice, 11*, 176–186.

Kivlighan, Jr., D.M., Miles, J.R., & Paquin, J.D. (2010). Therapeutic factors in group counseling: Asking new questions. In R. Conyne (Ed.), *Oxford handbook of group counseling* (pp. 121–136). New York: Oxford University Press.

Kivlighan, Jr, D.M., & Tibbits, B.M. (2012). Silence is mean and other misconceptions of group counseling trainees: Identifying errors of commission and omission in trainees' knowledge structures. *Group Dynamics: Theory, Research, and Practice*, 16(1), 14–34.

Kivlighan, D.M.I.I.I., & Chapman, N.A. (2018). Extending the multicultural orientation (MCO) framework to group psychotherapy: A clinical illustration. *Psychotherapy*, 55, 39–44.

Klein, R.H., Bernard, H.S., & Singer, D.L. (Eds.) (1992). *Handbook of contemporary group psychotherapy: Contributions from object relations, self psychology, and social systems theories* (pp. 27–54). Madison, CT: International University Press.

Kleinberg, J.L. (2015). *The Wiley-Blackwell handbook of group psychotherapy*. New York: Wiley.

Knapp, S., & VandeCreek, L. (2007). When values of different cultures conflict: Ethical decision making in a multicultural context. *Professional Psychology: Research and Practice*, 38(6), 660–666.

Knapp, S.J., VandeCreek, L.D., & Fingerhut, R. (2017). *Practical ethics for psychologists: A positive approach* (3rd ed.). Washington, DC: American Psychological Association.

Knauss, L.K. (2006). Ethical issues in recordkeeping in group psychotherapy. *International Journal of Group Psychotherapy*, 56(4), 415–430.

Kohout, J. L., Pate, W. E. II, & Maton, K. I. (2014). An updated profile of ethnic minority psychology: A pipeline perspective. In F. T. L. Leong, L. Comas-Díaz, G. C. Nagayama Hall, V. C. McLoyd, & J. E. Trimble (Eds.), *APA handbook of multicultural psychology, Vol. 1. Theory and research* (pp. 19–42). Washington, DC: American Psychological Association.

Koocher, G.P., & Keith-Spiegel, P. (2008). *Ethics in psychology and the mental health professions: Standards and cases*. Oxford University Press.

Kozan, S., & Blustein, D.L. (2018). Implementing social change: A qualitative analysis of counseling psychologists' engagement in advocacy. *The Counseling Psychologist*, 46(2), 154–189.

Krogel, J., Burlingame, G., Chapman, C., Renshaw, T., Gleave, R., Beecher, M., & MacNair-Semands, R. (2013). The Group Questionnaire: A clinical and empirically derived measure of group relationship. *Psychotherapy Research*, 23, 344–354.

Lambert, M. (2012). Helping clinicians to use and learn from research-based systems: The OQ-analyst. *Psychotherapy*, 49, 109–114.

Lawrence, W.G., Bain, A., & Gould, L. (1996). The fifth basic assumption. *Free Associations*, 6, 28–55.

Lawson, D.M. (2010). Comparing cognitive behavioral therapy and integrated cognitive behavioral therapy/psychodynamic therapy in group treatment for partner violent men. *Psychotherapy*, 47, 122–133.

Le Bon, G. (1960). *The Crowd: A Study of the Popular Mind (1895)*. New York: Viking.

Leong, F.T., & Kalibatseva, Z. (2011). Cross-cultural barriers to mental health services in the United States. *Cerebrum*, 2011, 5.

Leong, F.T.L., Comas-Díaz, L.E., Nagayama Hall, G.C., McLoyd, V.C., & Trimble, J.E. (2014). *APA handbook of multicultural psychology*. Washington, D.C: American Psychological Association.

Lese, K.P., & MacNair-Semands, R.R. (2000). The therapeutic factors inventory: Development of a scale. *Group*, 24, 303–317.

Leszcz, M. (2017a). *A relational approach to evidence-based group psychotherapy (audio recording), Louis R. Ormont lecture*. New York: American Group Psychotherapy Association.

Leszcz, M. (2017b). How understanding attachment enhances group therapist effectiveness. *International Journal of Group Psychotherapy*, 67(2), 280–287.

Leszcz, M. (2018). The evidence-based group psychotherapist. *Psychoanalytic Inquiry*, 38, 285–298.

Leszcz, M., & Kobos, J.C. (2008). Evidence based group psychotherapy: Using AGPA's practice guidelines to enhance clinical effectiveness. *Journal of Clinical Psychology*, 64(11), 1238–1260.

Levine, R. (2011). Progressing while regressing in relationships. *International Journal of Group Psychotherapy*, 61, 621–643.

Lewin, K. (1947). Group decision and social change. *Readings in Social Psychology*, 3(1), 197–211.

Lewin, K. (1951). Problems of research in social psychology. In D. Cartwright (Ed.), *Field theory in social science: Selected theoretical papers* (pp. 155–169). New York: Harper & Row.

Li, X., Kivlighan, Jr., D.M., & Gold, P.B. (2015). Errors of commission and omission in novice group counseling trainees' knowledge structures of group counseling situations. *Journal of Counseling Psychology*, 62, 159–172.

Lieberman, M.A., Yalom, I.D., & Miles, M.B. (1973). *Encounter groups: First facts.* New York: Basic Books.

Linehan, M. (2012). Back from the Edge. Retrieved from www.youtube.com/watch?v=967Ckat7f98

Linehan, M.M., & Wilks, C.R. (2015). The course and evolution of dialectical behavior therapy. *American Journal of Psychotherapy*, 69(2), 97–110.

Little, J., Hodari, K., Lavender, J., & Berg, A. (2008). Come as you are: Harm reduction drop-in groups for multi–diagnosed drug users. *Journal of Groups in Addiction and Recovery*, 3(3–4), 161–192.

Lo Coco, G., Gullo, S., Di Fratello, C., Giordano, C., & Kivlighan, Jr, D.M. (2016). Group relationships in early and late sessions and improvement in interpersonal problems. *Journal of Counseling Psychology*, 63(4), 419.

Lo Coco, G., Gullo, S., & Kivlighan, Jr., D.M. (2012). Examining patients' and other group members' agreement about their alliance to the group as a whole and changes in patient symptoms using response surface analysis. *Journal of Counseling Psychology*, 59, 197–207.

Lorentzen, S., Fjeldstad, A., Ruud, T., Marble, A., Klungsøyr, O., Ulberg, R., & Høglend, P.A. (2015). The effectiveness of short-and long-term psychodynamic group psychotherapy on self-concept: Three years follow-up of a randomized clinical trial. *International Journal of Group Psychotherapy*, 65(3), 362–385.

Luke, M., & Hackney, H. (2007). Group coleadership: A critical review. *Counselor Education and Supervision*, 46(4), 280–293.

MacIntosh, P. (1989). White privilege: Unpacking the invisible knapsack. *Peace and Freedom*, July/August, 10–12.

MacKenzie, K.R. (1983). The clinical application of a group climate measure. In R.R. Dies, & K.R. MacKenzie (Eds.), *Advances in group psychotherapy: Integrating research and practice* (pp. 159–170). Madison, CT: International Universities Press.

MacKenzie, K.R. (1997). Clinical application of group development ideas. *Group Dynamics*, 1, 275–287.

MacLean, P.D. (1990). *The triune brain in evolution: Role in paleocerebral functions.* New York: Springer Science & Business Media.

MacNair-Semands, R.R. (2002). Predicting attendance and expectations for group therapy. *Group Dynamics: Theory, Research, and Practice*, 6(3), 219–228.

MacNair-Semands, R.R. (2005). *Ethics in group psychotherapy.* New York: American Group Psychotherapy Association.

MacNair-Semands, R.R. (2007). Attending to the spirit of social justice as an ethical approach in group therapy. *International Journal of Group Psychotherapy*, 57(1), 61–66.

MacNair-Semands, R.R., Ogrodniczuk, J.S., & Joyce, A.S. (2010). Structure and initial validation of a short form of the therapeutic factors inventory. *International Journal of Group Psychotherapy*, 60, 245–281.

Malan, D.H., Balfour, F.H., Hood, V.G., & Shooter, A.M. (1976). Group psychotherapy: A long-term follow-up study. *Archives of General Psychiatry*, 33, 1303–1315.

Malcolm, J. (1982). *Psychoanalysis: The impossible profession.* New York: Vintage.

Mangione, L., Forti, R., & Iacuzzi, C.M. (2007). Ethics and endings in group psychotherapy: Saying good–Bye and saying it well. *International Journal of Group Psychotherapy*, 57(1), 25–40.

Markin, R.D. (2009). Exploring a method for transference assessment in group therapy using the social relations model: Suggestions for future research. *Journal for Specialists in Group Work, 34* (4), 307–325.

Markin, R.D., & Kivlighan, Jr., D.M. (2008). Central relationship themes in group psychotherapy: A social relations model analysis of transference. *Group Dynamics: Theory, Research, and Practice, 12*(4), 290–306.

Marmarosh, C.L. (2018). Introduction to special issue: Feedback in group psychotherapy. *Psychotherapy, 55,* 101–104.

Marmarosh, C.L., Markin, R.D., & Spiegel, E.B. (2013). Processes that foster secure attachment in group psychotherapy. In C.L. Marmarosh, R.D. Markin, & E.B. Spiegel (Eds.), *Attachment in group psychotherapy* (pp. 97–122). Washington, D.C: American Psychological Association.

Marsh, L.C. (1935). Group therapy and the psychiatric clinic. *The Journal of Nervous and Mental Disease, 82*(4), 381–393.

McAuliffe, G., & Eriksen, K. (2010). *Handbook of counselor preparation: Constructivist, developmental, and experiential approaches.* Thousand Oaks, CA: Sage.

McClanahan, K. (2014) Can confidentiality be maintained in group therapy? Retrieved from http://nationalpsychologist.com/2014/07/can-confidentiality-be-maintained-in-group-therapy/102566.html

McDougall, W. (1908). *Introduction to social psychology.* London: Methuen & Co.

McDougall, W. (1920). *The group mind: A sketch of the principles of collective psychology, with some attempt to apply them to the interpretation of national life and character.* London: GP Putnam's Sons.

McGilchrist, I. (2009). *The master and his emissary: The divided brain and the making of the western world.* New Haven, CT & London: Yale University Press.

McKensey, A., & Sullivan, L. (2016). Balint groups—Helping trainee psychiatrists make even better use of themselves. *Australasian Psychiatry, 24,* 84–87.

Mead, M. (1951). Group psychotherapy in the light of social anthropology. *International Journal of Group Psychotherapy, 1*(3), 193–199.

Menter, P. (2018). Training residents in empathic attunement and emotional process: Four group models. Presented at AGPAConnect 2018. Available at http://member.agpa.org/imis/agpa/store

Miles, J.R., & Kivlighan, Jr, D.M. (2010). Co-leader similarity and group climate in group interventions: Testing the co-leadership, team cognition-team diversity model. *Group Dynamics: Theory, Research, and Practice, 14*(2), 114–122.

Miles, J.R., & Paquin, J.D. (2014). Best practices in group counseling and psychotherapy research. In J.L. DeLucia-Waack, C.R. Kalodner, & M.T. Riva (Eds.), *The handbook of group counseling and psychotherapy* (2nd ed.). (pp. 178–192). Thousand Oaks, CA: Sage.

Miller, E. (Ed.) (1976). *Task and organization.* New York: Wiley.

Miller, E.J., & Rice, A.K. (1967). *Systems of organization.* London: Tavistock.

Miller-Bottome, M., Safran, J.D., Talia, A., & Muran, J.C. (2018). Therapeutic alliance, alliance ruptures, and the process of resolution. *Psychoanalytic Psychology, 35*(2), 175–183.

Minieri, A.M., Reese, R.J., Miserocchi, K.M., & Pascale-Hague, D. (2015). Using client feedback in training of future counseling psychologists: An evidence-based and social justice practice. *Counselling Psychology Quarterly, 28*(3), 305–323.

Mizock, L., & Page, K.V. (2016). Evaluating the ally role: Contributions, limitations, and the activist position in counseling and psychology. *Journal for Social Action in Counseling & Psychology, 8*(1), 17–33.

Morland, L.A., Greene, C.J., Rosen, C.S., Foy, D., Reilly, P., Shore, J., He, Q., & Frueh, B.C. (2010). Telemedicine for anger management therapy in a rural population of combat veterans with posttraumatic stress disorder: A randomized noninferiority trial. *Journal of Clinical Psychiatry, 71,* 850–863.

Motherwell, L., & Shay, J. J. (2014). *Complex dilemmas in group therapy: Pathways to resolution* (2nd ed.). New York: Routledge/Taylor & Francis Group.

Murphy, L., Leszcz, M., Collings, A.K., & Salvendy, J. (1996). Some observations on the subjective experience of neophyte group therapy trainees. *International Journal of Group Psychotherapy*, 46(4), 543–552.

Nadal, K.L. (2017). "Let's get in formation": On becoming a psychologist–Activist in the 21st century. *American Psychologist*, 72(9), 935.

Nettles, R., & Balter, R. (Eds.) (2012). *Multiple minority identities: Applications for practice, research, and training*. New York: Springer.

Neuropsychotherapy. (2016, August 22). The triune brain in 60 seconds [Video file]. Retrieved from www.youtube.com/watch?v=7uVSGbnEHOg

Nitsun, M. (1996). *The anti-group: Destructive forces in the group and their creative potential*. London: Routledge/Taylor & Francis Group.

Nitsun, M. (2000). The future of the group. *International Journal of Group Psychotherapy*, 50, 455–472.

Nitsun, M. (2014). *Beyond the anti-group: Survival and transformation*. London: Routledge/Taylor & Francis Group.

Norcross, J.C., & Guy, J.D. (2007). Psychotherapist self-care checklist. In J.C. Norcross, & J.D. Guy, *Leaving it at the office: A guide to psychotherapist self-care*. New York: Guilford. Retrieved from: www.researchgate.net/publication/300580928_Psychotherapist_Self-Care_Checklist

Ogden, T. (1979). On projective identification. *International Journal of Psychoanalysis*, 60, 357–373.

Ogrodniczuk, J.S., Joyce, A.S., & Piper, W.E. (2005). Strategies for reducing patient-initiated premature termination of psychotherapy. *Harvard Review of Psychiatry*, 13(2), 57–70.

Ormont, L. (1992). *The group therapy experience: From theory to practice*. New York: St. Martins.

Owen, J., Tao, K.W., Imel, Z.E., Wampold, B.E., & Rodolfa, E. (2014). Addressing racial and ethnic microaggressions in therapy. *Professional Psychology: Research and Practice*, 45(4), 283–290.

Paniagua, F.A. (2013). *Assessing and treating culturally diverse clients: A practical guide*. Thousand Oaks, CA: Sage.

Panksepp, J. (2014, January 13). The science of emotions. [Video file]. Retrieved from www.youtube.com/watch?v=65e2qScV_K8

Panksepp, J., & Biven, L. (2012). *The archaeology of mind: Neuroevolutionary origins of human emotions*. New York: Norton.

Paquin, J.D. (2017). Delivering the treatment so that the therapy occurs: Enhancing the effectiveness of time-limited, manualized group treatments. *International Journal of Group Psychotherapy*, 67 (sup1), S141-S153.

Paquin, J.D., & Kivlighan, Jr, D.M. (2016). All absences are not the same: What happens to the group climate when someone is absent from group? *International Journal of Group Psychotherapy*, 66(4), 506–525.

Pascual-Leone, A., & Andreescu, C. (2013). Repurposing process measures to train psychotherapists: Training outcomes using a new approach. *Counseling and Psychotherapy Research*, 13, 210–219.

Pease, B., Vreugdenhil, A., & Stanford, S. (Eds.) (2017). *Critical ethics of care in social work: Transforming the politics and practices of caring*. London: Routledge/Taylor & Francis Group.

Pennsylvania State University (producer). (2016). The Milgram experiment 1962 full documentary. Retrieved from www.youtube.com/watch?v=wdUu3u9Web4

Pierce, C.M. (1974). Psychiatric problems of the black minority. In S. Arieti (Ed.), *American handbook of psychiatry* (pp. 512–523). New York: Basic Books.

Piet, J., & Hougaard, E. (2011). The effect of mindfulness-based cognitive therapy for prevention of relapse in recurrent major depressive disorder: A systematic review and meta-analysis. *Clinical Psychology Review*, 31, 1032–1040.

Piper, W., Ogrodniczuk, J., Joyce, A., & Weideman, R. (2011). *Short-term group therapies for complicated grief.* Washington, D.C: American Psychological Association.

Pope, K.S., & Vasquez, M.J. (2016a). Creating and using strategies for self care. In K.S. Pope, & M.J. Vasquez (Eds.), *Ethics in psychotherapy and counseling: A practical guide* (pp. 114–122). Hoboken, NJ: John Wiley & Sons.

Pope, K.S., & Vasquez, M.J. (2016b). Sexual attraction to patients, therapist. In K.S. Pope, & M.J. Vasquez (Eds.), *Ethics in psychotherapy and counseling: A practical guide* (pp. 225–251). Hoboken, NJ: John Wiley & Sons.

Porges, S.W. (2011). *The polyvagal theory: Neurophysiological foundations of emotions, attachment, communication, and self-regulation.* New York: Norton.

Porges, S.W (2014). Human nature and early experience. Retrieved from www.youtube.com /watch?v=SRTkkYjQ_HU&t=639s

Powdermaker, F.B., & Frank, J.D. (1953). Group psychotherapy: studies in methodology of research and therapy. Report of a group psychotherapy research project of the US Veterans Administration.

Pratt, J. H. (1907a). The organization of tuberculosis classes. *Medical Communications of the Massachusetts Medical Society, 20,* 475–492.

Pratt, J. H. (1907b). *The class method of treating consumption in the homes of the poor. Journal of the American Medical Association, XLIX*(9), 755–759.

Racker, H. (1968). *Transference and countertransference.* New York: International Universities Press.

Ratts, M.J., Singh, A.A., Nassar-McMillian, S., Butler, S.K., & McCullough, J.R. (2016). Multicultural and social justice counseling competencies: Guidelines for the counseling profession. *Journal of Multicultural Counseling and Development, 44,* 28–48.

Ribeiro, M.D., & Turner, M.M. (2017). Racial and social justice implications on the practice of group psychotherapy. In M.D. Ribeiro, J. Gross, & M.M. Turner (Eds.), *The college counselor's guide to group psychotherapy* (pp. 36–55). New York City: Routledge/Taylor & Francis Group.

Rice, A.K. (1969). Individual, group and intergroup processes. *Human Relations, 22,* 565–584.

Rioch, M.J. (1970). The work of Wilfred Bion on groups. *Psychiatry, 33,* 56–66.

Riva, M.T. (2014). Supervision of group leaders. In J.L. DeLucia-Waack, D.A. Gerrity, C. R. Kalodner, & M.T. Riva (Eds.), *Handbook of group counseling and psychotherapy* (2nd ed.) (pp. 146–158). Thousand Oaks, CA: Sage.

Rivera, M., & Darke, J.L. (2012). Integrating empirically supported therapies for treating personality disorders: A synthesis of psychodynamic and cognitive-behavioral group treatments. *International Journal of Group Psychotherapy, 62,* 501–529.

Roth, A., & Fonagy, P. (2013). *What works for whom: A critical review of psychotherapy research* (2nd ed.). New York: Guilford.

Roth, B.E. (2009). Some problems with treatment: Destructive enactments in combined therapy. *International Journal of Group Psychotherapy, 59*(1), 47–66.

Rowe, M. (1974). Saturn's Rings: A study of the minutiae of sexism which maintain discrimination and inhibit affirmative action results in corporations and non-profit institutions. In *Graduate and Professional Education of Women* (pp. 1–9). Washington, DC: American Association of University Women.

Rubenfeld, S. (2001). Group therapy and complexity theory. *International Journal of Group Psychotherapy, 51*(4), 449–471.

Rutan, S., Stone, W., & Shay, J. (2014). *Psychodynamic group psychotherapy* (5th ed.). New York: Guilford.

Safran, J.D., Muran, J.C., & Eubanks-Carter, C. (2011). Repairing alliance ruptures. In J. C. Norcross (Ed.), *Psychotherapy relationships that work: Evidence-based responsiveness* (2nd ed.) (pp. 224–238). New York: Oxford University Press.

Scharff, J.S., & Scharff, D.E. (2017). Group affective learning in training for psychotherapy and psychoanalysis. *The International Journal of Psychoanalysis, 98*(6), 1619–1639.

Scheidlinger, S. (1974). On the concept of the "Mother-Group". *International Journal of Group Psychotherapy, 24*, 417–428.

Scheidlinger, S. (1982). Presidential address: On scapegoating in group psychotherapy. *International Journal of Group Psychotherapy, 32*, 131–143.

Scheidlinger, S. (1994). An overview of nine decades of group psychotherapy. *Hospital and Community Psychiatry, 45*, 217–225. Available at http://ps.psychiatryonline.org/doi/pdfplus/10.1176/ps.45.3.217

Scheidlinger, S. (2000). The group psychotherapy movement at the millennium: Some historical perspectives. *International Journal of Group Psychotherapy, 50*(3), 315–339.

Schermer, V. (2012). Group-as-a-whole and complexity theories: Areas of convergence. *Group Analysis, 45*, 275–288.

Schneider, K. (2015). Presence: The core contextual factor of effective psychotherapy. *Existential Analysis, 26*(2), 304–313.

Schore, A. (2002). Clinical implications of a psychoneurobiological model of projective identification. In S. Alhanati (Ed.), *Primitive mental states, Vol. II: Psychobiological and psychoanalytic perspectives on early trauma and personality development* (pp. 1–65). London: Karnac.

Schore, A.N. (2003). *Affect regulation and repair of the self*. New York: Norton.

Schore, A.N. (2010). The right brain implicit self: A central mechanism of the psychotherapy change process. In J. Petrucelli (Ed.), *Knowing, not-knowing and sort-of-knowing: Psychoanalysis and the experience of uncertainty* (pp. 177–202). London: Karnac.

Schore, A.N. (2012). *The science or the art of psychotherapy*. New York: Norton.

Schutz, W. (1958). *FIRO: A three-dimensional theory of interpersonal behavior*. New York: Rinehart.

Segal, H. (2006). *Dream, phantasy and art*. London: Routledge/Taylor & Francis Group.

Segal, Z.V., Williams, J.M.G., & Teasdale, J.D. (2001). *Mindfulness-based cognitive therapy for depression: A new approach to preventing relapse*. New York: Guilford.

Shapiro, E.L., & Gans, J.S. (2008). The courage of the group therapist. *International Journal of Group Psychotherapy, 58*(3), 345–361.

Shay, J. (2011). Projective identification simplified: Recruiting your shadow. *International Journal of Group Psychotherapy, 61*, 238–261.

Shay, J., & Motherwell, L. (2014). Why do we continue to do this work? The power of the group. In L. Motherwell, & J. Shay (Eds.), *Complex dilemmas in group therapy: Pathways to resolution* (2nd ed.). New York: Routledge.

Shehadeh, M.H., Heim, E., Chowdhary, N., Maercker, A., & Albanese, E. (2016). Cultural adaptation of minimally guided interventions for common mental disorders: A systematic review and meta-analysis. *JMIR Mental Health, 3*(3), e44.

Siegel, D.J. (2000). *The developing mind*. New York: Guilford.

Siegel, D.J. (2007). *The mindful brain*. New York: Norton.

Siegel, D.J. (2009). On integrating the two hemispheres of our brains. Retrieved from www.youtube.com/watch?v=xPjhfUVgvOQ

Siegel, D.J. (2010). Commentary on "Integrating interpersonal neurobiology with group psychotherapy": Reflections on mind, brain, and relationships in group psychotherapy. *International Journal of Group Psychotherapy, 60*(4), 483–485.

Siegel, D.J. (2012). *The developing mind: How relationships and the brain interact to shape who we are*. New York: Guilford.

Siegel, D.J. (2012, May 2). Mindfulness and neural integration. [Video file]. Retrieved from www.youtube.com/watch?v=LiyaSr5aeho

Siegel, D.J. (2013, April 16). Mindfulness. Brain hand model. [Video file]. Retrieved from www.youtube.com/watch?v=vESKrzvgA40

Siegel, D.J. (2013). *The mindful therapist: A clinician's guide to mindsight and neural integration*. Norton: New York City.

Sileo, F.J., & Kopala, M. (1993). An A-B-C-D-E worksheet for promoting beneficence when considering ethical issues. *Counseling and Values*, 37(2), 89–95.

Singer, D., Astrachan, B., Gould, L., & Klein, R. (1975). Boundary management in psychological work with groups. *Journal of Applied Behavioral Science*, 11, 137–176.

Singh, A.A., Merchant, N., Skudrzyk, B., & Ingene, D. (2012). Association for specialists in group work: Multicultural and social JUSTICE competence principles for group workers. *The Journal for Specialists in Group Work*, 37(4), 312–325.

Slone, N., Reese, R., Mathews-Duval, S., & Kodet, J. (2015). Evaluating the efficacy of client feedback in group psychotherapy. *Group Dynamics*, 19, 122–136.

Smith, B. D. (2007). Sifting through trauma: Compassion fatigue and HIV/AIDS. *Clinical Social Work Journal*, 35(3), 193–198.

Smith, P. (2017). How to manage compassion fatigue in caregiving | TEDxSanJuanIsland Talk. [video] Retrieved from www.youtube.com/watch?v=7keppA8XRas

Sochting, I. (2014). *Cognitive behavioral group therapy: Challenges and opportunities*. New York: Wiley.

Solomon, A., (2013) Depression: The secret we share. [Video file] Retrieved from: www.ted.com/talks/andrew_solomon_depression_the_secret_we_share

Springmann, R. (1976). Fragmentation in large groups. *Group Analysis*, 9, 185–188.

Stadler, H.A. (1986). Making hard choices: Clarifying controversial ethical issues. *Counseling and Human Development*, 19, 1–10.

Steffen, J. (2015). A paradigm shift from safe space to brave space: Dialogues in multicultural group therapy. *The Group Psychologist*, 25(1), 6–8.

Steinberg, P.I., & Ogrodniczuk, J.S. (2010). Hatred and fear: Projective identification in group psychotherapy. *Psychodynamic Practice*, 16(2), 201–205.

Steiner, A. (2011). The therapist's professional will: A backup plan every clinician needs. *Group*, 33–40.

Stevens, F.L., & Abernethy, A.D. (2018). Neuroscience and racism: The power of groups for overcoming implicit bias. *International Journal of Group Psychotherapy*, 68, 561–584.

Stockton, R., Morran, D.K., & Chang, S.-H. (2013). An overview of current research and best practices for training beginning group leaders. In J.L. DeLucia-Waack, D.A. Gerrity, C. R. Kalodner, & M.T. Riva (Eds.), *Handbook of group counseling and psychotherapy* (2nd ed.). (pp. 133–145). Thousand Oaks, CA: Sage.

Stone, W. (Ed.) (2010). Training in group psychotherapy (Special Issue). *Group*, 34(4).

Strauss, B., Burlingame, G.M., & Bormann, B. (2008). Using the CORE-R battery in group psychotherapy. *Journal of Clinical Psychology*, 64, 1225–1237.

Sue, D.W. (Ed.) (2010). *Microaggressions and marginality: Manifestation, dynamics, and impact*. New York: John Wiley.

Sue, D.W. (2013). Race talk: The psychology of racial dialogues. *American Psychologist*, 68(8), 663–672.

Sue, D.W. (2016). *Race talk and the conspiracy of silence: Understanding and facilitating difficult dialogues on race*. New York: John Wiley.

Sue, D.W., Arredondo, P., & McDavis, R.J. (1992). Multicultural counseling competencies and standards: A call to the profession. *Journal of Counseling and Development*, 70, 477–486.

Sue, D.W., Bernier, J.E., Durran, A., Feinberg, L., Pedersen, P., Smith, E.J., & Vasquez-Nuttall, E. (1982). Position paper: Cross-cultural counseling competencies. *The Counseling Psychologist*, 10, 45–52.

Sue, D.W., & Constantine, M.G. (2007). Racial microaggressions as instigators of difficult dialogues on race: Implications for student affairs educators and students. *College Student Affairs Journal*, 26(2), 136–143.

Sue, D.W., Gallardo, M.E., & Neville, H.A. (2013). *Case studies in multicultural counseling and therapy*. Hoboken, NJ: John Wiley.

Sue, D.W., & Sue, D. (2012). *Counseling the culturally diverse: Theory and practice*.

Sullivan, N., Mitchell, L., Goodman, D., Lang, N.C., & Mesbur, E.S. (2013). *Social work with groups: Social justice through personal, community, and societal change*. London: Routledge/Taylor & Francis Group.

Tao, K.W., Owen, J., Pace, B. T., & Imel, Z. E. (2015). A meta-analysis of multicultural competencies and psychotherapy process and outcome. *Journal of Counseling Psychology, 62*(3), 337–350.

Tasca, G.A., Cabrera, C., Kristjansson, E., MacNair-Semands, R., Joyce, A.S., & Ogrodniczuk, J.S. (2016). The therapeutic factors inventory-8: Using item response theory to create a brief scale for continuous process monitoring for group psychotherapy. *Psychotherapy Research, 26*, 131–145.

Tasca, G.A., Francis, K., & Balfour, L. (2014). Group psychotherapy levels of interventions: A clinical process commentary. *Psychotherapy, 51*, 25–29.

Taube-Schiff, M., Suvak, M.K., Antony, M.M., Bieling, P.J., & McCabe, R.E. (2007). Group cohesion in cognitive-behavioral group therapy for social phobia. *Behaviour Research and Therapy, 45*, 687–698.

Taylor, R., & Gazda, G. M. (1991). Concurrent individual and group therapy: The ethical issues. *Journal of Group Psychotherapy, Psychodrama & Sociometry, 44*(2), 51–59.

Tervalon, M., & Murray-Garcia, J. (1998). Cultural humility versus cultural competence: A critical distinction in defining physician training outcomes in multicultural education. *Journal of Health Care for the Poor and Underserved, 9*(2), 117–125.

Thorgeirsdottir, M.T., Bjornsson, A.S., & Arnkelsson, G.B. (2015). Group climate development in brief group therapies: A comparison between cognitive-behavioral group therapy and group psychotherapy for social anxiety disorder. *Group Dynamics: Theory, Research, and Practice, 19* (3), 200.

Triplett, N. (1898). The dynamogenic factors in pacemaking and competition. *The American Journal of Psychology, 9*(4), 507–533.

Tuckman, B.W. (1965). Development sequence in small groups. *Psychological Bulletin, 63*, 384–399.

Tuckman, B.W., & Jensen, M. (1977). Stages of small-group development revisited. *Group and Organization Studies, 2*, 419–427.

Turner, M.M. (2017). Nuts and bolts: The group screen. In M.D. Ribeiro, J. Gross, & M. M. Turner (Eds.), *The college counselor's guide to group psychotherapy* (pp. 145–155). New York: Routledge/Taylor & Francis Group.

Turquet, P. (1974). Leadership: The individual and the group. In G.S. Gibbard, J.J. Hartman, & R. D. Mann (Eds.), *Analysis of groups* (pp. 337–371). San Francisco, CA: Jossey-Bass.

Turquet, P. (1975). Threats to identity in the large groups. In L. Kreeger (Ed.), *The large group: Dynamics and therapy* (pp. 87–144). London: Constable.

Van Hoose, W.H., & Paradise, L.V. (1979). *Ethics in counseling and psychotherapy: Perspectives in issues and decision making*. Cranston, RI: The Carroll Press.

Van Wagoner, S.L. (2012). From empathically immersed inquiry to discrete intervention: Are there limits to theoretical purity? In J.L. Kleinberg (Ed.), *The Wiley-Blackwell handbook of group psychotherapy* (pp. 249–270). New York: Wiley.

Walser, R.D., & Pistorello, J. (2005). ACT in group format. In S. Hayes, & K. Strosahl (Eds.), *A practical guide to acceptance and commitment therapy* (pp. 347–372). New York: Springer Science.

Wampold, B.E., & Imel, Z.E. (2015). *The great psychotherapy debate: The evidence for what makes psychotherapy work*. New York: Routledge/Taylor & Francis Group.

Waters, A., & Asbill, L. (2013). *Reflections on cultural humility*. Washington, DC: American Psychological Association.

Weber, R. (2014). Unraveling projective identification and enactment. In L. Motherwell, & J. Shay (Eds.), *Complex dilemmas in group therapy: Pathways to resolution* (2nd ed., pp. 95–107). New York: Routledge/Taylor & Francis Group.

Weber, R.L., & Gans, J.S. (2003). The group therapist's shame: A much undiscussed topic. *International Journal of Group Psychotherapy, 53,* 395–416.

Weinberg, H. (2001). Group process and group phenomena on the Internet. *International Journal of Group Psychotherapy, 51*(3), 361–378.

Weinberg, H. (2014). *The paradox of internet groups: Alone in the presence of others.* London: Karnac.

Westra, H.A., & Norouzian, N. (2018). Using motivational interviewing to manage process markers of ambivalence and resistance in cognitive behavioral therapy. *Cognitive Therapy and Research, 42*(2), 193–203.

Wheelan, S.A. (2005). *Group processes: A developmental perspective.* Auckland: Pearson Education New Zealand.

White, J.L. (1969). Guidelines for Black psychologists. *The Black Scholar, 1,* 52–57.

White, J.L. (1970, August). Toward a black psychology. *Ebony, 25,* 44–45, 48–50, 52.

Whittingham, M. (2018). Innovations in group assessment: How focused brief group therapy integrates formal measures to enhance treatment preparation, process, and outcomes. *Psychotherapy, 55,* 186–190.

Wolf, A., & Schwartz, E. (1962). *Psychoanalysis in groups.* New York: Grune & Stratton.

Woods, J., & Ruzek, N. (2017). Ethics in Group Psychotherapy. In M.D. Ribeiro, J. Gross, & M. M. Turner (Eds.), *The college counselor's guide to group psychotherapy* (pp. 83–100). New York: Routledge/Taylor & Francis Group.

Yalom, I., & Leszcz, M. (2005). *The theory and practice of group psychotherapy.* New York: Basic Books.

Zaharopoulos, M., & Chen, E.C. (2018). Racial-cultural events in group therapy as perceived by group therapists. *International Journal of Group Psychotherapy, 68*(4), 629–653.

Zaslav, M.R. (1988). A model of group therapist development. *International Journal of Group Psychotherapy, 38,* 511–519.

Zukor, T. (2017). Trainee development in group psychotherapy. In M.D. Ribeiro, J. Gross, & M. M. Turner (Eds.), *The college counselor's guide to group psychotherapy* (pp. 101–113). New York: Routledge/Taylor & Francis Group.

Index